DISCARDED BY
DURHAM COUNTY LIBRARY

DURHAM COUNTY LIBRARY
DURHAM, NORTH CAROLINA

PHILOSOPHY: WHO NEEDS IT

❋ Ayn Rand ❋

PHILOSOPHY: WHO NEEDS IT

Introduction by
Leonard Peikoff

THE BOBBS-MERRILL COMPANY, INC
Indianapolis / New York

COPYRIGHT © 1982 Leonard Peikoff, Executor, Estate of Ayn Rand

Introduction COPYRIGHT © 1982 Leonard Peikoff

All rights reserved.
No part of this publication may be reproduced, stored in a retrieval system or transmitted in any form or by any means, mechanical, electronic, photo-copying, recording or otherwise without the prior written permission of the publisher. For information, address The Bobbs-Merrill Co., Inc., 630 Third Avenue, New York, NY 10017.

Published by The Bobbs-Merrill Co., Inc.
Indianapolis/New York
Manufactured in the United States of America

Second Paperback Printing

Designed by Sheila Lynch

Library of Congress Cataloging in Publication Data

Rand, Ayn.
    Philosophy, who needs it.

    Includes index.
    1. Philosophy—Addresses, essays, lectures.
I. Title.
B29.R26   100   82-4320
ISBN 0-672-52725-1   AACR2
    0-672-52795-2 (pbk.)

Contents

Introduction

Ayn Rand was not only a novelist and philosopher; she was also a salesman of philosophy—the greatest salesman philosophy has ever had.

Who else could write a Romantic best seller such as *Atlas Shrugged*—in which the heroes and the villains are differentiated fundamentally by their metaphysics; in which the wrong epistemology is shown to lead to train wrecks, furnace breakouts, and sexual impotence; in which the right ethics is shown to be the indispensable means to the rebuilding of New York City and of man's soul? Who else today could write a book called *Philosophy: Who Needs It*—and have an answer to offer?

Ayn Rand's power to sell philosophy is a consequence of her particular philosophy, Objectivism.

" . . . I am not *primarily* an advocate of capitalism, but of egoism," she wrote a decade ago; "and I am not *primarily* an advocate of egoism, but of reason. If one recognizes the supremacy of reason and applies it consistently, all the rest follows. This—the supremacy of reason—was, is and will be the primary concern of my work, and the essence of Objectivism." (*The Objectivist*, September 1971.)

Reason, according to Objectivism, is not merely a distinguishing attribute of man; it is his fundamental attribute—his basic means of survival. Therefore, whatever reason requires in order to function is a necessity of human life.

Reason functions by integrating perceptual data into concepts. This process, Ayn Rand holds, ultimately requires the widest integrations—those which give man knowledge of the universe in which he acts, of his means of knowledge, and of his proper values.

Man, therefore, needs metaphysics, epistemology and ethics; i.e., he needs philosophy. He needs it by his essential nature and for a practical purpose: in order to be able to think, to act, to live.

In today's world, this view of the role of philosophy is unique—just as, in today's neo-mystic culture, Objectivism's advocacy of reason is all but unique.

To Ayn Rand, philosophy is not a senseless parade of abstractions created to fill out the ritual at cocktail parties or in Sunday morning services. It is not a ponderous Continental wail of futility resonating with Oriental overtones. It is not a chess game divorced from reality designed by British professors for otherwise unemployable colleagues. To Ayn Rand, philosophy is the fundamental factor in human life; it is the basic force that shapes the mind and character of men and the destiny of nations. It shapes them for good or for evil, depending on the kind of philosophy men accept.

A man's choice, according to Ayn Rand, is not whether to have a philosophy, but only which philosophy to have. His choice is whether his philosophy will be conscious, explicit, logical, and therefore practical—or random, unidentified, contradictory, and therefore lethal.

In these essays, Ayn Rand explains some of the steps necessary to achieve a conscious, rational philosophy. She teaches the reader how to identify, and then evaluate, the hidden premises at work in his own soul or nation. She makes clear the mechanism by which philosophy rules men and societies, the forms that abstract theory takes in daily life, and the profound existential consequences that flow from even the most abstruse ideas, ideas which may seem at first glance to be of merely academic concern. She shows that, when an idea is rational, its consequence, ultimately, is the preservation of man's life; and that when an idea is irrational, its consequence is the opposite.

Contrary to the injunctions issued to men for millennia, Ayn Rand did not equate objectivity with "disinterest"; she was *interested* in philosophy, in the Objectivist sense of "self-interest"; she wanted—selfishly, for the sake of her own actions and life—to know which ideas are right. If man needs philosophy, she held, he needs one that is *true*, i.e., in accordance with reality.

Philosophy: Who Needs It is the last work planned by Ayn Rand before her death in March of this year.

The book was first suggested by a Canadian Objectivist, Walter Huebscher. In the fall of 1981, he wrote to Miss Rand: "In [your articles], you detail dramatically how everyone, through each statement he makes, uses philosophical premises. . . . If [such] articles were published in a single volume, I believe that it would focus direct attention on philosophy's powerful influence, identify the philosophical roots of some of today's most dangerous trends, [and] indicate that it is possible to reverse a cultural trend, that everyone can and should get involved in doing just that."

Miss Rand was pleased with Mr. Huebscher's idea of a collection taken largely from her newsletter, *The Ayn Rand Letter*, and featuring as its title piece one of her favorites among her own articles, "Philosophy: Who Needs It"—originally a speech given at the United States Military Academy at West Point. In subsequent months—with her publisher at Bobbs-Merrill, Grace Shaw, and with friends and associates—she several times discussed her concept of the book. She indicated its content and structure in general terms. She mentioned articles whose inclusion would be mandatory, and others that she regarded as optional. She did not live long enough, however, to determine the final selection of pieces or their sequence. It has fallen to me to make these decisions, guided, wherever possible, by Miss Rand's stated wishes.

Following her policy in other anthologies, I have placed the more theoretical articles in the first part of the book, and followed them by more concrete applications and/or essentially critical articles. None of the pieces has been published before in book form.

The title article is followed by one written originally as its companion piece. Next comes a group dealing with the Objectivist philosophy. The first of these (Chapter 3), her analysis of what is or is not open to change, represents Ayn Rand's fullest discussion in print of one element of the Objectivist metaphysics—the primacy of existence. The following discussions of the anti-conceptual mentality (Chapters 4 and 5) are a demonstration, in reverse, of one element of the Objectivist epistemology: they show what happens to men who never fully develop the *human* form of knowledge—concepts. The open letter to Boris Spassky (Chapter 6), the Soviet chessmaster, is a tour de force summarizing, in the form of a single startling example, the role in man's life of every branch of philosophy.

With one exception, all the articles in this book were written between 1970 and 1975. The exception is "Faith and Force: The Destroyers of the Modern World" (Chapter 7), a speech given initially at Yale University in 1960, a few years after the publication of *Atlas Shrugged*. This speech is an excellent, simple introduction to Objectivism and to Ayn Rand's view of today's world. Until now, it has not been easily available. Those unfamiliar with Miss Rand's work might be well advised to begin their reading with this chapter.

There follows an essentially critical section (Chapters 8–13) dealing with Kant, and with some of his heirs, such as the egalitarian movement and B. F. Skinner.

Miss Rand was frequently asked why there are so few advocates of good ideas in positions of power today. To indicate her answer, at least in part, I have included two political pieces (Chapters 14 and 15); they discuss some current methods used by the government to corrupt our cultural life.

These are followed by two pieces (Chapters 16 and 17) relating to another question Ayn Rand was repeatedly asked: What can anyone do about the state of today's world?

I have ended the book as, I think, Miss Rand would have ended it. "Don't Let It Go" presents the American sense of life as the basis of hope for this country's future.

When articles written years apart are published in book form, editorial changes are occasionally necessary. I have enclosed such changes in square brackets. In a few cases, where Miss Rand uses a term that would be unfamiliar to new readers, I have offered a brief definition, also in square brackets. Otherwise, aside from minor copy-editing, the text is exactly as worded (and in some cases later reworded) by Ayn Rand herself. (Please note that square brackets *within a quotation* are in every case Miss Rand's, and represent her own additions to or comments on the quotation.)

Since Miss Rand's death, her associates in New York have received a great deal of mail inquiring how one can learn more about her ideas; how one can obtain back issues of her magazines; what current publications, schools, courses now carry on her philosophy; what work is done by the Foundation for the New Intellectual; etc. If you are interested in any of the above, I suggest that you write to: Objectivism PW, P.O. Box 177, Murray Hill Station, New York, N.Y. 10016. I regret that, owing to the volume of mail, you will probably not receive a personal reply; but in due course you will receive literature from several sources indicating the direction to pursue if you wish to investigate Ayn Rand's ideas further, or to support them.

Meanwhile, if you are about to read these essays for the first time, I envy you, because of what you still have in store for you. Ayn Rand has changed many people's minds and lives. Perhaps she will change yours, too.

LEONARD PEIKOFF
New York City
May 1982

1

Philosophy: Who Needs It

1974

(An address given to the graduating class of the United States Military Academy at West Point on March 6, 1974.)

Since I am a fiction writer, let us start with a short short story. Suppose that you are an astronaut whose spaceship gets out of control and crashes on an unknown planet. When you regain consciousness and find that you are not hurt badly, the first three questions in your mind would be: Where am I? How can I discover it? What should I do?

You see unfamiliar vegetation outside, and there is air to breathe; the sunlight seems paler than you remember it and colder. You turn to look at the sky, but stop. You are struck by a sudden feeling: if you don't look, you won't have to know that you are, perhaps, too far from the earth and no return is possible; so long as you don't know it, you are free to believe what you wish—and you experience a foggy, pleasant, but somehow guilty, kind of hope.

You turn to your instruments: they may be damaged, you don't know how seriously. But you stop, struck by a sudden fear: how can you trust these instruments? How can you be sure that they won't mislead you? How can you know whether they will work in a different world? You turn away from the instruments.

Now you begin to wonder why you have no desire to do anything. It seems so much safer just to wait for something to turn up somehow; it is better, you tell yourself, not to rock the spaceship. Far in the distance, you see some sort of living creatures approaching; you don't know whether they are human, but they walk on two feet. *They*, you decide, will tell you what to do.

You are never heard from again.

This is fantasy, you say? You would not act like that and no astronaut ever would? Perhaps not. But this is the way most men live their lives, here, on earth.

Most men spend their days struggling to evade three questions, the answers to which underlie man's every thought, feeling and action, whether he is consciously aware of it or not: Where am I? How do I know it? What should I do?

By the time they are old enough to understand these questions, men believe that they know the answers. Where am I? Say, in New York City. How do I know it? It's self-evident. What should I do? Here, they are not too sure—but the usual answer is: whatever everybody does. The only trouble seems to be that they are not very active, not very confident, not very happy—and they experience, at times, a causeless fear and an undefined guilt, which they cannot explain or get rid of.

They have never discovered the fact that the trouble comes from the three unanswered questions—and that there is only one science that can answer them: *philosophy*.

Philosophy studies the *fundamental* nature of existence, of man, and of man's relationship to existence. As against the special sciences, which deal only with particular aspects, philosophy deals with those aspects of the universe which pertain to everything that exists. In the realm of cognition, the special sciences are the trees, but philosophy is the soil which makes the forest possible.

Philosophy would not tell you, for instance, whether you are in New York City or in Zanzibar (though it would give you the means to find out). But here is what it *would* tell you: Are you in a universe which is ruled by natural laws and, therefore, is stable, firm, absolute—and knowable? Or are you in an incomprehensible chaos, a realm of inexplicable miracles, an unpredictable, unknowable flux, which your mind is impotent to grasp? Are the things you see around you real—or are they only an illusion? Do they exist independent of any observer—or are they created by the observer? Are they the object or the subject of man's consciousness? Are they *what they are*—or can they be changed by a mere act of your consciousness, such as a wish?

The nature of your actions—and of your ambition—will be different, according to which set of answers you come to accept. These answers are the province of *metaphysics*—the study of existence as such or, in Aristotle's words, of "being qua being"—the basic branch of philosophy.

No matter what conclusions you reach, you will be confronted by the necessity to answer another, *corollary* question: How do I know it? Since man is not omniscient or infallible, you have to discover what you can claim as knowledge and how to *prove* the validity of your conclusions. Does man acquire knowledge by a process of reason—or by sudden revelation from a supernatural power? Is reason a faculty that identifies and integrates the material provided by man's senses—or is it fed by innate ideas, implanted in man's mind before he was born? Is reason competent to perceive reality—or does man possess some other cognitive faculty which is superior to reason? Can man achieve certainty—or is he doomed to perpetual doubt?

The extent of your self-confidence—and of your success—will be different, according to which set of answers you accept. These answers are the province of *epistemology*, the theory of knowledge, which studies man's means of cognition.

These two branches are the theoretical foundation of philosophy. The third branch—*ethics*—may be regarded as its technology. Ethics does not apply to everything that exists, only to man, but it applies to every aspect of man's life: his character, his actions, his values, his relationship to all of existence. Ethics, or morality, defines a code of values to guide man's choices and actions—the choices and actions that determine the course of his life.

Just as the astronaut in my story did not know what he should do, because he refused to know where he was and how to discover it, so you cannot know what you should do until you know the nature of the universe you deal with, the nature of your means of cognition—and your own nature. Before you come to ethics, you must answer the questions posed by metaphysics and epistemology: Is man a rational being, able to deal with reality—or is he a helplessly blind misfit, a chip buffeted by the universal flux? Are achievement and enjoyment possible to man on earth—or is he doomed to failure and disaster? Depending on the answers, you can proceed to consider the questions posed by ethics: What is good or evil for man—and why? Should man's primary concern be a quest for joy—or an escape from suffering? Should man hold self-fulfillment—or self-destruction—as the goal of his life? Should man pursue his values—or should he place the interests of others above his own? Should man seek happiness—or self-sacrifice?

I do not have to point out the different consequences of these two sets of answers. You can see them everywhere—within you and around you.

The answers given by ethics determine how man should treat other men, and this determines the fourth branch of philosophy: *politics*, which defines the principles of a proper social system. As an example of philosophy's function, political philosophy will not tell you how much rationed gas you should be given and on which day of the week—it will tell you whether the government has the right to impose any rationing on anything.

The fifth and last branch of philosophy is *esthetics*, the study of art, which is based on metaphysics, epistemology and ethics. Art deals with the needs—the refueling—of man's consciousness.

Now some of you might say, as many people do: "Aw, I never think in such abstract terms—I want to deal with concrete, particular, real-life problems—what do I need philosophy for?" My answer is: In order to be able to deal with concrete, particular, real-life problems—i.e., in order to be able to live on earth.

You might claim—as most people do—that you have never been influenced by philosophy. I will ask you to check that claim. Have you ever thought or said the following? "Don't be so sure—nobody can be certain of anything." You got that notion from David Hume (and many, many others), even though you might never have heard of him. Or: "This may be good in theory, but it doesn't work in practice." You got that from Plato. Or: "That was a rotten thing to do, but it's only human, nobody is perfect in this world." You got it from Augustine. Or: "It may be true for you, but it's not true for me." You got it from William James. Or: "I couldn't help it! Nobody can help anything he does." You got it from Hegel. Or: "I can't prove it, but I *feel* that it's true." You got it from Kant. Or: "It's logical, but logic has nothing to do with reality." You got it from Kant. Or: "It's evil, because it's selfish." You got it from Kant. Have you heard the modern activists say: "Act first, think afterward"? They got it from John Dewey.

Some people might answer: "Sure, I've said those things at different times, but I don't have to believe that stuff *all* of the time. It may have been true yesterday, but it's not true today." They got it from Hegel. They might say: "Consistency is the hobgoblin of little minds." They got it from a very little mind, Emerson. They might say: "But can't one compromise and borrow different ideas from different philosophies according to the expediency of the moment?" They got it from Richard Nixon—who got it from William James.

Now ask yourself: if you are not interested in abstract

ideas, why do you (and all men) feel compelled to use them? The fact is that abstract ideas are conceptual integrations which subsume an incalculable number of concretes—and that without abstract ideas you would not be able to deal with concrete, particular, real-life problems. You would be in the position of a newborn infant, to whom every object is a unique, unprecedented phenomenon. The difference between his mental state and yours lies in the number of conceptual integrations your mind has performed.

You have no choice about the necessity to integrate your observations, your experiences, your knowledge into abstract ideas, i.e., into principles. Your only choice is whether these principles are true or false, whether they represent your conscious, rational convictions—or a grab-bag of notions snatched at random, whose sources, validity, context and consequences you do not know, notions which, more often than not, you would drop like a hot potato if you knew.

But the principles you accept (consciously or subconsciously) may clash with or contradict one another; they, too, have to be integrated. What integrates them? Philosophy. A philosophic system is an integrated view of existence. As a human being, you have no choice about the fact that you need a philosophy. Your only choice is whether you define your philosophy by a conscious, rational, disciplined process of thought and scrupulously logical deliberation—or let your subconscious accumulate a junk heap of unwarranted conclusions, false generalizations, undefined contradictions, undigested slogans, unidentified wishes, doubts and fears, thrown together by chance, but integrated by your subconscious into a kind of mongrel philosophy and fused into a single, solid weight: *self-doubt*, like a ball and chain in the place where your mind's wings should have grown.

You might say, as many people do, that it is not easy always to act on abstract principles. No, it is not easy. But how much harder is it, to have to act on them without knowing what they are?

Your subconscious is like a computer—more complex a computer than men can build—and its main function is the integration of your ideas. Who programs it? Your conscious mind. If you default, if you don't reach any firm convictions, your subconscious is programmed by chance—and you deliver yourself into the power of ideas you do not know you have accepted. But one way or the other, your computer gives you print-outs, daily and hourly, in the form of *emotions*— which are lightning-like estimates of the things around you, calculated according to your values. If you programmed your computer by conscious thinking, you know the nature of your values and emotions. If you didn't, you don't.

Many people, particularly today, claim that man cannot live by logic alone, that there's the emotional element of his nature to consider, and that they rely on the guidance of their emotions. Well, so did the astronaut in my story. The joke is on him—and on them: man's values and emotions are determined by his fundamental view of life. The ultimate programmer of his subconscious is *philosophy*—the science which, according to the emotionalists, is impotent to affect or penetrate the murky mysteries of their feelings.

The quality of a computer's output is determined by the quality of its input. If your subconscious is programmed by chance, its output will have a corresponding character. You have probably heard the computer operators' eloquent term "gigo"—which means: "Garbage in, garbage out." The same formula applies to the relationship between a man's thinking and his emotions.

A man who is run by emotions is like a man who is run by a computer whose print-outs he cannot read. He does not know whether its programming is true or false, right or wrong, whether it's set to lead him to success or destruction, whether it serves his goals or those of some evil, unknowable power. He is blind on two fronts: blind to the world around him and to his own inner world, unable to grasp reality or his own motives, and he is in chronic terror of both. Emotions are not tools of cognition. The men who are not interested in philosophy need it most urgently: they are most helplessly in its power.

The men who are not interested in philosophy absorb its principles from the cultural atmosphere around them—from schools, colleges, books, magazines, newspapers, movies, television, etc. Who sets the tone of a culture? A small handful of men: the philosophers. Others follow their lead, either by conviction or by default. For some two hundred years, under the influence of Immanuel Kant, the dominant trend of philosophy has been directed to a single goal: the destruction of man's mind, of his confidence in the power of reason. Today, we are seeing the climax of that trend.

When men abandon reason, they find not only that their emotions cannot guide them, but that they can experience no emotions save one: terror. The spread of drug addiction among young people brought up on today's intellectual fashions, demonstrates the unbearable inner state of men who are deprived of their means of cognition and who seek escape from reality—from the terror of their impotence to deal with existence. Observe these young people's dread of independence and their frantic desire to "belong," to attach themselves to some group, clique or gang. Most of them have never heard of philosophy, but they sense that they need some fundamental answers to questions they dare not ask— and they hope that the tribe will tell them *how to live*. They are ready to be taken over by any witch doctor, guru, or dictator. One of the most dangerous things a man can do is to surrender his *moral* autonomy to others: like the astronaut in my story, he does not know whether they are human, even though they walk on two feet.

Now you may ask: If philosophy can be that evil, why should one study it? Particularly, why should one study the philosophical theories which are blatantly false, make no sense, and bear no relation to real life?

My answer is: In self-protection—and in defense of truth, justice, freedom, and any value you ever held or may ever hold.

Not all philosophies are evil, though too many of them are, particularly in modern history. On the other hand, at the root of every civilized achievement, such as science, technology, progress, freedom—at the root of every value we enjoy today, including the birth of this country—you will find the achievement of *one man*, who lived over two thousand years ago: Aristotle.

If you feel nothing but boredom when reading the virtually unintelligible theories of *some* philosophers, you have my deepest sympathy. But if you brush them aside, saying: "Why should I study that stuff when I *know* it's nonsense?"—you are mistaken. It *is* nonsense, but you *don't* know it—not so long as you go on accepting all their conclusions, all the vicious catch phrases generated by those philosophers. And not so long as you are unable to *refute* them.

That nonsense deals with the most crucial, the life-or-death issues of man's existence. At the root of every significant philosophic theory, there is a legitimate issue—in the sense that there is an authentic need of man's consciousness, which some theories struggle to clarify and others struggle to obfuscate, to corrupt, to prevent man from ever discovering. The battle of philosophers is a battle for man's mind. If you do not understand their theories, you are vulnerable to the worst among them.

The best way to study philosophy is to approach it as one approaches a detective story: follow every trail, clue and implication, in order to discover who is a murderer and who is a hero. The criterion of detection is two questions: Why? and How? If a given tenet seems to be true—why? If another tenet seems to be false—why? and how is it being put over? You will not find all the answers immediately, but you will acquire an invaluable characteristic: the ability to think in terms of essentials.

Nothing is given to man automatically, neither knowledge, nor self-confidence, nor inner serenity, nor the right way to use his mind. Every value he needs or wants has to be discovered, learned and acquired—even the proper posture of his body. In this context, I want to say that I have always admired the posture of West Point graduates, a posture that projects man in proud, disciplined control of his body. Well, philosophical training gives man the proper *intellectual* posture—a proud, disciplined control of his mind.

In your own profession, in military science, you know the importance of keeping track of the enemy's weapons, strategy and tactics—and of being prepared to counter them. The same is true in philosophy: you have to understand the enemy's ideas and be prepared to refute them, you have to know his basic arguments and be able to blast them.

In physical warfare, you would not send your men into a booby trap: you would make every effort to discover its location. Well, Kant's system is the biggest and most intricate booby trap in the history of philosophy—but it's so full of holes that once you grasp its gimmick, you can defuse it without any trouble and walk forward over it in perfect safety. And, once it is defused, the lesser Kantians—the lower ranks of his army, the philosophical sergeants, buck privates, and mercenaries of today—will fall of their own weightlessness, by chain reaction.

There is a special reason why you, the future leaders of the United States Army, need to be philosophically armed today. You are the target of a special attack by the Kantian-Hegelian-collectivist establishment that dominates our cultural institutions at present. You are the army of the last semi-free country left on earth, yet you are accused of being a tool of imperialism—and "imperialism" is the name given to the foreign policy of this country, which has never engaged in military conquest and has never profited from the two world wars, which she did not initiate, but entered and won. (It was, incidentally, a foolishly overgenerous policy, which made this country waste her wealth on helping both her allies and her former enemies.) Something called "the military-industrial complex"—which is a myth or worse—is being blamed for all of this country's troubles. Bloody college hoodlums scream demands that R.O.T.C. units be banned from college campuses. Our defense budget is being attacked, denounced and undercut by people who claim that financial priority should be given to ecological rose gardens and to classes in esthetic self-expression for the residents of the slums.

Some of you may be bewildered by this campaign and may be wondering, in good faith, what errors you committed to bring it about. If so, it is urgently important for you to understand the nature of the enemy. You are attacked, not for any errors or flaws, but for your virtues. You are denounced, not for any weaknesses, but for your strength and your competence. You are penalized for being the protectors of the United States. On a lower level of the same issue, a similar kind of campaign is conducted against the police force. Those who seek to destroy this country, seek to disarm it—intellectually and physically. But it is not a mere political issue; politics is not the cause, but the last consequence of philosophical ideas. It is not a communist conspiracy, though some communists may be involved—as maggots cashing in on a disaster they had no power to originate. The motive of the destroyers is not love for communism, but hatred for America. Why hatred? Because America is the living refutation of a Kantian universe.

Today's mawkish concern with and compassion for the feeble, the flawed, the suffering, the guilty, is a cover for the profoundly Kantian hatred of the innocent, the strong, the able, the successful, the virtuous, the confident, the happy. A philosophy out to destroy man's mind is necessarily a philosophy of hatred for man, for man's life, and for every human value. Hatred of the good for being the good, is the hallmark of the twentieth century. *This* is the enemy you are facing.

A battle of this kind requires special weapons. It has to be fought with a full understanding of your cause, a full confidence in yourself, and the fullest certainty of the *moral* rightness of both. Only philosophy can provide you with these weapons.

The assignment I gave myself for tonight is not to sell you on *my* philosophy, but on philosophy as such. I have, however, been speaking implicitly of my philosophy in every sentence—since none of us and no statement can escape from philosophical premises. What is my *selfish* interest in the matter? I am confident enough to think that if you accept the importance of philosophy and the task of examining it critically, it is *my* philosophy that you will come to accept. Formally, I call it Objectivism, but informally I call it a philosophy for living on earth. You will find an explicit presentation of it in my books, particularly in *Atlas Shrugged*.

In conclusion, allow me to speak in personal terms. This evening means a great deal to me. I feel deeply honored by the opportunity to address you. I can say—not as a patriotic bromide, but with full knowledge of the necessary metaphysical, epistemological, ethical, political and esthetic roots— that the United States of America is the greatest, the noblest and, in its original founding principles, the *only* moral country in the history of the world. There is a kind of quiet radiance associated in my mind with the name West Point—because you have preserved the spirit of those original founding principles and you are their symbol. There were contradictions and omissions in those principles, and there may be in yours—but I am speaking of the essentials. There may be individuals in your history who did not live up to your highest standards—as there are in every institution—since no institution and no social system can guarantee the automatic perfection of all its members; this depends on an individual's free will. I am speaking of your standards. You have preserved three qualities of character which were typical at the time of America's birth, but are virtually nonexistent today: earnestness—dedication—a sense of honor. Honor is self-esteem made visible in action.

You have chosen to risk your lives for the defense of this country. I will not insult you by saying that you are dedicated to selfless service—it is not a virtue in *my* morality. In my morality, the defense of one's country means that a man is personally unwilling to live as the conquered slave of any enemy, foreign or domestic. *This* is an enormous virtue. Some of you may not be consciously aware of it. I want to help you to realize it.

The army of a free country has a great responsibility: the right to use force, but not as an instrument of compulsion and brute conquest—as the armies of other countries have done in their histories—only as an instrument of a free nation's self-defense, which means: the defense of a man's individual rights. The principle of using force only in retaliation against those who initiate its use, is the principle of subordinating might to right. The highest integrity and sense of honor are required for such a task. No other army in the world has achieved it. You have.

West Point has given America a long line of heroes, known and unknown. You, this year's graduates, have a glorious tradition to carry on—which I admire profoundly, not because it is a tradition, but because it *is* glorious.

Since I came from a country guilty of the worst tyranny on earth, I am particularly able to appreciate the meaning, the greatness and the supreme value of that which you are defending. So, in my own name and in the name of many people who think as I do, I want to say, to all the men of West Point, past, present and future: Thank you.

2

Philosophical Detection

1974

My [lecture at West Point was] devoted to a brief presentation of an enormous subject: "Philosophy: Who Needs It." I covered the essentials, but a more detailed discussion of certain points will be helpful to those who wish to study philosophy (particularly today, because philosophy has been abolished by the two currently fashionable schools, Linguistic Analysis and Existentialism).

I said that the best way to study philosophy is to approach it as one approaches a detective story. A detective seeks to discover the truth about a crime. A philosophical detective must seek to determine the truth or falsehood of an abstract system and thus discover whether he is dealing with a great achievement or an intellectual crime. A detective knows what to look for, or what clues to regard as significant. A philosophical detective must remember that all human knowledge has a hierarchical structure; he must learn to distinguish the *fundamental* from the derivative, and in judging a given philosopher's system, he must look—first and above all else—at its fundamentals. If the foundation does not hold, neither will anything else.

In philosophy, the fundamentals are metaphysics and epistemology. On the basis of a knowable universe and of a rational faculty's competence to grasp it, you can define man's proper ethics, politics and esthetics. (And if you make an error, you retain the means and the frame of reference necessary to correct it.) But what will you accomplish if you advocate honesty in ethics, while telling men that there is no such thing as truth, fact or reality? What will you do if you advocate political freedom on the grounds that you *feel* it is good, and find yourself confronting an ambitious thug who declares that he feels quite differently?

The layman's error, in regard to philosophy, is the tendency to accept consequences while ignoring their causes—to take the end result of a long sequence of thought as the given and to regard it as "self-evident" or as an irreducible primary, while negating its preconditions. Examples can be seen all around us, particularly in politics. There are liberals who want to preserve individual freedom while denying its source: individual rights. There are religious conservatives who claim to advocate capitalism while attacking its root: reason. There are sundry "libertarians" who plagiarize the Objectivist theory of politics, while rejecting the metaphysics, epistemology and ethics on which it rests. That attitude, of course, is not confined to philosophy: its simplest example is the people who scream that they need more gas and that the oil industry should be taxed out of existence.

As a philosophical detective, you must remember that nothing is self-evident except the material of sensory perception—and that an irreducible primary is a fact which cannot be analyzed (i.e., broken into components) or derived from antecedent facts. You must examine your own convictions and any idea or theory you study, by asking: Is this an irreducible primary—and, if not, what does it depend on? You must ask the same question about any answer you obtain, until you do come to an irreducible primary: if a given idea contradicts a primary, the idea is false. This process will lead you to the field of metaphysics and epistemology—and you will discover in what way every aspect of man's knowledge depends on that field and stands or falls with it.

There is an old fable which I read in Russian (I do not know whether it exists in English). A pig comes upon an oak tree, devours the acorns strewn on the ground and, when his belly is full, starts digging the soil to undercut the oak tree's roots. A bird perched on a high branch upbraids him, saying: "If you could lift your snoot, you would discover that the acorns grow on this tree."

In order to avoid that pig's role in the forest of the intellect, one must know and protect the metaphysical-epistemological tree that produces the acorns of one's convictions, goals and desires. And, conversely, one must not gobble up any brightly colored fruit one finds, without bothering to discover that it comes from a deadly yew tree. If laymen did no more than learn to identify the nature of such fruit and stop munching it or passing it around, they would stop being the victims and the unwary transmission belts of philosophical poison. But a minimal grasp of philosophy is required in order to do it.

If an intelligent and honest layman were to translate his implicit, common-sense rationality (which he takes for granted) into explicit philosophical premises, he would hold that the world he perceives is real (existence exists), that things are what they are (the Law of Identity), that reason is the only means of gaining knowledge and logic is the method of using reason. Assuming this base, let me give you an example of what a philosophical detective would do with some of the catch phrases I cited in ["Philosophy: Who Needs It"].

"It may be true for you, but it's not true for me." What is the meaning of the concept "truth"? Truth is the recognition of reality. (This is known as the correspondence theory of truth.) The same thing cannot be true and untrue at the same time and in the same respect. That catch phrase, therefore, means: a. that the Law of Identity is invalid; b. that there is no objectively perceivable reality, only some indeterminate flux which is nothing in particular, i.e., that there is no reality (in which case, there can be no such thing as truth); or c. that the two debaters perceive two different universes (in which case, no debate is possible). (The purpose of the catch phrase is the destruction of objectivity.)

"Don't be so sure—nobody can be certain of anything." Bertrand Russell's gibberish to the contrary notwithstanding, that pronouncement includes itself; therefore, one cannot be sure that one cannot be sure of anything. The pronouncement means that no knowledge of any kind is possible to man, i.e., that man is not conscious. Furthermore, if one tried to accept that catch phrase, one would find that its second part contradicts its first: if nobody can be certain of anything, then everybody can be certain of everything he pleases—since it cannot be refuted, and he can claim he is not certain he is certain (which is the purpose of that notion).

"This may be good in theory, but it doesn't work in practice." What is a theory? It is a set of abstract principles purporting to be either a correct description of reality or a set of guidelines for man's actions. Correspondence to reality is the standard of value by which one estimates a theory. If a theory is inapplicable to reality, by what standard can it be estimated as "good"? If one were to accept that notion, it would mean: a. that the activity of man's mind is unrelated to reality; b. that the purpose of thinking is neither to acquire knowledge nor to guide man's actions. (The purpose of that catch phrase is to invalidate man's conceptual faculty.)

"It's logical, but logic has nothing to do with reality." Logic is the art or skill of non-contradictory identification. Logic has a single law, the Law of Identity, and its various corollaries. If logic has nothing to do with reality, it means that the Law of Identity is inapplicable to reality. If so, then: a. things are not what they are; b. things can be and not be at the same time, in the same respect, i.e., reality is made up of contradictions. If so, by what means did anyone discover it? By illogical means. (This last is for sure.) The purpose of that notion is crudely obvious. Its actual meaning is not: "Logic has nothing to do with reality," but: "I, the speaker, have nothing to do with logic (or with reality)." When people use that catch phrase, they mean either: "It's logical, but I don't choose to be logical" or: "It's logical, but people are not logical, they don't think—and I intend to pander to their irrationality."

This is a clue to the kind of error (or epistemological sloppiness) that permits the spread of such catch phrases. Most people use them in regard to some concrete, particular instance and are not aware of the fact that they are uttering a devastating metaphysical generalization. When they say: "It may be true for you, but it's not true for me," they usually mean some optional matter of taste, involving some minor value-judgment. The meaning they intend to convey is closer to: "You may like it, but I don't." The unchallenged idea that value-preferences and emotions are unaccountable primaries, is at the root of their statement. And, in defense of their failure of introspection, they are recklessly willing to wipe the universe out of existence.

When people hear the catch phrase: "It may have been true yesterday, but it's not true today," they usually think of man-made issues or customs, such as: "Men fought duels yesterday, but not today" or: "Women wore hoop skirts yesterday, but not today" or: "We're not in the horse-and-buggy age any longer." The proponents of that catch phrase are seldom innocent, and the examples they give are usually of the above kind. So their victims—who have never discovered the difference between the metaphysical and the man-made—find themselves, in helpless bewilderment, unable to refute such conclusions as: "Freedom was a value yesterday, but not today" or: "Work was a human necessity yesterday, but not today" or: "Reason was valid yesterday, but not today."

Now observe the method I used to analyze those catch phrases. You must attach clear, specific meanings to words, i.e., be able to identify their referents in reality. This is a precondition, without which neither critical judgment nor thinking of any kind is possible. All philosophical con games count on your using words as vague approximations. You must not take a catch phrase—or any abstract statement—as if it were approximate. Take it literally. Don't translate it, don't glamorize it, don't make the mistake of thinking, as many people do: "Oh, nobody could possibly mean this!" and then proceed to endow it with some whitewashed meaning of your own. Take it straight, for what it *does* say and mean.

Instead of dismissing the catch phrase, *accept* it—for a few brief moments. Tell yourself, in effect: "If I were to accept it as true, what would follow?" This is the best way of unmasking any philosophical fraud. The old saying of plain con men holds true for intellectual ones: "You can't cheat an honest man." Intellectual honesty consists in taking ideas seriously. To take ideas seriously means that you intend to live by, to *practice*, any idea you accept as true. Philosophy provides man with a comprehensive view of life. In order to evaluate it properly, ask yourself what a given theory, if accepted, would do to a human life, starting with your own.

Most people would be astonished by this method. They think that abstract thinking must be "impersonal"—which means that ideas must hold no personal meaning, value or importance to the thinker. This notion rests on the premise that a personal interest is an agent of distortion. But "personal" does not mean "non-objective"; it depends on the kind of person you are. If your thinking is determined by your emotions, then you will not be able to judge anything personally or impersonally. But if you are the kind of person who knows that reality is not your enemy, that truth and knowledge are of crucial, personal, *selfish* importance to you and to your own life—then, the more passionately personal the thinking, the clearer and truer.

Would *you* be willing and able to act, daily and consistently, on the belief that reality is an illusion? That the things you see around you, do not exist? That it makes no difference whether you drive your car down a road or over the edge of an abyss —whether you eat or starve—whether you save the life of a person you love or push him into a blazing fire? It is particularly important to apply this test to any moral theory. Would *you* be willing and able to act on the belief that altruism is a moral ideal? That you must sacrifice everything—everything you love, seek, own, or desire, including your life—for the benefit of any and every stranger?

Do not evade such issues by means of self-abasement—by saying: "Maybe reality is unreal, but I'm not wise enough to transcend my low-grade, materialistic bondage" or: "Yes, altruism is an ideal, but I'm not good enough to practice it." Self-abasement is not an answer—and it is not a license to apply to others the precepts from which you exempt yourself; it is merely a trap set by the very philosophers you are trying to judge. They have spent a prodigious effort to teach you to assume an unearned guilt. Once you assume it, you pronounce your mind incompetent to judge, you renounce morality, integrity and thought, and you condemn yourself to the gray fog of the approximate, the uncertain, the uninspiring, the flameless, through which most men drag their lives—which is the purpose of that trap.

The acceptance of unearned guilt is a major cause of philosophical passivity. There are other causes—and other kinds of guilt which *are* earned.

A major source of men's *earned* guilt in regard to philosophy—as well as in regard to their own minds and lives—is failure of introspection. Specifically, it is the failure to identify the nature and causes of their emotions.

An emotion as such tells you nothing about reality, beyond the fact that something makes you feel something. Without a ruthlessly honest commitment to introspection—to the conceptual identification of your inner states—you will not discover what you feel, what arouses the feeling, and whether your feeling is an appropriate response to the facts of reality, or a mistaken response, or a vicious illusion produced by years of self-deception. The men who scorn or dread introspection take their inner states for granted, as an irreducible and irresistible primary, and let their emotions determine their actions. This means that they choose to act without knowing the context (reality), the causes (motives), and the consequences (goals) of their actions.

The field of extrospection is based on two cardinal questions: "What do I know?" and "How do I know it?" In the field of introspection, the two guiding questions are: "*What* do I feel?" and "*Why* do I feel it?"

Most men can give themselves only some primitively superficial answers—and they spend their lives struggling with incomprehensible inner conflicts, alternately repressing their emotions and indulging in emotional fits, regretting it, losing control again, rebelling against the mystery of their inner chaos, trying to unravel it, giving up, deciding to feel nothing—and feeling the growing pressure of fear, guilt, self-doubt, which makes the answers progressively harder to find.

Since an emotion is experienced as an immediate primary, but is, in fact, a complex, derivative sum, it permits men to practice one of the ugliest of psychological phenomena: *rationalization*. Rationalization is a cover-up, a process of providing one's emotions with a false identity, of giving them spurious explanations and justifications—in order to hide one's motives, not just from others, but primarily from oneself. The price of rationalizing is the hampering, the distortion and, ultimately, the destruction of one's cognitive faculty. Rationalization is a process not of perceiving reality, but of attempting to make reality fit one's emotions.

Philosophical catch phrases are handy means of rationalization. They are quoted, repeated and perpetuated in order to justify feelings which men are unwilling to admit.

"Nobody can be certain of anything" is a rationalization for a feeling of envy and hatred toward those who *are* certain. "It may be true for you, but it's not true for me" is a rationalization for one's inability and unwillingness to prove the validity of one's contentions. "Nobody is perfect in this world" is a rationalization for the desire to continue indulging in one's imperfections, i.e., the desire to escape morality. "Nobody

can help anything he does" is a rationalization for the escape
from moral responsibility. "It may have been true yesterday,
but it's not true today" is a rationalization for the desire to get
away with contradictions. "Logic has nothing to do with reality" is a crude rationalization for a desire to subordinate reality to one's whims.

"I can't prove it, but I *feel* that it's true" is more than a
rationalization: it is a description of the process of rationalizing. Men do not accept a catch phrase by a process of
thought, they seize upon a catch phrase—*any* catch phrase
—because it fits their emotions. Such men do not judge the
truth of a statement by its correspondence to reality—they
judge reality by its correspondence to their feelings.

If, in the course of philosophical detection, you find yourself, at times, stopped by the indignantly bewildered question: "How could anyone arrive at such nonsense?"—you will
begin to understand it when you discover that *evil philosophies are systems of rationalization.*

The nonsense is never accidental, if you observe what subjects it deals with. The elaborate structures in which it is presented are never purposeless. You may find a grim proof of
reality's power in the fact that the most virulently rabid ir-
rationalist senses the derivative nature of emotions and will
not proclaim their primacy, their sovereign causelessness, but
will seek to justify them as responses to reality—and if reality
contradicts them, he will invent another reality of which they
are the humble reflectors, not the rulers.

In modern history, the philosophy of Kant is a systematic
rationalization of every major psychological vice. The metaphysical inferiority of this world (as a "phenomenal" world of
mere "appearances"), is a rationalization for the hatred of
reality. The notion that reason is unable to perceive reality
and deals only with "appearances," is a rationalization for the
hatred of reason; it is also a rationalization for a profound
kind of epistemological egalitarianism which reduces reason
to equality with the futile puttering of "idealistic" dreamers.

The metaphysical superiority of the "noumenal" world, is a rationalization for the supremacy of emotions, which are thus given the power to know the unknowable by ineffable means.

The complaint that man can perceive things only through his own consciousness, not through any other kinds of consciousnesses, is a rationalization for the most profound type of second-handedness ever confessed in print: it is the whine of a man tortured by perpetual concern with what others think and by inability to decide which others he should conform to. The wish to perceive "things in themselves" unprocessed by any consciousness, is a rationalization for the wish to escape the effort and responsibility of cognition—by means of the automatic omniscience a whim-worshiper ascribes to his emotions. The moral imperative of the duty to sacrifice oneself to duty, a sacrifice without beneficiaries, is a gross rationalization for the image (and soul) of an austere, ascetic monk who winks at you with an obscenely sadistic pleasure—the pleasure of breaking man's spirit, ambition, success, self-esteem, and enjoyment of life on earth. Et cetera. These are just some of the highlights.

Observe that the history of philosophy reproduces—in slow motion, on a macrocosmic screen—the workings of ideas in an individual man's mind. A man who has accepted false premises is free to reject them, but until and unless he does, they do not lie still in his mind, they grow without his conscious participation and reach their ultimate logical conclusions. A similar process takes place in a culture: if the false premises of an influential philosopher are not challenged, generations of his followers—acting as the culture's subconscious—milk them down to their ultimate consequences.

Since Kant substituted the collective for the objective (in the form of "categories" collectively creating a "phenomenal" world), the next step was the philosophy of Hegel—which is a rationalization for *subjectivism*, for the power-lust of an ambitious elite who would create a *"noumenal,"* non-material world (by means of establishing the brute force of an absolute

state in the "phenomenal," material one). Since those outside
the elite could not be counted upon to obey or accept such a
future, the next side step was Pragmatism—which is a rationalization for the concrete-bound, range-of-the-moment,
anti-conceptual mentalities that long for liberation from principles and future.

Today, there is the philosophy of Linguistic Analysis—
which is a rationalization for men who are able to focus on
single words, but unable to integrate them into sentences,
paragraphs or philosophical systems, yet who wish to be philosophers. And there is the philosophy of Existentialism—
which discards the politeness of rationalization, takes Kant
straight, and proclaims the supremacy of emotions in an unknowable, incomprehensible, inexplicable, nauseating non-
world.

Observe that, in spite of their differences, altruism is the
untouched, unchallenged common denominator in the ethics
of all these philosophies. It is the single richest source of rationalizations. A morality that cannot be practiced is an unlimited cover for any practice. Altruism is the rationalization
for the mass slaughter in Soviet Russia—for the legalized
looting in the welfare state—for the power-lust of politicians
seeking to serve the "common good"—for the concept of a
"common good"—for envy, hatred, malice, brutality—for
the arson, robbery, highjacking, kidnapping, murder perpetrated by the selfless advocates of sundry collectivist
causes—for sacrifice and more sacrifice and an infinity of
sacrificial victims. When a theory achieves nothing but the
opposite of its alleged goals, yet its advocates remain unde-
terred, you may be certain that it is not a conviction or an
"ideal," but a rationalization.

Philosophical rationalizations are not always easy to detect.
Some of them are so complex that an innocent man may be
taken in and paralyzed by intellectual confusion. At their first
encounter with modern philosophy, many people make the
mistake of dropping it and running, with the thought: "I *know*

it's false, but I can't prove it. I know something's wrong there, but I can't waste my time and effort trying to untangle it." Here is the danger of such a policy: you might forget all about Kant's "categories" and his "noumenal" world, but someday, under the pressure of facing some painfully difficult choice, when you feel tempted to evade the responsibility or to make a dishonest decision, when you need all of your inner strength, confidence and courage, you will find yourself thinking: "How do I know what's true? Nobody knows it. Nobody can be certain of anything." *This* is all Kant wanted of you.

A thinker like Kant does not want you to agree with him: all he wants is that you give him the benefit of the doubt. He knows that your own subconscious does the rest. What he dreads is your conscious mind: once you understand the meaning of his theories, they lose their power to threaten you, like a Halloween mask in bright sunlight.

One further suggestion: if you undertake the task of philosophical detection, drop the dangerous little catch phrase which advises you to keep an "open mind." This is a very ambiguous term—as demonstrated by a man who once accused a famous politician of having "a wide open mind." That term is an anti-concept: it is usually taken to mean an objective, unbiased approach to ideas, but it is used as a call for perpetual skepticism, for holding no firm convictions and granting plausibility to anything. A "closed mind" is usually taken to mean the attitude of a man impervious to ideas, arguments, facts and logic, who clings stubbornly to some mixture of unwarranted assumptions, fashionable catch phrases, tribal prejudices—and emotions. But this is not a "closed" mind, it is a *passive* one. It is a mind that has dispensed with (or never acquired) the practice of thinking or judging, and feels threatened by any request to consider anything.

What objectivity and the study of philosophy require is not an "open mind," but an *active mind*—a mind able and eagerly willing to examine ideas, but to examine them *critically*.

An active mind does not grant equal status to truth and false-hood; it does not remain floating forever in a stagnant vacuum of neutrality and uncertainty; by assuming the responsibility of judgment, it reaches firm convictions and holds to them. Since it is able to prove its convictions, an active mind achieves an unassailable certainty in confrontations with assailants—a certainty untainted by spots of blind faith, ap-proximation, evasion and fear.

If you keep an active mind, you will discover (assuming that you started with common-sense rationality) that every chal-lenge you examine will strengthen your convictions, that the conscious, reasoned rejection of false theories will help you to clarify and amplify the true ones, that your ideological enemies will make you invulnerable by providing countless demonstrations of their own impotence.

No, you will not have to keep your mind eternally open to the task of examining every new variant of the same old false-hoods. You will discover that they are variants or attacks on certain philosophical essentials—and that the entire, gigantic battle of philosophy (and of human history) revolves around the upholding or the destruction of these essentials. You will learn to recognize at a glance a given theory's stand on these essentials, and to reject the attacks without lengthy consid-eration—because you will know (and will be able to *prove*) in what way any given attack, old or new, is made of contradic-tions and "stolen concepts."*

I will list these essentials for your future reference. But do not attempt the shortcut of accepting them on faith (or as semi-grasped approximations and floating abstractions). That would be a fundamental contradiction and it would not work.

The essentials are: in metaphysics, *the Law of Identity*—in epistemology, *the supremacy of reason*—in ethics, *rational*

*[The "stolen concept" fallacy, first identified by Ayn Rand, is the fallacy of using a concept while denying the validity of its genetic roots, i.e., of an earlier concept(s) on which it logically depends. See *The Objectivist Newslet-ter*, Vol. II, No. 1, January 1963.]

egoism—in politics, *individual rights* (i.e., capitalism)—in esthetics, *metaphysical values.*

If you reach the day when these essentials become your absolutes, you will have entered Atlantis—at least psychologically; which is a precondition of the possibility ever to enter it existentially.

3

The Metaphysical Versus The Man-Made
1973

"God grant me the serenity to accept things I cannot change, courage to change things I can, and wisdom to know the difference."

This remarkable statement is attributed to a theologian with whose ideas I disagree in every fundamental respect: Reinhold Niebuhr. But—omitting the form of a prayer, i.e., the implication that one's mental-emotional states are a gift from God—that statement is profoundly true, as a summary and a guideline: it names the mental attitude which a rational man must seek to achieve. The statement is beautiful in its eloquent simplicity; but the achievement of that attitude involves philosophy's deepest metaphysical-moral issues.

I was startled to learn that that statement has been adopted as a prayer by Alcoholics Anonymous, which is not exactly a philosophical organization. In view of the fact that today's social-psychological theories stress emotional, not intellectual, needs and frustrations as the cause of human suffering (e.g., the lack of "love"), that organization deserves credit for discovering that such a prayer is relevant to the problems of alcoholics—that the misery of confusion on those issues has devastating consequences and is one of the factors driving men to drink—i.e., to seek escape from reality. This is just one more example of the way in which philosophy rules the lives of men who have never heard or cared to hear about it.

Most men spend their lives in futile rebellion against things they cannot change, in passive resignation to things they can, and—never attempting to learn the difference—in chronic guilt and self-doubt on both counts.

Observe what philosophical premises are implicit in that advice and are required for an attempt to live up to it. If there are things that man can change, it means that he possesses the power of choice, i.e., the faculty of volition. If he does not possess it, he can change nothing, including his own actions and characteristics, such as courage or lack of it. If there are things that man cannot change, it means that there are things that cannot be affected by his actions and are not open to his choice. This leads to the basic metaphysical issue that lies at the root of any system of philosophy: *the primacy of existence* or *the primacy of consciousness*.

The primacy of existence (of realty) is the axiom that existence exists, i.e., that the universe exists independent of consciousness (of *any* consciousness), that things are what they are, that they possess the specific nature, an *identity*. The epistemological corollary is the axiom that consciousness is the faculty of perceiving that which exists—and that man gains knowledge of reality by looking outward. The rejection of these axioms represents a reversal: the primacy of consciousness—the notion that the universe has no independent existence, that it is the product of a consciousness (either human or divine or both). The epistemological corollary is the notion that man gains knowledge of reality by looking inward (either at his own consciousness or at the revelations it receives from another, superior consciousness).

The source of this reversal is the inability or unwillingness fully to grasp the difference between one's inner state and the outer world, i.e., between the perceiver and the perceived (thus blending consciousness and existence into one indeterminate package-deal).* This crucial distinction is not given to man automatically; it has to be learned. It is implicit in any awareness, but it has to be grasped conceptually and held as an absolute. As far as can be observed, infants and savages do not grasp it (they may, perhaps, have some rudimentary glimmer of it). Very few men ever choose to grasp it and fully to accept it. The majority keep swinging from side to side, implicitly recognizing the primacy of existence in some cases and denying it in others, adopting a kind of hit-or-miss, rule-of-thumb epistemological agnosticism, through ignorance and/or by intention—the result of which is the shrinking of their intellectual range, i.e., of their capacity to deal with abstractions. And although few people today believe that the singing of mystic incantations will bring rain, most people still regard as valid an argument such as: "If there is no God, who created the universe?"

To grasp the axiom that existence exists, means to grasp the fact that nature, i.e., the universe as a whole, cannot be created or annihilated, that it cannot come into or go out of existence. Whether its basic constituent elements are atoms, or subatomic particles, or some yet undiscovered forms of energy, it is not ruled by a consciousness or by will or by chance, but by the Law of Identity. All the countless forms, motions, combinations and dissolutions of elements within the universe—from a floating speck of dust to the formation of a galaxy to the emergence of life—are caused and determined by the identities of the elements involved. Nature is the *metaphysically given*—i.e., the nature of nature is outside the power of any volition.

Man's volition is an attribute of his consciousness (of his rational faculty) and consists in the choice to perceive existence or to evade it. To perceive existence, to discover the

*["Package-dealing" is the fallacy of failing to discriminate crucial differences. It consists of treating together, as parts of a single conceptual whole or "package," elements which differ essentially in nature, truth-status, importance or value.]

characteristics or properties (the identities) of the things that exist, means to discover and accept the metaphysically given. Only on the basis of this knowledge is man able to learn how the things given in nature can be rearranged to serve his needs (which is his method of survival).

The power to rearrange the combinations of natural elements is the only creative power man possesses. It is an enormous and glorious power—and it is the only meaning of the concept "creative." "Creation" does not (and metaphysically cannot) mean the power to bring something into existence out of nothing. "Creation" means the power to bring into existence an arrangement (or combination or integration) of natural elements that had not existed before. (This is true of any human product, scientific or esthetic: man's imagination is nothing more than the ability to rearrange the things he has observed in reality.) The best and briefest identification of man's power in regard to nature is Francis Bacon's "Nature, to be commanded, must be obeyed." In this context, "to be commanded" means to be made to serve man's purposes; "to be obeyed" means that they cannot be served unless man discovers the properties of natural elements and uses them accordingly.

For example, two hundred years ago, men would have said that it is impossible to hear a human voice at a distance of 238,000 miles. It is as impossible today as it was then. But if we are able to hear an astronaut's voice coming from the moon, it is by means of the science of electronics, which discovered certain natural phenomena and enabled men to build the kind of equipment that picks up the vibrations of that voice, transmits them, and reproduces them on earth. Without this knowledge and this equipment, centuries of wishing, praying, screaming and foot-stamping would not make a man's voice heard at the distance of ten miles.

Today, this is (implicitly) understood and (more or less) accepted in regard to the physical sciences (hence their progress). It is neither understood nor accepted—and is, in fact, vociferously denied—in regard to the humanities, the sciences dealing with man (hence their stagnant barbarism). Almost unanimously, man is regarded as an *unnatural* phenomenon: either as a *supernatural* entity, whose mystic (divine) endowment, the mind ("soul"), is above nature—or as a *subnatural* entity, whose mystic (demoniacal) endowment, the mind, is an enemy of nature ("ecology"). The purpose of all such theories is to exempt man from the Law of Identity.

But man exists and his mind exists. Both are part of nature, both possess a specific identity. The attribute of volition does not contradict the fact of identity, just as the existence of living organisms does not contradict the existence of inanimate matter. Living organisms possess the power of self-initiated motion, which inanimate matter does not possess; man's consciousness possesses the power of self-initiated motion in the realm of cognition (thinking), which the consciousnesses of other living species do not possess. But just as animals are able to move only in accordance with the nature of their bodies, so man is able to initiate and direct his mental action only in accordance with the nature (the *identity*) of his consciousness. His volition is limited to his cognitive processes; he has the power to identify (and to conceive of rearranging) the elements of reality, but not the power to alter them. He has the power to use his cognitive faculty as its nature requires, but not the power to alter it nor to escape the consequences of its misuse. He has the power to suspend, evade, corrupt or subvert his perception of reality, but not the power to escape the existential and psychological disasters that follow. (The use or misuse of his cognitive faculty determines a man's choice of values, which determine his emotions and his character. It is in this sense that man is a being of self-made soul.)

Man's faculty of volition as such is not a contradiction of nature, but it opens the way for a host of contradictions—when and if men do not grasp *the crucial difference between the metaphysically given and any object, institution, procedure, or rule of conduct made by man.*

It is the metaphysically given that must be accepted: it cannot be changed. It is the man-made that must never be accepted uncritically: it must be judged, then accepted or rejected and changed when necessary. Man is not omniscient or infallible: he can make innocent errors through lack of knowledge, or he can lie, cheat and fake. The man-made may be a product of genius, perceptiveness, ingenuity—or it may be a product of stupidity, deception, malice, evil. One man may be right and everyone else wrong, or vice versa (or any numerical division in between). Nature does not give man any automatic guarantee of the truth of his judgments (and *this* is a metaphysically given fact, which must be accepted). Who, then, is to judge? Each man, to the best of his ability and honesty. What is his standard of judgment? *The metaphysically given.*

The metaphysically given cannot be true or false, it simply *is*—and man determines the truth or falsehood of his judgments by whether they correspond to or contradict the facts of reality. The metaphysically given cannot be right or wrong—it is the standard of right or wrong, by which a (rational) man judges his goals, his values, his choices. The metaphysically given is, was, will be, and had to be. Nothing made by man *had to be:* it was made by choice.

To rebel against the metaphysically given is to engage in a futile attempt to negate existence. To accept the man-made as beyond challenge is to engage in a successful attempt to negate one's own consciousness. Serenity comes from the ability to say "Yes" to existence. Courage comes from the ability to say "No" to the wrong choices made by others.

Any natural phenomenon, i.e., any event which occurs without human participation, is the metaphysically given, and could not have occurred differently or failed to occur; any phenomenon involving human action is the man-made, and could have been different. For example, a flood occurring in an uninhabited land, is the metaphysically given; a dam built to contain the flood water, is the man-made; if the builders miscalculate and the dam breaks, the disaster is metaphysical in its origin, but intensified by man in its consequences. To correct the situation, men must obey nature by studying the causes and potentialities of the flood, then command nature by building better flood controls.

But to declare that all of man's efforts to improve the conditions of his existence are futile, to declare that nature is unknowable because we cannot prove that there will be a flood next year, even though there has been one every year in memory, to declare that human knowledge is an illusion because the original dam builders were certain that the dam would hold, but it did not—is to drive men back to the primordial confusion on the relationship of consciousness to existence, and thus to rob men of serenity and courage (as well as of many other things). Yet this is what modern philosophy has been declaring for two hundred years or longer.

Observe that the philosophical system based on the axiom of the primacy of existence (i.e., on recognizing the absolutism of reality) led to the recognition of man's identity and *rights*. But the philosophical systems based on the primacy of consciousness (i.e., on the seemingly megalomaniacal notion that nature is whatever man wants it to be) lead to the view that man possesses no identity, that he is infinitely flexible, malleable, usable and disposable. Ask yourself why.

A major part of the philosophers' attack on man's mind is devoted to attempts to obliterate the difference between the metaphysically given and the man-made. The confusion on this issue started as an ancient error (to which even Aristotle contributed in some of his Platonist aspects); but today it is running deliberately and inexcusably wild.

A typical package-deal, used by professors of philosophy, runs as follows: to prove the assertion that there is no such thing as "necessity" in the universe, a professor declares that just as this country did not *have to* have fifty states, there could have been forty-eight or fifty-two—so the solar system did not *have to* have nine planets, there could have been seven or eleven. It is not sufficient, he declares, to prove that something *is*, one must also prove that it *had to be*—and since nothing had to be, nothing is certain and anything goes.

The technique of undercutting man's mind consists in palming off the man-made as if it were the metaphysically given, then ascribing to nature the concepts that refer only to men's lack of knowledge, such as "chance" or "contingency," then reversing the two elements of the package-deal. From the assertion: "Man is unpredictable, therefore nature is unpredictable," the argument goes to: "Nature possesses volition, man does not—nature is free, man is ruled by unknowable forces—nature is not to be conquered, man is."

Most people believe that an issue of this kind is empty academic talk, of no practical significance to anyone—which blinds them to its consequences in their own lives. If one were to tell them that the package-deal made of this issue is part of the nagging uncertainty, the quiet hopelessness, the gray despair of their daily inner state, they would deny it: they would not recognize it introspectively. But the inability to introspect is one of the consequences of this package-deal.

Most men have no knowledge of the nature or the functioning of a human consciousness and, consequently, no knowledge of what is or is not possible to them, what one can or cannot demand of oneself and of others, what is or is not one's fault. On the implicit premise that consciousness has no identity, men alternate between the feeling that they possess some sort of omnipotent power over their consciousness and can abuse it with impunity ("It doesn't matter, it's only in my mind")—and the feeling that they have no choice, no control, that the content of consciousness is innately predetermined, that they are victims of the impenetrable mystery inside their own skulls, prisoners of an unknowable enemy, helpless automatons driven by inexplicable emotions ("I can't help it, that's the way I am").

Many men are crippled by the influence of this uncertainty. When such a man considers a goal or desire he wants to achieve, the first question in his mind is: "Can *I* do it?"—

not: "What is required to do it?" His question means: "Do I
have the innate ability?" For example: "I want to be a composer more than anything else on earth, but I have no idea of
how it's done. Do I have that mysterious gift which will do it
for me, somehow?" He has never heard of a premise such as
the primacy of consciousness, but that is the premise moving
him as he embarks on a hopeless search through the dark
labyrinth of his consciousness (hopeless, because without reference to existence, nothing can be learned about one's consciousness).

If he does not give up his desire right then, he stumbles
uncertainly to attempt to achieve it. Any small success aug-
ments his anxiety: he does not know what caused it and
whether he can repeat it. Any small failure is a crushing blow:
he takes it as proof that he lacks the mystic endowment.
When he makes a mistake, he does not ask himself: "What
do I need to learn?"—he asks: "What's wrong with me?" He
waits for an automatic and omnipotent inspiration, which
never comes. He spends years on a cheerless struggle, with
his eyes focused inward, on the growing, leering monster of
self-doubt, while existence drifts by, unseen, on the periphery
of his mental vision. Eventually, he gives up.

Substitute for "composer" any other profession, goal or
desire—to be a scientist, a businessman, a reporter or a
headwaiter, to get rich, to find friends, to lose weight—and
the pattern remains the same. Some of the pattern's victims
are phonies, but not all. It is impossible to tell what amount of
authentic intelligence, particularly in the arts, has been ham-
pered, stunted or crushed by the myth of "innate endowment."

Unable to determine what they can or cannot change, some
men attempt to "rewrite reality," i.e., to alter the nature of
the metaphysically given. Some dream of a universe in which
man experiences nothing but happiness—no pain, no frustration, no illness—and wonder why they lose the desire to improve their life on earth. Some feel that they would be brave,
honest, ambitious in a world where everyone automatically

shared these virtues—but not in the world as it is. Some dread the thought of eventual death—and never undertake the task of living. Some grant omniscience to the passage of time and regard tradition as the equivalent of nature: if people have believed an idea for centuries, they feel, it must be true. Some grant omnipotence and the status of the metaphysically given, not even to people's ideas, but to people's *feelings*, and pander to the irrationality of others, to their blind emotions (such as prejudices, superstitions, envy), regardless of the truth or falsehood of the issues involved—on the premise that "It doesn't matter whether this is true if people *feel* that it's true."

Some men switch to others (who were helpless in the matter) the blame for their own actions; some men, who were helpless in the matter, accept the blame for the actions of others. Some feel guilty because they do not know what they have no way of knowing. Some feel guilty for not having known yesterday what they have learned today. Some feel guilty for not being able to convert the whole world to their own ideas effortlessly and overnight.

The question of how to deal with nature is partially understood, at least by some people; but the question of how to deal with men and how to judge them is still in the state of a primeval jungle. It is man's faculty of volition that sets him apart (even in the eyes of those who deny the existence of that faculty), and makes men regard themselves and others as unintelligible, unknowable, exempt from the Law of Identity.

But nothing is exempt from the Law of Identity. A manmade product did not have to exist, but, once made, it *does* exist. A man's actions did not have to be performed, but, once performed, they are *facts* of reality. The same is true of a man's character: he did not have to make the choices he made, but, once he has formed his character, it is a *fact*, and it is his personal *identity*. (Man's volition gives him great, but not unlimited, latitude to change his character; if he does, the change becomes a *fact*.)

Things of human origin (whether physical or psychological)

may be designated as "man-made facts"—as distinguished from the metaphysically given facts. A skyscraper is a man-made fact, a mountain is a metaphysically given fact. One can alter a skyscraper or blow it up (just as one can alter or blow up a mountain), but so long as it exists, one cannot pretend that it is not there or that it is not what it is. The same principle applies to men's actions and characters. A man does not have to be a worthless scoundrel, but so long as he chooses to be, he *is* a worthless scoundrel and must be treated accordingly; to treat him otherwise is to contradict a *fact*. A man does not have to be a heroic achiever; but so long as he chooses to be, he *is* a heroic achiever and must be treated accordingly; to treat him otherwise is to contradict a *fact*. Men did not have to build a skyscraper; but, once they did, it is worse than a contradiction to regard a skyscraper as a mountain, as a metaphysically given fact which, on this view, "just happened to happen."

The faculty of volition gives man a special status in two crucial respects: 1. unlike the metaphysically given, man's products, whether material or intellectual, are not to be accepted uncritically—and 2. by *its metaphysically given nature*, a man's volition is outside the power of other men. What the unalterable basic constituents are to nature, the attribute of a volitional consciousness is to the entity "man." Nothing can force a man to think. Others may offer him incentives or impediments, rewards or punishments, they may destroy his brain by drugs or by the blow of a club, but they cannot order his mind to function: *this* is in his exclusive, sovereign power. Man is neither to be obeyed nor to be commanded.

What has to be "obeyed" is man's metaphysically given nature—in the sense in which one "obeys" the nature of all existents; this means, in man's case, that one must recognize the fact that his mind is not to be "commanded" in any sense, including the sense applicable to the rest of nature. Natural objects can be reshaped to serve men's goals and are to be regarded as means to men's ends, but man himself cannot and is not.

In regard to nature, "to accept what I cannot change" means to accept the metaphysically given; "to change what I can" means to strive to rearrange the given by acquiring knowledge—as science and technology (e.g., medicine) are doing; "to know the difference" means to know that one cannot rebel against nature and, when no action is possible, one must accept nature serenely.

In regard to man, "to accept" does not mean *to agree*, and "to change" does not mean *to force*. What one must accept is the fact that the minds of other men are not in one's power, as one's own mind is not in theirs; one must accept their right to make their own choices, and one must agree or disagree, accept or reject, join or oppose them, as one's mind dictates. The only means of "changing" men is the same as the means of "changing" nature: knowledge—which, in regard to men, is to be used as a process of *persuasion*, when and if their minds are active; when they are not, one must leave them to the consequences of their own errors. "To know the difference" means that one must never accept man-made evils (there are no others) in silent resignation, one must never submit to them voluntarily—and even if one is imprisoned in some ghastly dictatorship's jail, where no action is possible, serenity comes from the knowledge that one does *not* accept it.

To deal with men by force is as impractical as to deal with nature by persuasion—which is the policy of savages, who rule men by force and plead with nature bv prayers, incantations and bribes (sacrifices). It does not work and has not worked in any human society in history. Yet this is the policy to which modern philosophers are urging mankind to revert —as they have reverted to the notion of the primacy of consciousness. They urge a passive, mystic, "ecological" submission to nature—and the rule of brute force for men.

The philosophers' denial of the Law of Identity permits them to evade man's identity and the requirements of his survival. It permits them to evade the fact that man cannot survive for long in a state of nature, that reason is his tool of survival, that he survives by means of man-made products, and that the source of man-made products is man's *intelligence*. Intelligence is the ability to grasp the facts of reality and to deal with them long-range (i.e., conceptually). On the axiom of the primacy of existence, intelligence is man's most precious attribute. But it has no place in a society ruled by the primacy of consciousness: it is such a society's deadliest enemy.

Today, intelligence is neither recognized nor rewarded, but is being systematically extinguished in a growing flood of brazenly flaunted irrationality. As just one example of the extent to which today's culture is dominated by the primacy of consciousness, observe the following: in politics, people hold a ruthless, absolutist, either-or attitude toward elections, they expect a man either to win or not and are concerned only with the winner, ignoring the loser altogether (even though, in some cases, the loser was right)—while in economics, in the realm of production, they evade the absolutism of reality, of the fact that man either produces or not, and destroy the winners in favor of the losers. To them, men's decisions are an absolute; reality's demands are not.

The climax of that trend, the ultimate cashing-in on the package-deal of the metaphysical and the man-made, is the egalitarian movement and its philosophical manifesto, John Rawls's *A Theory of Justice*.* This obscenely evil theory proposes to subordinate man's nature and mind to the desires (including the envy), not merely of the lowest human specimens, but of the lowest non-existents—to the emotions these would have felt before they were born—and requires that men make lifelong choices on the premise that they are all equally devoid of brains. The fact that a brain cannot project an alteration of its own nature and power, that a genius cannot project himself into the state of a moron, and vice versa, that the needs and desires of a genius and a moron are not

*[A fuller discussion of Rawls's viewpoint is offered in Chapter 11.]

identical, that a genius reduced to the existential level of a moron would perish in unspeakable agony, and a moron raised to the existential level of a genius would paint graffiti on the sides of a computer, then die of starvation—all this does not enter the skulls of men who have dispensed with the Law of Identity (and, therefore, with reality), who demand "equal results" regardless of unequal causes, and who propose to alter metaphysical facts by the power of whims and guns.

This is being preached, touted and demanded today. There can be no intellectual—or moral—neutrality on such an issue. The moral cowards who try to evade it by pleading ignorance, confusion or helplessness, who keep silent and avoid the battle, yet feel a growing sense of guilty terror over the question of what they can or cannot change, are paving the way for the egalitarians' atrocities, and will end up like the derelicts whom Alcoholics Anonymous is struggling to help.

The least that any decent man can do today is to fight that book's doctrine—to fight it intransigently on *moral* grounds. A proposal to annihilate intelligence by slow torture cannot be treated as a difference of civilized opinion.

If any man feels that the world is too complex and its evil is too big to cope with, let him remember that it is too big to drown in a glass of whiskey.

4

The Missing Link
1973

I shall begin by giving you four examples and asking you to identify what psychological element they have in common.

1. I once knew a businessman in a large Midwestern city, who was an unusually hard-working, active, energetic person. He had built a small business of his own and had risen from poverty to affluence. He was the adviser and protector of an enormous conglomeration of relatives, friends, and friends of friends, who ran to him, not merely for loans, but for help with problems of any kind. He was in his late thirties, but acted as a sort of tribal patriarch.

It was hard to tell whether he enjoyed or resented his role; he seemed to take it for granted, as a kind of metaphysical duty: he had probably never thought of questioning it. He did enjoy acting as a small big shot, however, and doing favors for people, about which he was very generous. He had, apparently, some marginal connections with his particular district's political machine and he loved obtaining for his friends the sort of favors that were unobtainable without special pull, such as extra ration coupons (in World War II) or the fixing of traffic tickets. The concept of "friends" had some peculiar significance to him. He watched their *intentions* like a hypochondriac watches his health—in a manner that projected a touchy suspiciousness and a fierce loyalty to some unwritten moral code.

Politically, he tended to be a conservative, and was usually complaining about this country's trends. One day, he launched into a passionate denunciation of the liberals, the government, the unfairness to businessmen, the arbitrary power of political machines. "Do you know how powerful they are?" he asked bitterly, and proceeded to tell me that he had tried to run for some minuscule city office, but "they" had ordered him to withdraw his candidacy "or else," and he had complied.

I said that such problems would always exist so long as government controls existed, and that the only solution was a system of full, laissez-faire capitalism, under which no groups could acquire economic privileges or special pull, so that everyone would have to stand on his own. "That's impossible!" he snapped; his voice was peculiarly tense, abrupt, defensive, as if he were slamming a mental door on some barely glimpsed fact; the voice conveyed fear. I did not pursue the subject: I had grasped a psychological issue that was new to me.

2. A well-known lady novelist once wrote an essay on the nature of fiction. Adopting an extreme Naturalist position, she declared: "The distinctive mark of the novel is its concern with the actual world, the world of fact . . ." And by "fact," she meant the immediately available facts—"the empiric element in experience." "The novel does not permit occurrences outside the order of nature—miracles. . . . You remember how in *The Brothers Karamazov* when Father Zossima dies, his faction (most of the sympathetic characters in the book) expects a miracle: that his body will stay sweet and fresh because he died 'in the odor of sanctity.' But instead he begins to stink. The stink of Father Zossima is the natural, generic smell of the novel. By the same law, a novel cannot be laid in the future, since the future, until it happens, is outside the order of nature . . ."

She declared that "the novel's characteristic tone is one of gossip and tittletattle. . . . Here is another criterion: if the breath of scandal has not touched it, the book is not a novel.

. . . The scandals of a village or a province, the scandals of a nation or of the high seas feed on facts and breed speculation. But it is of the essence of a scandal that it be finite . . . It is impossible, except for theologians, to conceive of a world-wide scandal or a universe-wide scandal; the proof of this is the way people have settled down to living with nuclear fission, radiation poisoning, hydrogen bombs, satellites, and space rockets." Why facts of this kind should be regarded as the province of theology, she did not explain. "Yet these 'scandals,' in the theological sense, of the large world and the universe have dwarfed the finite scandals of the village and the province . . ."

She then proceeded to explain what she regards as "the dilemma of the novelist": we forget or ignore the events of the modern world, "because their special quality is to stagger belief." But if we think of them, "our daily life becomes incredible to us. . . . The coexistence of the great world and us, when contemplated, appears impossible." From this, she drew a conclusion: since the novelist is motivated by his love of truth, "ordinary common truth recognizable to everyone," the novel is "of all forms the least adapted to encompass the modern world, whose leading characteristic is irreality. And that, so far as I can understand, is why the novel is dying."

3. The following story was told to me by an American businessman. In his youth, he took a job as efficiency-expert adviser to the manager of a factory in South America. The factory was using U.S. machines, but was getting only 45 percent of the machines' potential productivity. Observing the low wage scale, he concluded that the men were given no incentive to work—and suggested the introduction of pay by piecework. The elderly manager told him, with a skeptical smile, that this would be futile, but agreed to try it.

In the first three weeks of the new plan, productivity soared. In the fourth week, no one showed up for work: virtually the entire labor force vanished—and did not come back until a week later Having earned a month's wages in three weeks, the workers saw no reason to work that extra week; they had no desire to earn more than they had been earning. No arguments could persuade them; the plan was discontinued.

4. A professor of philosophy once invited me to address his class on ethics; they were studying the subject of "justice," and he asked me to present the Objectivist view of justice. The format he proposed was a fifteen-minute presentation, followed by a question period. I pointed out to him that it would be very difficult to present, in fifteen minutes, the basis of the Objectivist ethics and thus give the reasons for my definition of justice. "Oh, you don't have to give the reasons," he said, "just present your views." (I did not comply.)

The circumstances and the people in these four examples are different; the type of mentality they display is the same. This mentality is self-made, but many different factors can contribute to its formation. These factors may be social, as in the case of the South American workers—or personal, as in the case of the lady novelist—or both, as in the case of the Midwestern businessman. As to the professor of philosophy, the modern trend of his profession is the factor responsible for all the rest.

These cases are examples of the *anti-conceptual* mentality.

The main characteristic of this mentality is a special kind of passivity: not passivity as such and not across-the-board, but passivity beyond a certain limit—i.e., passivity in regard to the process of conceptualization and, therefore, in regard to fundamental principles. It is a mentality which decided, at a certain point of development, that it knows enough and does not care to look further. What does it accept as "enough"? The immediately given, directly perceivable concretes of its background—"the empiric element in experience."

To grasp and deal with such concretes, a human being needs a certain degree of conceptual development, a process which the brain of an animal cannot perform. But after the initial feat of learning to speak, a child can counterfeit this process, by memorization and imitation. The anti-conceptual mentality stops on this level of development—on the first levels of abstractions, which identify perceptual material consisting predominantly of physical objects—and does not choose to take the next, crucial, fully volitional step: the higher levels of abstraction from abstractions, which cannot be learned by imitation. (See my book *Introduction to Objectivist Epistemology*.) Such a mind can grasp the scandals of a village or a province or (at secondhand) a nation; it cannot grasp the concepts of "world" or "universe"—or the fact that their events are not "scandals."

The anti-conceptual mentality takes most things as irreducible primaries and regards them as "self-evident." It treats concepts as if they were (memorized) percepts; it treats abstractions as if they were *perceptual* concretes. To such a mentality, everything is the given: the passage of time, the four seasons, the institution of marriage, the weather, the breeding of children, a flood, a fire, an earthquake, a revolution, a book are phenomena of the same order. The distinction between the metaphysical and the man-made is not merely unknown to this mentality, it is incommunicable.

The two cardinal questions, the prime movers of a human mind—"Why?" and "What for?"—are alien to an anti-conceptual mentality. If asked, they elicit nothing beyond the conventionally accepted answers. The answers are usually some equivalent of "Such is life" or "One is supposed to." *Whose* life? Blank out. Supposed—by *whom*? Blank out.

The absence of concern with the "Why?" eliminates the concept of causality and cuts off the past. The absence of concern with the "What for?" eliminates long-range purpose and cuts off the future. Thus only the present is fully real to an anti-conceptual mentality. Something of the past remains with it, in the form of stagnant bits of a random chronicle, like a kind of small talk of memory, without goal or meaning. But the future is a blank; the future cannot be grasped perceptually.

In this respect, paradoxically enough, the hidebound tradi-

tionalist and the modern college activist are two sides of the
same psycho-epistemological coin.* The first seeks to escape
the terror of an unknowable future by seeking safety in the
alleged wisdom of the past. ("What was good enough for my
father, is good enough for me!") The second seeks to escape
the terror of an unintelligible past by screaming his way into
an indefinable future. ("If it's not good for my father, it's good
enough for me!") And, paradoxically enough, neither of them
is able to live in the present—because man's life span is a
continuum whose only integrator is his *conceptual* faculty.

In the brain of an anti-conceptual person, the process of
integration is largely replaced by a process of association.
What his subconscious stores and automatizes is not ideas,
but an indiscriminate accumulation of sundry concretes, random facts, and unidentified feelings, piled into unlabeled
mental file folders. This works, up to a certain point—i.e., so
long as such a person deals with other persons whose folders
are stuffed similarly, and thus no search through the entire
filing system is ever required. Within such limits, the person
can be active and willing to work hard—like the Midwestern
businessman, who exercised a great deal of initiative and ingenuity, within the limits set by his particular city district—
like the lady novelist, who wrote many books, within the
terms set by her college teachers—like the professor of philosophy, who spent his time analyzing results, without bothering about their causes.

A person of this mentality may uphold some abstract principles or profess some intellectual convictions (without re-
membering where or how he picked them up). But if one asks
him what he means by a given idea, he will not be able to
answer. If one asks him the *reasons* of his convictions, one

*["Psycho-epistemology," a term coined by Ayn Rand, pertains not to the
content of a man's ideas, but to his method of awareness, i.e., the method
by which his mind habitually deals with its content. "Psycho-epistemology
is the study of man's cognitive processes from the aspect of the interaction
between man's conscious mind and the automatic functions of his subconscious." See "The Comprachicos" in *The New Left: The Anti-Industrial
Revolution*.]

will discover that his convictions are a thin, fragile film floating over a vacuum, like an oil slick in empty space—and one
will be shocked by the number of questions it had never occurred to him to ask.

This kind of psycho-epistemology works so long as no part
of it is challenged. But all hell breaks loose when it is—
because what is threatened then is not a particular idea, but
that mind's whole structure. The hell ranges from fear to resentment to stubborn evasion to hostility to panic to malice to
hatred.

The best illustration of an anti-conceptual mentality is a
small incident in a novel published years ago, whose title, un-
fortunately, I do not remember. A commonplace kind of
blonde goes out on a date with a college boy; when she is
asked later whether she had a good time, she answers: "No.
He was awfully boring. He never said anything I'd ever heard
before."

The concrete-bound, anti-conceptual mentality can cope
only with men who are bound by the same concretes—by the
same kind of "finite" world. To this mentality, it means a
world in which men do not have to deal with abstract principles: principles are replaced by memorized rules of behavior,
which are accepted uncritically as the given. What is "finite"
in such a world is not its extension, but the degree of mental
effort required of its inhabitants. When they say "finite," they
mean "perceptual."

Within the limits of their rules (which are usually called
"traditions"), the inhabitants of such worlds are free to
function—i.e., to deal with concretes without worrying about
consequences, to deal with results without bothering about
causes, to deal with "facts" as discrete phenomena, unham-
pered by the "intangibles" of theory—and to feel *safe*. Safe
from what? Consciously, they would answer: "Safe from outsiders." Actually, the answer is: safe from the necessity of
dealing with fundamental principles (and, consequently, safe
from full responsibility for one's own life).

It is the fundamentals of philosophy (particularly, of ethics) that an anti-conceptual person dreads above all else. To understand and to apply them requires a long conceptual chain, which he has made his mind incapable of holding beyond the first, rudimentary links. If his professed beliefs— i.e., the rules and slogans of his group—are challenged, he feels his consciousness dissolving in fog. Hence, his fear of outsiders. The word "outsiders," to him, means the whole wide world beyond the confines of his village or town or gang—the world of all those people who do not live by his "rules." He does not know why he feels that outsiders are a deadly threat to him and why they fill him with helpless terror. The threat is not existential, but psycho-epistemological: to deal with them requires that he rise above his "rules" to the level of abstract principles. He would die rather than attempt it.

"Protection from outsiders" is the benefit he seeks in clinging to his group. What the group demands in return is obedience to its rules, which he is eager to obey: those rules *are* his protection—from the dreaded realm of abstract thought. By whom are those rules established? In theory, by tradition. In fact, by those who happen to be the leaders of his group; the way it stands in his mind is: by those who know the mysteries he does not have to know.

Thus, his survival depends on the substitution of *men* for ideas—and on the subordination of the metaphysical to the man-made. The metaphysical is beyond his grasp—laws of nature cannot be grasped perceptually—but man-made rules are absolutes that protect him from the unknowable, psychologically and existentially. The group comes to his rescue if he gets into trouble—and he does not have to *earn* their help, it is given to him automatically, it is not at the precarious mercy of his own virtues, flaws or errors, it is his by grace of the fact that he belongs to the group.

As an example of the principle that the rational is the moral, observe that the anti-conceptual is the profoundly anti-moral. The basic commandment of all such groups, which takes precedence over any other rules, is: *loyalty to the group*—not to ideas, but to people; not to the group's beliefs, which are minimal and chiefly ritualistic, but to the group's members and leaders. Whether a given member is right or wrong, the others must protect him from outsiders; whether he is innocent or guilty, the others must stand by him against outsiders; whether he is competent or not, the others must employ him or trade with him in preference to outsiders. Thus a physical qualification—the accident of birth in a given village or tribe—takes precedence over morality and justice. (But the physical is only the most frequently apparent and superficial qualification, since such groups reject the non-conforming children of their own members. The actual qualification is psycho-epistemological: men bound by the same concretes.)

Primitive tribes are an obvious example of the anti-conceptual mentality—perhaps, with some justification: savages, like children, are on the preconceptual level of development. Their later counterparts, however, demonstrate that this mentality is not the product of ignorance (nor is it caused by lack of intelligence): it is self-made, i.e., self-arrested. It has resisted the rise of civilization and has manifested itself in countless forms throughout history. Its symptom is always an attempt to circumvent reality by substituting men for ideas, the man-made for the metaphysical, favors for rights, special pull for merit—i.e., an attempt to reduce man's life to a small backyard (or rat hole) exempt from the absolutism of reason. (The driving motive of these attempts is deeper than power-lust: the rulers of such groups seek protection from reality as anxiously as the followers.)

Racism is an obvious manifestation of the anti-conceptual mentality. So is xenophobia—the fear or hatred of foreigners ("outsiders"). So is any caste system, which prescribes a man's status (i.e., assigns him to a tribe) according to his birth; a caste system is perpetuated by a special kind of snobbishness (i.e., group loyalty) not merely among the aristocrats, but, perhaps more fiercely, among the commoners or even the serfs, who like to "know their place" and to guard it jealously against the outsiders from above or from below. So is guild socialism. So is any kind of ancestor worship or of family "solidarity" (the family including uncles, aunts and third cousins). So is any criminal gang.

Tribalism (which is the best name to give to all the group manifestations of the anti-conceptual mentality) is a dominant element in Europe, as a reciprocally reinforcing cause and result of Europe's long history of caste systems, of national and local (provincial) chauvinism, of rule by brute force and endless, bloody wars. As an example, observe the Balkan nations, which are perennially bent upon exterminating one another over minuscule differences of tradition or language. Tribalism had no place in the United States—until recent decades. It could not take root here, its imported seedlings were withering away and turning to slag in the melting pot whose fire was fed by two inexhaustible sources of energy: individual rights and objective law; these two were the only protection man needed.

The remnants of European tribalism, imported by the more timid immigrants, took the innocuous form of "ethnic" neighborhoods in cities, each neighborhood offering its own customs, traditional festivals, old-country restaurants, and words in its native language on battered store-signs. Those signs were battered, because the men who clung to the tribal rule of giving trade priorities to fellow-tribesmen, remained in the backwaters of impoverished neighborhoods, while the torrent of productive energy that placed merit above tribe, swept past them, carrying away the best of their children.

There was no harm in such backwaters, so long as no one was forced to remain in them. The pressure of enlightenment by example was undercutting the group loyalty of the most stubbornly anti-conceptual mentalities, urging them to venture out into the great world where no man is an "outsider" (or all men are, as far as special privileges are concerned).

The disintegration of philosophy reversed this trend.

Tribalism is a product of fear, and fear is the dominant emotion of any person, culture or society that rejects man's power of survival: reason. As philosophy slithered into the primitive swamp of irrationalism, men were driven—existentially and psychologically—into its primordial corollary: tribalism. Existentially, the rise of the welfare state broke up the country into pressure groups, each fighting for special privileges at the expense of the others—so that an individual unaffiliated with any group became fair game for tribal predators. Psychologically, Pragmatism lobotomized the country's intellectuals: John Dewey's theory of "Progressive" education (which has dominated the schools for close to half a century), established a method of crippling a child's conceptual faculty and replacing cognition with "social adjustment." It was and is a systematic attempt to manufacture tribal mentalities. (See my article "The Comprachicos" in *The New Left: The Anti-Industrial Revolution.*)

Observe that today's resurgence of tribalism is not a product of the lower classes—of the poor, the helpless, the ignorant—but of the intellectuals, the college-educated "elitists" (which is a purely tribalistic term). Observe the proliferation of grotesque herds or gangs—hippies, yippies, beatniks, peaceniks, Women's Libs, Gay Libs, Jesus Freaks, Earth Children—which are not tribes, but shifting aggregates of people desperately seeking tribal "protection."

The common denominator of all such gangs is the belief in motion (mass demonstrations), not action—in chanting, not arguing—in demanding, not achieving—in feeling, not thinking—in denouncing "outsiders," not in pursuing values—in focusing only on the "now," the "today" without a "tomorrow"—in seeking to return to "nature," to "the earth," to the mud, to physical labor, i.e., to all the things which a *perceptual* mentality is able to handle. You don't see advocates of reason and science clogging a street in the belief that using their bodies to stop traffic, will solve any problem.

Most of those embryonic tribal gangs are leftist or collectivist. But, as a demonstration of the fact that the cause of tribalism is deeper than politics, there are tribalists still further removed from reality, who claim to be rightists. They are champions of individualism, they claim, which they define as the right to form one's own gang and use physical force against others—and they intend to preserve capitalism, they claim, by replacing it with anarchism (establishing "private" or "competing" governments, i.e., tribal rule). The common denominator of such individualists is the desire to escape from *objectivity* (objectivity requires a very long conceptual chain and very abstract principles), to act on whim, and to deal with men rather than with ideas—i.e., with the men of their own gang bound by the same concretes.

These rightists' distance from reality may be gauged by the fact that they are unable to recognize the actual examples of their ideals in practice, One such example is the Mafia. The Mafia (or "family") is a "private government," with subjects who chose to join it voluntarily, with a rigid set of rules rigidly, efficiently and bloodily enforced, a "government" that undertakes to protect you from "outsiders" and to enforce your immediate interests—at the price of your selling your soul, i.e., of your total obedience to any "favor" it may demand. Another example of a "government" without territorial sovereignty is offered by the Palestinian guerrillas, who have no country of their own, but who engage in terroristic attacks and slaughter of "outsiders" anywhere on earth.

The activist manifestations of modern tribalism, of Left or "Right," are crude extremes. It is the subtler manifestations of the anti-conceptual mentality that are more tragic and harder to deal with. These are the "mixed economies" of the spirit—the men torn inwardly between tribal emotions and scattered fragments of thought—the products of modern education who do not like the nature of what they feel, but have never learned to think.

Since early childhood, their emotions have been conditioned by the tribal premise that one must "belong," one must be "in," one must swim with the "mainstream," one must follow the lead of "those who know." A man's frustrated mind adds another emotion to the tribal conditioning: a blindly bitter resentment of his own intellectual subservience. Modern men are gregarious and antisocial at the same time. They have no inkling of what constitutes a rational human association.

There is a crucial difference between an association and a tribe. Just as a proper society is ruled by laws, not by men, so a proper association is united by ideas, not by men, and its members are loyal to the ideas, not to the group. It is eminently reasonable that men should seek to associate with those who share their convictions and values. It is impossible to deal or even to communicate with men whose ideas are fundamentally opposed to one's own (and one should be free not to deal with them). All proper associations are formed or joined by individual choice and on conscious, intellectual grounds (philosophical, political, professional, etc.)—not by the physiological or geographical accident of birth, and not on the ground of tradition. When men are united by ideas, i.e., by explicit principles, there is no room for favors, whims, or arbitrary power: the principles serve as an *objective* criterion for determining actions and for *judging* men, whether leaders or members.

This requires a high degree of conceptual development and independence, which the anti-conceptual mentality is desperately struggling to avoid. But this is the only way men can work together justly, benevolently and *safely*. There is no way for men to survive on the perceptual level of consciousness.

I am not a student of the theory of evolution and, therefore, I am neither its supporter nor its opponent. But a certain hypothesis has haunted me for years; I want to stress that it is only a hypothesis. There is an enormous breach of continuity between man and all the other living species. The difference lies in the nature of man's consciousness, in its distinctive characteristic: his conceptual faculty. It is as if, after aeons of physiological development, the evolutionary process altered its course, and the higher stages of development focused primarily on the consciousness of living species, not their bodies. But the development of a man's consciousness is volitional: no matter what the innate degree of his intelligence, *he* must develop it, *he* must learn how to use it, *he* must become a human being by choice. What if he does not choose to? Then he becomes a transitional phenomenon—a desperate creature that struggles frantically against his own nature, longing for the effortless "safety" of an animal's consciousness, which he cannot recapture, and rebelling against a human consciousness, which he is afraid to achieve.

For years, scientists have been looking for a "missing link" between man and animals. Perhaps that missing link is the anti-conceptual mentality.

5

Selfishness
Without a Self
1973

In ["The Missing Link"], I discussed the anti-conceptual mentality and its social (tribal) manifestations. All tribalists are anti-conceptual in various degrees, but not all anti-conceptual mentalities are tribalists. Some are lone *wolves* (stressing that species' most predatory characteristics).

The majority of such wolves are frustrated tribalists, i.e., persons rejected by the tribe (or by the people of their immediate environment): they are too unreliable to abide by conventional rules, and too crudely manipulative to compete for tribal power. Since a perceptual mentality cannot provide a man with a way of survival, such a person, left to his own devices, becomes a kind of intellectual hobo, roaming about as an eclectic second-hander or brainpicker, snatching bits of ideas at random, switching them at whim, with only one constant in his behavior: the drifting from group to group, the need to cling to people, any sort of people, and to manipulate them.

Whatever theoretical constructs he may be able to spin and juggle in various fields, it is the field of ethics that fills him with the deepest sense of terror and of his own impotence. Ethics is a conceptual discipline; loyalty to a code of values requires the ability to grasp abstract principles and to apply them to concrete situations and actions (even on the most

primitive level of practicing some rudimentary moral commandments). The tribal lone wolf has no firsthand grasp of
values. He senses that this is a lack he must conceal at any
price—and that this issue, for him, is the hardest one to fake.
The whims that guide him and switch from moment to moment or from year to year, cannot help him to conceive of an
inner state of lifelong dedication to one's chosen values. His
whims condition him to the opposite: they automatize his
avoidance of any permanent commitment to anything or anyone. Without personal values, a man can have no sense of
right or wrong. The tribal lone wolf is an *amoralist* all the way
down.

The clearest symptom by which one can recognize this type
of person, is his total inability to judge himself, his actions, or
his work by any sort of standard. The normal pattern of self-
appraisal requires a reference to some abstract value or
virtue—e.g., "I am good because I am rational," "I am good
because I am honest," even the second-hander's notion of "I
am good because people like me." Regardless of whether the
value-standards involved are true or false, these examples
imply the recognition of an essential moral principle: that
one's own value has to be *earned*.

The amoralist's implicit pattern of self-appraisal (which he
seldom identifies or admits) is: "I am good because it's *me*."

Beyond the age of about three to five (i.e., beyond the perceptual level of mental development), this is not an expression
of pride or self-esteem, but of the opposite: of a vacuum—of
a stagnant, arrested mentality confessing its impotence to
achieve any personal value or virtue.

Do not confuse this pattern with psychological subjectivism. A psychological subjectivist is unable fully to identify
his values or to prove their objective validity, but he may be
profoundly consistent and loyal to them in practice (though
with terrible psycho-epistemological difficulty). The amoralist
does not hold subjective values; he does not hold *any* values.
The implicit pattern of all his estimates is: "It's good because

I like it"—"It's right because *I* did it"—"It's true because *I* want it to be true." What is the "I" in these statements? A physical hulk driven by chronic anxiety.

The frequently encountered examples of this pattern are: the writer who rehashes some ancient bromides and feels that his work is new, because *he* wrote it—the non-objective artist who feels that his smears are superior to those made by a monkey's tail, because *he* made them—the businessman who hires mediocrities because *he* likes them—the political "idealist" who claims that racism is good if practiced by a minority (of *his* choice), but evil if practiced by a majority—and any advocate of any sort of double standard.

But even such shoddy substitutes for morality are only a pretense: the amoralist does not believe that "I am good because it's *me.*" That implicit policy is his protection against his deepest, never-to-be-identified conviction: *"I am no good through and through."*

Love is a response to values. The amoralist's actual self-appraisal is revealed in his abnormal need to be loved (but not in the rational sense of the word)—to be "loved for himself," ı.e., *causelessly.* James Taggart reveals the nature of such a need: "I don't want to be loved *for* anything. I want to be loved for myself—not for anything I do or have or say or think. For myself—not for my body or mind or words or works or actions." *(Atlas Shrugged.)* When his wife asks: "But then . . . what *is* yourself?" he has no answer.

As a real-life example: Years ago, I knew an older woman who was a writer and very intelligent, but inclined toward mysticism, embittered, hostile, lonely, and very unhappy. Her views of love and friendship were similar to James Taggart's. At the time of the publication of *The Fountainhead,* I told her that I was very grateful to Archibald Ogden, the editor who had threatened to resign if his employers did not publish it. She listened with a peculiar kind of skeptical or disapproving look, then said: "You don't have to feel grateful to him. He did not do it for *you.* He did it to further his own career,

because he thought it was a good book." I was truly appalled.
I asked: "Do you mean that his action would be better—and
that I should prefer it—if he thought it was a worthless book,
but fought for its publication out of *charity* to me?" She would
not answer and changed the subject. I was unable to get any
explanation out of her. It took me many years to begin to
understand.

A similar phenomenon, which had puzzled me for a long
time, can be observed in politics. Commentators often exhort
some politician to place the interests of the country above his
own (or his party's) and to compromise with his opponents—
and such exhortations are not addressed to petty grafters, but
to reputable men. What does this mean? If the politician is
convinced that his ideas are right, it is the country that he
would betray by compromising. If he is convinced that his
opponents' ideas are wrong, it is the country that he would be
harming. If he is not certain of either, then he should check
his views for his own sake, not merely the country's—
because the truth or falsehood of his ideas should be of the
utmost *personal* interest to him.

But these considerations presuppose a conceptual consciousness that takes ideas seriously—i.e., that derives its
views from principles derived from reality. A perceptual consciousness is unable to believe that ideas can be of *personal*
importance to anyone; it regards ideas as a matter of arbitrary
choice, as means to some immediate ends. On this view, a
man does not seek to be elected to a public office in order to
carry out certain policies—he advocates certain policies in
order to be elected. If so, then why on earth should he want to
be elected? Perceptual mentalities never ask such a question:
the concept of a long-range goal is outside their limits. (There
are a great many politicians and a great many commentators
of that type—and since that mentality is taken for granted as
proper and normal, what does this indicate about the intellectual state of today's culture?)

If a man subordinates ideas and principles to his "personal

interests," what are his personal interests and by what means does he determine them? Consider the senseless, selfless drudgery to which a politician condemns himself if the goal of his work—the proper administration of the country—is of no personal interest to him (or a lawyer, if justice is of no personal interest to him; or a writer, if the objective value of his books is of no personal interest to him, as the woman I quoted was suggesting). But a perceptual mentality is incapable of generating values or goals, and has to pick them secondhand, as the given, then go through the expected motions. (Not all such men are tribal lone wolves—some are faithful, bewildered tribalists out of their psycho-epistemological depth—but all are anti-conceptual mentalities.)

With all of his emphasis on "himself" (and on being "loved for himself"), the tribal lone wolf has no self and no personal interests, only momentary whims. He is aware of his own immediate sensations and of very little else. Observe that whenever he ventures to speak of spiritual (i.e., intellectual) values—of the things he personally loves or admires—one is shocked by the triteness, the vulgarity, the borrowed trashiness of what comes out of him.

A tribal lone wolf feels that his "self" is dissociated from his actions, his work, his pursuits, his ideas. All these, he feels, are things that some outside power—society or reality or the material universe—has somehow forced on him. His real "self," he feels, is some ineffable entity devoid of attributes. One thing is true: his "self" *is* ineffable, i.e., non-existent. A man's self is his mind—the faculty that perceives reality, forms judgments, chooses values. To a tribal lone wolf, "reality" is a meaningless term; his metaphysics consists in the chronic feeling that life, somehow, is a conspiracy of people and things against *him*, and he will walk over piles of corpses—in order to assert himself? no—in order to hide (or fill) the nagging inner vacuum left by his aborted self.

The grim joke on mankind is the fact that *he* is held up as a symbol of *selfishness*. This encourages him in his depredations: it gives him the hope of success in faking a stature he knows to be beyond his power. Selfishness is a profoundly philosophical, *conceptual* achievement. Anyone who holds a tribal lone wolf as an image of selfishness, is merely confessing the perceptual nature of his own mental functioning.

Yet the tribalists keep proclaiming that morality is an exclusively social phenomenon and that adherence to a tribe— any tribe—is the only way to keep men moral. But the docile members of a tribe are no better than their rejected wolfish brother and fully as amoral: their standard is "We're good because it's *us*."

The abdication and shriveling of the self is a salient characteristic of all perceptual mentalities, tribalist or lonewolfish. All of them dread self-reliance; all of them dread the responsibilities which only a self (i.e., a conceptual consciousness) can perform, and they seek escape from the two activities which an actually selfish man would defend with his life: judgment and choice. They fear reason (which is exercised volitionally) and trust their emotions (which are automatic)—they prefer relatives (an accident of birth) to friends (a matter of choice)—they prefer the tribe (the given) to outsiders (the new)—they prefer commandments (the memorized) to principles (the understood)—they welcome every theory of determinism, every notion that permits them to cry: "I couldn't help it!"

It is obvious why the morality of *altruism* is a tribal phenomenon. Prehistorical men were physically unable to survive without clinging to a tribe for leadership and protection against other tribes. The cause of altruism's perpetuation into civilized eras is not physical, but psycho-epistemological: the men of self-arrested, perceptual mentality are unable to survive without tribal leadership and "protection" against reality. The doctrine of self-sacrifice does not offend them: they have no sense of self or of personal value—they do not know what it is that they are asked to sacrifice—they have no firsthand inkling of such things as intellectual integrity, love of truth, personally chosen values, or a passionate dedication to an idea. When they hear injunctions against "selfishness," they believe that what they must renounce is the brute, mindless whim-worship of a tribal lone wolf. But their leaders—the theoreticians of altruism—know better. Immanuel Kant knew it; John Dewey knew it; B. F. Skinner knows it; John Rawls knows it. Observe that it is not the mindless brute, but reason, intelligence, ability, merit, self-confidence, self-esteem that they are out to destroy.

Today, we are seeing a ghastly spectacle: a magnificent scientific civilization dominated by the morality of prehistorical savagery. The phenomenon that makes it possible is the split psycho-epistemology of "compartmentalized" minds. Its best example are men who *escape* into the physical sciences (or technology or industry or business), hoping to find protection from human irrationality, and abandoning the field of ideas to the enemies of reason. Such refugees include some of mankind's best brains. But no such refuge is possible. These men, who perform feats of conceptual integration and rational thinking in their work, become helplessly anti-conceptual in all the other aspects of their lives, particularly in human relationships and in social issues. (E.g., compare Einstein's scientific achievement to his political views.)

Man's progress requires specialization. But a division-of-labor society cannot survive without a rational philosophy—without a firm base of fundamental principles whose task is to train a human mind to be human, i.e., *conceptual*.

6

An Open Letter to Boris Spassky
1972

Dear Comrade Spassky:

I have been watching with great interest your world chess championship match with Bobby Fischer. I am not a chess enthusiast or even a player, and know only the rudiments of the game. I am a novelist-philosopher by profession.

But I watched some of your games, reproduced play by play on television, and found them to be a fascinating demonstration of the enormous complexity of thought and planning required of a chess player—a demonstration of how many considerations he has to bear in mind, how many factors to integrate, how many contingencies to be prepared for, how far ahead to see and plan. It was obvious that you and your opponent had to have an unusual intellectual capacity.

Then I was struck by the realization that the game itself and the players' exercise of mental virtuosity are made possible by the *metaphysical absolutism* of the reality with which they deal. The game is ruled by the Law of Identity and its corollary, the Law of Causality. Each piece is what it is: a queen is a queen, a bishop is a bishop—and the actions each can perform are determined by its nature: a queen can move any distance in any open line, straight or diagonal, a bishop cannot; a rook can move from one side of the board to the other, a pawn cannot; etc. Their identities and the rules of their movements are immutable—and this enables the player's mind to devise a complex, long-range strategy, so that the game depends on nothing but the power of his (and his opponent's) ingenuity.

This led me to some questions that I should like to ask you.

1. Would you be able to play if, at a crucial moment—when, after hours of brain-wrenching effort, you had succeeded in cornering your opponent—an unknown, arbitrary power suddenly changed the rules of the game in his favor, allowing, say, his bishops to move like queens? You would not be able to continue? Yet out in the living world, this is the law of your country—and this is the condition in which your countrymen are expected, not to play, but to live.

2. Would you be able to play if the rules of chess were updated to conform to a dialectic reality, in which opposites merge—so that, at a crucial moment, your queen turned suddenly from White to Black, becoming the queen of your opponent, and then turned Gray, belonging to both of you? You would not be able to continue? Yet in the living world, this is the view of reality your countrymen are taught to accept, to absorb, and to live by.

3. Would you be able to play if you had to play by teamwork—i.e., if you were forbidden to think or act alone and had to play not with a group of advisers, but with a team that determined your every move by vote? Since, as champion, you would be the best mind among them, how much time and effort would you have to spend persuading the team that *your* strategy is the best? Would you be likely to succeed? And what would you do if some pragmatist, range-of-the-moment mentalities voted to grab an opponent's knight at the price of a checkmate to you three moves later? You would not be able to continue? Yet in the living world, this is the theoretical ideal of your country, and this is the method by which it proposes to deal (someday) with scientific research, industrial production, and every other kind of activity required for man's survival.

4. Would you be able to play if the cumbersome mechanism of teamwork were streamlined, and your moves were dictated simply by a man standing behind you, with a gun pressed to your back—a man who would not explain or argue, his gun being his only argument and sole qualification? You would not be able to start, let alone continue, playing? Yet in the living world, this is the practical policy under which men live—and die—in your country.

5. Would you be able to play—or to enjoy the professional understanding, interest and acclaim of an international Chess Federation—if the rules of the game were splintered, and you played by "proletarian" rules while your opponent played by "bourgeois" rules? Would you say that such "polyrulism" is more preposterous than polylogism? Yet in the living world, your country professes to seek global harmony and understanding, while proclaiming that she follows "proletarian" logic and that others follow "bourgeois" logic, or "Aryan" logic, or "third-world" logic, etc.

6. Would you be able to play if the rules of the game remained as they are at present, with one exception: that the pawns were declared to be the most valuable and non-expendable pieces (since they may symbolize the masses) which had to be protected at the price of sacrificing the more efficacious pieces (the individuals)? You might claim a draw on the answer to this one—since it is not only your country, but the whole living world that accepts this sort of rule in morality.

7. Would you *care* to play, if the rules of the game remained unchanged, but the distribution of rewards were altered in accordance with egalitarian principles: if the prizes, the honors, the fame were given not to the winner, but to the loser—if winning were regarded as a symptom of selfishness, and the winner were penalized for the crime of possessing a superior intelligence, the penalty consisting in suspension for a year, in order to give others a chance? Would you and your opponent try playing not to win, but to lose? What would this do to your mind?

You do not have to answer me, Comrade. You are not free to speak or even to think of such questions—and I know the answers. No, you would not be able to play under any of the conditions listed above. It is to escape this category of phenomena that you fled into the world of chess.

Oh yes, Comrade, chess is an escape—an escape from reality. It is an "out," a kind of "make-work" for a man of higher than average intelligence who was afraid to live, but could not leave his mind unemployed and devoted it to a placebo—thus surrendering to others the living world he had rejected as too hard to understand.

Please do not take this to mean that I object to games as such: games are an important part of man's life, they provide a necessary rest, and chess may do so for men who live under the constant pressure of purposeful work. Besides, some games—such as sports contests, for instance—offer us an opportunity to see certain human skills developed to a level of perfection. But what would you think of a world champion runner who, in real life, moved about in a wheelchair? Or of a champion high jumper who crawled about on all fours? You, the chess professionals, are taken as exponents of the most precious of human skills: intellectual power—yet that power deserts you beyond the confines of the sixty-four squares of a chessboard, leaving you confused, anxious, and helplessly unfocused. Because, you see, the chessboard is not a training ground, but a *substitute* for reality.

A gifted, precocious youth often finds himself bewildered by the world: it is *people* that he cannot understand, it is their inexplicable, contradictory, messy behavior that frightens him. The enemy he rightly senses, but does not choose to fight, is human *irrationality*. He withdraws, gives up, and runs, looking for some sanctuary where his mind would be appreciated—and he falls into the booby trap of chess.

You, the chess professionals, live in a special world—a safe, protected, orderly world, in which all the great, fundamental principles of existence are so firmly established and obeyed that you do not even have to be aware of them. (They are the principles involved in my seven questions.) You do not know that these principles are the preconditions of your game—and you do not have to recognize them when you encounter them, or their breach, in reality. In *your* world, you do not have to be concerned with them: all you have to do is *think*.

The process of thinking is man's basic means of survival. The pleasure of performing this process successfully—of experiencing the efficacy of one's own mind—is the most profound pleasure possible to men, and it is their deepest need, on any level of intelligence, great or small. So one can understand what attracts you to chess: you believe that you have found a world in which all irrelevant obstacles have been eliminated, and nothing matters but the pure, triumphant exercise of your mind's power. But have you, Comrade?

Unlike algebra, chess does not represent the *abstraction*— the basic pattern—of mental effort; it represents the opposite: it focuses mental effort on a set of concretes, and demands such complex calculations that a mind has no room for anything else. By creating an illusion of action and struggle, chess reduces the professional player's mind to an uncritical, unvaluing passivity toward life. Chess removes the motor of intellectual effort—the question "What for?"—and leaves a somewhat frightening phenomenon: intellectual effort devoid of purpose.

If—for any number of reasons, psychological or existential—a man comes to believe that the living world is closed to him, that he has nothing to seek or to achieve, that no action is possible, then chess becomes his antidote, the means of drugging his own rebellious mind that refuses fully to believe it and to stand still. This, Comrade, is the reason why chess has always been so popular in your country, before and since its present regime—and why there have not been many American masters. You see, in this country, men are still free to act.

Because the rulers of your country have proclaimed this

championship match to be an ideological issue, a contest between Russia and America, I am rooting for Bobby to win—and so are all my friends. The reason why this match has aroused an unprecedented interest in our country is the longstanding frustration and indignation of the American people at your country's policy of attacks, provocations, and hooligan insolence—and at our own government's overtolerant, overcourteous patience. There is a widespread desire in our country to see Soviet Russia beaten in any way, shape or form, and—since we are all sick and tired of the global clashes among the faceless, anonymous masses of collectives—the almost medieval drama of two individual knights fighting the battle of good against evil, appeals to us symbolically. (But this, of course, is only a symbol; you are not necessarily the voluntary defender of evil—for all we know, you might be as much its victim as the rest of the world.)

Bobby Fischer's behavior, however, mars the symbolism—but it is a clear example of the clash between a chess expert's mind, and reality. This confident, disciplined, obviously brilliant player falls to pieces when he has to deal with the real world. He throws tantrums like a child, breaks agreements, makes arbitrary demands, and indulges in the kind of whim-worship one touch of which in the playing of chess would disqualify him for a high-school tournament. Thus he brings to the real world the very evil that made him escape it: *irrationality*. A man who is afraid to sign a letter, who fears any firm commitment, who seeks the guidance of the arbitrary edicts of a mystic sect in order to learn how to live his life—is not a great, confident mind, but a tragically helpless victim, torn by acute anxiety and, perhaps, by a sense of treason to what might have been a great potential.

But, you may wish to say, the principles of reason are not applicable beyond the limit of a chessboard, they are merely a human invention, they are impotent against the chaos outside, they have no chance in the real world. If this were true, none of us would have survived nor even been born, because the human species would have perished long ago. If, under irrational rules, like the ones I listed above, men could not even play a game, how could they live? It is not reason, but irrationality that is a human invention—or, rather, a default.

Nature (reality) is just as absolutist as chess, and her rules (laws) are just as immutable (more so)—but her rules and their applications are much, much more complex, and have to be discovered by man. And just as a man may memorize the rules of chess, but has to use his own mind in order to apply them, i.e., in order to play well—so each man has to use his own mind in order to apply the rules of nature, i.e., in order to live successfully. A long time ago, the grandmaster of all grandmasters gave us the basic principles of the method by which one discovers the rules of nature and of life. His name was Aristotle.

Would you have wanted to escape into chess, if you lived in a society based on Aristotelian principles? It would be a country where the rules were objective, firm and clear, where you could use the power of your mind to its fullest extent, on any scale you wished, where you would gain rewards for your achievements, and men who chose to be irrational would not have the power to stop you nor to harm anyone but themselves. Such a social system could not be devised, you say? But it *was* devised, and it came close to full existence—only, the mentalities whose level was playing jacks or craps, the men with the guns and their witch doctors, did not want mankind to know it. It was called *Capitalism*.

But on this issue, Comrade, you may claim a draw: your country does not know the meaning of that word—and, today, most people in our country do not know it, either.

Sincerely,
AYN RAND

7

Faith and Force: The Destroyers of the Modern World
1960

(A lecture delivered at Yale University on February 17, 1960; at Brooklyn College on April 4, 1960; and at Columbia University on May 5, 1960.)

If you want me to name in one sentence what is wrong with the modern world, I will say that never before has the world been clamoring so desperately for answers to crucial problems—and never before has the world been so frantically committed to the belief that no answers are possible.

Observe the peculiar nature of this contradiction and the peculiar emotional atmosphere of our age. There have been periods in history when men failed to find answers because they evaded the existence of the problems, pretended that nothing threatened them and denounced anyone who spoke of approaching disaster. This is not the predominant attitude of our age. Today, the voices proclaiming disaster are so fashionable a bromide that people are battered into apathy by their monotonous insistence; but the anxiety under that apathy is real. Consciously or subconsciously, intellectually or emotionally, most people today know that the world is in a terrible state and that it cannot continue on its present course much longer.

The existence of the problems is acknowledged, yet we

hear nothing but meaningless generalities and shameful evasions from our so-called intellectual leaders. Wherever you
look—whether in philosophical publications, or intellectual
magazines, or newspaper editorials or political speeches of
either party—you find the same mental attitude, made of two
characteristics: staleness and superficiality. People seem to
insist on talking—and on carefully saying nothing. The evasiveness, the dullness, the gray conformity of today's intellectual expressions sound like the voices of men under censorship—where no censorship exists. Never before has there
been an age characterized by such a grotesque combination of
qualities as *despair* and *boredom*.

You might say that this is the honest exhaustion of men who
have done their best in the struggle to find answers, and have
failed. But the dignity of an honestly helpless resignation is
certainly not the emotional atmosphere of our age. An honest
resignation would not be served or expressed by repeating the
same worn-out bromides over and over again, while going
through the motions of a quest. A man who is honestly convinced that he can find no answers, would not feel the need to
pretend that he is looking for them.

You might say that the explanation lies in our modern cynicism and that people fail to find answers because they really
don't care. It is true that people are cynical today, but this is
merely a symptom, not a cause. Today's cynicism has a special twist: we are dealing with cynics who *do* care—and the
ugly secret of our age lies in that which they do care about,
that which they are seeking.

The truth about the intellectual state of the modern world,
the characteristic peculiar to the twentieth century, which
distinguishes it from other periods of cultural crises, is the
fact that what people are seeking is *not* the answers to problems, but the *reassurance that no answers are possible*.

A friend of mine once said that today's attitude, paraphras-
ing the Bible, is: "Forgive me, Father, for I know not what
I'm doing—and please don't tell me."

Observe how noisily the modern intellectuals are seeking

solutions for problems—and how swiftly they blank out the existence of any theory or idea, past or present, that offers the lead to a solution. Observe that these modern relativists—with their credo of intellectual tolerance, of the open mind, of the anti-absolute—turn into howling dogmatists to denounce anyone who claims to possess knowledge. Observe that they tolerate anything, except certainty—and approve of anything, except values. Observe that they profess to love mankind, and drool with sympathy over any literary study of murderers, dipsomaniacs, drug addicts and psychotics, over any presentation of their loved object's depravity—and scream with anger when anyone dares to claim that man is *not* depraved. Observe that they profess to be moved by compassion for human suffering—and close their ears indignantly to any suggestion that man does not *have to* suffer.

What you see around you today, among modern intellectuals, is the grotesque spectacle of such attributes as militant uncertainty, crusading cynicism, dogmatic agnosticism, boastful self-abasement and self-righteous depravity. The two absolutes of today's non-absolutists are that ignorance consists of claiming knowledge, and that immorality consists of pronouncing moral judgments.

Now why would people want to cling to the conviction that doom, darkness, depravity and ultimate disaster are inevitable? Well, psychologists will tell you that when a man suffers from neurotic anxiety, he seizes upon any rationalization available to explain his fear to himself, and he clings to that rationalization in defiance of logic, reason, reality or any argument assuring him that the danger can be averted. He does not *want* it to be averted because the rationalization serves as a screen to hide from himself the real cause of his fear, the cause he does not dare to face.

Ladies and gentlemen, what you are seeing today is the neurotic anxiety of an entire culture. People do not want to find any answers to avert their danger: all they want, all they're looking for, is only some excuse to yell: "I couldn't help it!"

If certain centuries are to be identified by their dominant

characteristics, like the Age of Reason or the Age of Enlightenment, then ours is *the Age of Guilt*.

What *is* it that people dread—and what do they feel guilty of?

They dread the unadmitted knowledge that their culture is bankrupt. They feel guilty, because they know that *they* have brought it to bankruptcy and that they lack the courage to make a fresh start.

They dread the knowledge that they have reached the dead end of the traditional evasions of the centuries behind them, that the contradictions of Western civilization have caught up with them, that no compromises or middle-of-the-roads will work any longer and that the responsibility of resolving those contradictions by making a fundamental choice is theirs, now, today. They are temporizing, in order to evade the fact that we have to check our basic premises, or pay the price of all unresolved contradictions, which is: destruction.

The three values which men had held for centuries and which have now collapsed are: mysticism, collectivism, altrusim. Mysticism—as a cultural power—died at the time of the Renaissance. Collectivism—as a political ideal—died in World War II. As to altruism—it has never been alive. It is the poison of death in the blood of Western civilization, and men survived it only to the extent to which they neither believed nor practiced it. But it has caught up with them—and *that* is the killer which they now have to face and to defeat. *That* is the basic choice they have to make. If any civilization is to survive, it is the morality of altruism that men have to reject.

Some of you will recognize my next sentences. Yes, this *is* an age of moral crisis. Yes, you *are* bearing punishment for your evil. Your moral code has reached its climax, the blind alley at the end of its course. And if you wish to go on living, what you now need is not to *return* to morality, but to *discover* it.

What *is* morality? It is a code of values to guide man's

choices and actions—the choices which determine the *pur-pose* and the course of his life. It is a code by means of which he judges what is right or wrong, good or evil.

What is the moral code of altruism? The basic principle of altruism is that man has no right to exist for his own sake, that service to others is the only justification of his existence, and that self-sacrifice is his highest moral duty, virtue and value.

Do not confuse altruism with kindness, good will or respect for the rights of others. These are not primaries, but conse-quences, which, in fact, altruism makes impossible. The ir-reducible primary of altruism, the basic absolute, is *self-sacrifice*—which means: self-immolation, self-abnegation, self-denial, self-destruction—which means: the *self* as a standard of evil, the *selfless* as a standard of the good.

Do not hide behind such superficialities as whether you should or should not give a dime to a beggar. That is not the issue. The issue is whether you *do* or do *not* have the right to exist *without* giving him that dime. The issue is whether you must keep buying your life, dime by dime, from any beggar who might choose to approach you. The issue is whether the need of others is the first mortgage on your life and the moral purpose of your existence. The issue is whether man is to be regarded as a sacrificial animal. Any man of self-esteem will answer: "*No.*" Altruism says: "*Yes.*"

Now there is one word—a single word—which can blast the morality of altruism out of existence and which it cannot withstand—the word: "*Why?*" *Why* must man live for the sake of others? *Why* must he be a sacrificial animal? *Why* is that the good? There is no earthly reason for it—and, ladies and gentlemen, in the whole history of philosophy no *earthly* reason has ever been given.

It is only *mysticism* that can permit moralists to get away with it. It was mysticism, the *un*earthly, the supernatural, the irrational that has always been called upon to justify it—or, to be exact, to escape the necessity of justification. One does not justify the irrational, one just takes it on faith. What most moralists—and few of their victims—realize is that reason and altruism are incompatible. And *this* is the basic contradiction of Western civilization: reason versus altruism. This is the conflict that had to explode sooner or later.

The real conflict, of course, is reason versus mysticism. But if it weren't for the altruist morality, mysticism would have died when it did die—at the Renaissance—leaving no vampire to haunt Western culture. A "vampire" is supposed to be a dead creature that comes out of its grave only at night— only in the darkness—and drains the blood of the living. The description, applied to altruism, is exact.

Western civilization was the child and product of reason—via ancient Greece. In all other civilizations, reason has always been the menial servant—the handmaiden—of mysticism. You may observe the results. It is only Western culture that has ever been dominated—imperfectly, incompletely, precariously and at rare intervals—but still, dominated by reason. You may observe the results of that.

The conflict of reason versus mysticism is the issue of life or death—of freedom or slavery—of progress or stagnant brutality. Or, to put it another way, it is the conflict of consciousness versus unconsciousness.

Let us define our terms. What is reason? Reason is the faculty which perceives, identifies and integrates the material provided by man's senses. Reason integrates man's perceptions by means of forming abstractions or conceptions, thus raising man's knowledge from the *perceptual* level, which he shares with animals, to the *conceptual* level, which he alone can reach. The *method* which reason employs in this process is *logic*—and logic is the art of *non-contradictory identification*.

What is mysticism? Mysticism is the acceptance of allegations without evidence or proof, either apart from or *against* the evidence of one's senses and one's reason. Mysticism is the claim to some non-sensory, non-rational, non-definable, non-identifiable means of knowledge, such as "instinct," "intuition," "revelation," or any form of "just knowing."

Reason is the perception of reality, and rests on a single axiom: the Law of Identity.

Mysticism is the claim to the perception of some other reality—other than the one in which we live—whose definition is only that it is *not* natural, it is supernatural, and is to be perceived by some form of unnatural or supernatural means.

You realize, of course, that *epistemology*—the theory of knowledge—is the most complex branch of philosophy, which cannot be covered exhaustively in a single lecture. So I will not attempt to cover it. I will say only that those who wish a fuller discussion will find it in *Atlas Shrugged*. For the purposes of tonight's discussion, the definitions I have given you contain the *essence* of the issue, regardless of whose theory, argument or philosophy you choose to accept.

I will repeat: *Reason* is the faculty which perceives, identifies and integrates the material provided by man's senses. *Mysticism* is the claim to a non-sensory means of knowledge.

In Western civilization, the period ruled by mysticism is known as the Dark Ages and the Middle Ages. I will assume that you know the nature of that period and the state of human existence in those ages. The Renaissance broke the rule of the mystics. "Renaissance" means "rebirth." Few people today will care to remind you that it was a rebirth of *reason*—of man's mind.

In the light of what followed—most particularly, in the light of the industrial revolution—nobody can now take faith, or religion, or revelation, or any form of mysticism as his basic and exclusive guide to existence, not in the way it was taken in the Middle Ages. This does not mean that the Renaissance has automatically converted everybody to rationality; far from it. It means only that so long as a single automobile, a single skyscraper or a single copy of Aristotle's Logic remains in existence, nobody will be able to arouse men's hope, eagerness and joyous enthusiasm by telling them to ditch their mind and rely on mystic faith. This is why I said that mysticism, as a cultural power, is dead. Observe that in the attempts at a mystic revival today, it is not an appeal to life, hope and joy that the mystics are making, but an appeal to fear, doom and despair. "Give up, your mind is impotent, life is only a foxhole," is not a motto that can revive a culture.

Now, if you ask me to name the man most responsible for the present state of the world, the man whose influence has almost succeeded in destroying the achievements of the Renaissance—I will name Immanuel Kant. He was the philosopher who saved the morality of altruism, and who knew that what it had to be saved from was—reason.

This is not a mere hypothesis. It is a known historical fact that Kant's interest and purpose in philosophy was to save the morality of altruism, which could not survive without a mystic base. His metaphysics and his epistemology were devised for that purpose. He did not, of course, announce himself as a mystic—few of them have, since the Renaissance. He announced himself as a champion of reason—of *"pure"* reason.

There are two ways to destroy the power of a concept: one, by an open attack in open discussion—the other, by subversion, from the inside; that is: by subverting the meaning of the concept, setting up a straw man and then refuting it. Kant did the second. He did not attack reason—he merely constructed such a version of what *is* reason that it made mysticism look like plain, rational common sense by comparison. He did not deny the validity of reason—he merely claimed that reason is "limited," that it leads us to impossible contradictions, that everything we perceive is an illusion and that we can never perceive reality or "things as they are." He claimed, in effect, that the things we perceive are not real, *because* we perceive them.

A "straw man" is an odd metaphor to apply to such an enormous, cumbersome, ponderous construction as Kant's system of epistemology. Nevertheless, a straw man is what it was—and the doubts, the uncertainty, the skepticism that followed, skepticism about man's ability ever to know anything, were not, in fact, applicable to human consciousness, because it was not a human consciousness that Kant's robot represented. But philosophers accepted it as such. And while they cried that reason had been invalidated, they did not notice that reason had been pushed off the philosophical scene altogether and that the faculty they were arguing about was *not* reason.

No, Kant did not destroy reason; he merely did as thorough a job of undercutting as anyone could ever do.

If you trace the roots of all our current philosophies—such as Pragmatism, Logical Positivism, and all the rest of the neo-mystics who announce happily that you cannot *prove* that you exist—you will find that they all grew out of Kant.

As to Kant's version of the altruist morality, he claimed that it was derived from "pure reason," not from revelation—except that it rested on a special instinct for *duty*, a "categorical imperative" which one "just knows." *His* version of morality makes the Christian one sound like a healthy, cheerful, benevolent code of selfishness. Christianity merely told man to love his neighbor as himself; that's not exactly rational—but at least it does not forbid man to love himself. What Kant propounded was full, total, abject selflessness: he held that an action is moral *only* if you perform it out of a sense of duty and derive no benefit from it of any kind, neither material nor spiritual; if you derive any benefit, your action is not moral any longer. *This* is the ultimate form of demanding that man turn himself into a "shmoo"—the mystic little animal of the Li'l Abner comic strip, that went around seeking to be eaten by somebody.

It is Kant's version of altruism that is generally accepted today, not practiced—who can practice it?—but guiltily accepted. It is Kant's version of altruism that people, who have never heard of Kant, profess when they equate self-interest with evil. It is Kant's version of altruism that's working whenever people are afraid to admit the pursuit of any personal pleasure or gain or motive—whenever men are afraid to confess that they are seeking their own happiness—whenever businessmen are afraid to say that they are making profits—whenever the victims of an advancing dictatorship are afraid to assert their "selfish" rights.

The ultimate monument to Kant and to the whole altruist morality is Soviet Russia.

If you want to prove to yourself the power of ideas and, particularly, of morality—the intellectual history of the nineteenth century would be a good example to study. The greatest, unprecedented, undreamed of events and achievements were taking place before men's eyes—but men did not see them and did not understand their meaning, as they do not understand it to this day. I am speaking of the industrial revolution, of the United States and of capitalism. For the first time in history, men gained control over physical nature and threw off the control of men over men—that is: men discovered science and political freedom. The creative energy, the abundance, the wealth, the rising standard of living for *every* level of the population were such that the nineteenth century looks like a fiction-Utopia, like a blinding burst of sunlight, in the drab progression of most of human history. If life on earth is one's standard of value, then the nineteenth century moved mankind forward more than all the other centuries combined.

Did anyone appreciate it? Does anyone appreciate it now? Has anyone identified the causes of that historical miracle?

They did not and have not. What blinded them? The morality of altruism.

Let me explain this. There are, fundamentally, only two causes of the progress of the nineteenth century—the same two causes which you will find at the root of any happy, benevolent, progressive era in human history. One cause is psychological, the other existential—or: one pertains to man's consciousness, the other to the physical conditions of his existence. The first is *reason*, the second is *freedom*. And when I say *"freedom,"* I do not mean poetic sloppiness, such as "freedom from want" or "freedom from fear" or "freedom from the necessity of earning a living." I mean *"freedom from compulsion*—freedom from rule by *physical force."* Which means: *political* freedom.

These two—reason and freedom—are corollaries, and their relationship is reciprocal: when men are rational, freedom wins; when men are free, reason wins.

Their antagonists are: *faith* and *force*. These, also, are corollaries: every period of history dominated by mysticism, was a period of statism, of dictatorship, of tyranny. Look at the Middle Ages—and look at the political systems of today.

The nineteenth century was the ultimate product and expression of the intellectual trend of the Renaissance and the Age of Reason, which means: of a predominantly Aristotelian philosophy. And, for the first time in history, it created a new economic system, the necessary corollary of political freedom, a system of free trade on a free market: *capitalism.*

No, it was not a full, perfect, unregulated, totally laissez-faire capitalism—as it should have been. Various degrees of government interference and control still remained, even in America—and *this* is what led to the eventual destruction of capitalism. But the extent to which certain countries were free was the exact extent of their economic progress. America, the freest, achieved the most.

Never mind the low wages and the harsh living conditions of the early years of capitalism. They were all that the national economies of the time could afford. Capitalism did not create poverty—it inherited it. Compared to the centuries of precapitalist starvation, the living conditions of the poor in the early years of capitalism were the first chance the poor had ever had to survive. As proof—the enormous growth of the European population during the nineteenth century, a growth of over 300 percent, as compared to the previous growth of something like 3 percent per century.

Now why was this not appreciated? Why did capitalism, the truly magnificent benefactor of mankind, arouse nothing but resentment, denunciations and hatred, then and now? Why did the so-called defenders of capitalism keep apologizing for it, then and now? Because, ladies and gentlemen, *capitalism and altruism are incompatible*.

Make no mistake about it—and tell it to your Republican friends: capitalism and altruism cannot coexist in the same man or in the same society.

Tell it to anyone who attempts to justify capitalism on the ground of the "public good" or the "general welfare" or "service to society" or the benefit it brings to the poor. All these things are true, but they are the by-products, the secondary consequences of capitalism—not its goal, purpose or moral justification. The moral justification of capitalism is man's right to exist for his own sake, neither sacrificing himself to others nor sacrificing others to himself; it is the recognition that man—every man—is an end in himself, not a means to the ends of others, not a sacrificial animal serving anyone's need.

This is implicit in the function of capitalism, but, until now, it has never been stated explicity, in *moral* terms. Why not? Because this is the base of a morality diametrically opposed to the morality of altruism which, to this day, people are afraid to challenge.

There is a tragic, twisted sort of compliment to mankind involved in this issue: in spite of all their irrationalities, inconsistencies, hypocrisies and evasions, the majority of men will not act, in major issues, without a sense of being *morally right* and will not oppose the morality they have accepted. They will break it, they will cheat on it, but they will not oppose it; and when they break it, they take the blame on themselves. The power of morality is the greatest of all intellectual powers—and mankind's tragedy lies in the fact that the vicious moral code men have accepted destroys them by means of the best within them.

So long as altruism was their moral ideal, men had to regard capitalism as immoral; capitalism certainly does not and cannot work on the principle of selfless service and sacrifice. This was the reason why the majority of the nineteenth-century intellectuals regarded capitalism as a vulgar, uninspiring, materialistic necessity of this earth, and continued to long for their unearthly moral ideal. From the start, while capitalism was creating the splendor of its achievements, creating it in silence, unacknowledged and undefended (*morally* undefended), the intellectuals were moving in greater and greater numbers towards a new dream: socialism.

Just as a small illustration of how ineffectual a defense of capitalism was offered by its most famous advocates, let me mention that the British socialists, the Fabians, were predominantly students and admirers of John Stuart Mill and Jeremy Bentham.

The socialists had a certain kind of logic on their side: if the collective sacrifice of all to all *is* the moral ideal, then they wanted to establish this ideal in practice, here and on this earth. The arguments that socialism would not and could not work, did not stop them: neither has altruism ever worked, but this has not caused men to stop and question it. Only *reason* can ask such questions—and *reason*, they were told on all sides, has nothing to do with morality, morality lies outside the realm of reason, no *rational* morality can ever be defined.

The fallacies and contradictions in the economic theories of socialism were exposed and refuted time and time again, in the nineteenth century as well as today. This did not and does not stop anyone: it is not an issue of economics, but of morality. The intellectuals and the so-called idealists were determined to make socialism work. How? By that magic means of all irrationalists: *somehow*.

It was not the tycoons of big business, it was not the labor unions, it was not the working classes, it was the intellectuals who reversed the trend toward political freedom and revived the doctrines of the absolute State, of totalitarian government rule, of the government's right to control the lives of the citizens in any manner it pleases. This time, it was not in the name of the "divine right of kings," but in the name of the divine right of the masses. The basic principle was the same: the right to enforce at the point of a gun the moral doctrines of whoever happens to seize control of the machinery of government.

There are only two means by which men can deal with one another: guns or logic. Force or persuasion. Those who know that they cannot win by means of logic, have always resorted to guns.

Well, ladies and gentlemen, the socialists got their dream. They got it in the twentieth century and they got it in triplicate, plus a great many lesser carbon copies; they got it in every possible form and variant, so that now there can be no mistake about its nature: Soviet Russia—Nazi Germany—Socialist England.

This was the collapse of the modern intellectuals' most cherished tradition. It was World War II that destroyed collectivism as a political ideal. Oh, yes, people still mouth its slogans, by routine, by social conformity and by default—but it is *not* a moral crusade any longer. It is an ugly, horrifying reality—and part of the modern intellectuals' guilt is the knowledge that *they* have created it. They have seen for themselves the bloody slaughterhouse which they had once greeted as a noble experiment—Soviet Russia. They have seen Nazi Germany—and they know that "Nazi" means "National Socialism." Perhaps the worst blow to them, the greatest disillusionment, was Socialist England: here was their literal dream, a bloodless socialism, where force was not used for murder, only for expropriation, where lives were not taken, only the products, the meaning and the future of lives, here was a country that had not been murdered, but had voted itself into suicide. Most of the modern intellectuals, even the more evasive ones, have now understood what socialism—or any form of political and economic collectivism—actually means.

Today, their perfunctory advocacy of collectivism is as fee-

ble, futile and evasive as the alleged conservatives' defense of
capitalism. The fire and the moral fervor have gone out of it.
And when you hear the liberals mumble that Russia is not
really socialistic, or that it was all Stalin's fault, or that
socialism never had a *real* chance in England, or that what
they advocate is something that's different *somehow*—you
know that you are hearing the voices of men who haven't a leg
to stand on, men who are reduced to some vague hope that
"somehow, *my* gang would have done it better."

The secret dread of modern intellectuals, liberals and conservatives alike, the unadmitted terror at the root of their anxiety, which all of their current irrationalities are intended to
stave off and to disguise, is the unstated knowledge that
Soviet Russia is the full, actual, literal, consistent embodiment of the morality of altruism, that Stalin did *not* corrupt a
noble ideal, that this is the only way altruism has to be or can
ever be practiced. If service and self-sacrifice are a moral
ideal, and if the "selfishness" of human nature prevents men
from leaping into sacrificial furnaces, there is no reason—no
reason that a mystic moralist could name—why a dictator
should not push them in at the point of bayonets—for their
own good, or the good of humanity, or the good of posterity,
or the good of the latest bureaucrat's latest five-year plan.
There is no reason that they can name to oppose *any* atrocity.
The value of a man's life? His right to exist? His right to pursue his own happiness? These are concepts that belong to
individualism and capitalism—to the antithesis of the altruist
morality.

Twenty years ago, the conservatives were uncertain, evasive, morally disarmed before the aggressive moral self-
righteousness of the liberals. Today, *both* are uncertain,
evasive, morally disarmed before the aggressiveness of the
communists. It is not a *moral* aggressiveness any longer, it is
the plain aggressiveness of a thug—but what disarms the
modern intellectuals is the secret realization that a *thug* is the
inevitable, ultimate and *only* product of their cherished morality.

I have said that faith and force are corollaries, and that mysticism will always lead to the rule of brutality. The cause of it is contained in the very nature of mysticism. *Reason* is the only *objective* means of communication and of understanding among men; when men deal with one another by means of reason, reality is their *objective* standard and frame of reference. But when men claim to possess supernatural means of knowledge, no persuasion, communication or understanding are impossible. Why do we kill wild animals in the jungle? Because no other way of dealing with them is open to us. And *that* is the state to which mysticism reduces mankind—a state where, in case of disagreement, men have no recourse except to physical violence. And more: no man or mystical elite can hold a whole society subjugated to their arbitrary assertions, edicts and whims, without the use of force. Anyone who resorts to the formula: "It's so, because I say so," will have to reach for a gun, sooner or later. Communists, like all materialists, are neo-mystics: it does not matter whether one rejects the mind in favor of revelations or in favor of conditioned reflexes. The basic premise and the results are the same.

Such is the nature of the evil which modern intellectuals have helped to let loose in the world—and such is the nature of their guilt.

Now take a look at the state of the world. The signs and symptoms of the Dark Ages are rising again all over the earth. Slave labor, executions without trial, torture chambers, concentration camps, mass slaughter—all the things which the capitalism of the nineteenth century had abolished in the civilized world, are now brought back by the rule of the neo-mystics.

Look at the state of our intellectual life. In philosophy, the climax of the Kantian version of reason has brought us to the point where alleged philosophers, forgetting the existence of dictionaries and grammar primers, run around studying such questions as: "What do we mean when we say 'The cat is on the mat'?"—while other philosophers proclaim that nouns are an illusion, but such terms as "if-then," "but" and "or" have profound philosophical significance—while still others toy with the idea of an "index of prohibited words" and desire to place on it such words as—I quote—"entity—essence—mind—matter—reality—thing."

In psychology, one school holds that man, by nature, is a helpless, guilt-ridden, instinct-driven automaton—while another school objects that this is not true, because there is no scientific evidence to prove that man is conscious.

In literature, man is presented as a mindless cripple, inhabiting garbage cans. In art, people announce that they do not paint objects, they paint *emotions*. In youth movements—if that's what it can be called—young men attract attention by openly announcing that they are "beat."

The spirit of it all, both the cause of it and the final climax, is contained in a quotation which I am going to read to you. I will preface it by saying that in *Atlas Shrugged* I stated that the world is being destroyed by mysticism and altruism, which are anti-man, anti-mind and anti-life. You have undoubtedly heard me being accused of exaggeration. I shall now read to you an excerpt from the paper of a professor, published by an alumni faculty seminar of a prominent university.

"Perhaps in the future reason will cease to be important. Perhaps for guidance in time of trouble, people will turn not to human thought, but to the human capacity for suffering. Not the universities with their thinkers, but the places and people in distress, the inmates of asylums and concentration camps, the helpless decision makers in bureaucracy and the helpless soldiers in foxholes—these will be the ones to lighten man's way, to refashion his knowledge of disaster into something creative. We may be entering a new age. Our heroes may not be intellectual giants like Isaac Newton or Albert Einstein, but victims like Anne Frank, who will show us a greater miracle than thought. They will teach us how to endure—how to create good in the midst of evil and how to nurture love in the presence of death. Should this happen, however, the university will still have its place. Even the intellectual man can be an example of creative suffering."

Observe that we are not to question "the helpless decision makers in bureaucracy"—we are not to discover that *they* are the cause of the concentration camps, of the foxholes and of victims like Anne Frank—we are not to help such victims, we are merely to feel suffering and to learn to suffer some more—we can't help it, the helpless bureaucrats can't help it, nobody can help it—the inmates of asylums will guide us, not intellectual giants—suffering is the supreme value, not reason.

This, ladies and gentlemen, is cultural bankruptcy.

Since *"challenge"* is your slogan, I will say that if you are looking for a challenge, you are facing the greatest one in history. A *moral* revolution is the most difficult, the most demanding, the most radical form of rebellion, but that is the task to be done today, if you choose to accept it. When I say "radical," I mean it in its literal and reputable sense: fundamental. Civilization does not have to perish. The brutes are winning only by default. But in order to fight them to the finish and with full rectitude, it is the altruist morality that you have to reject.

Now, if you want to know what my philosophy, Objectivism, offers you—I will give you a brief indication. I will not attempt, in one lecture, to present my whole philosophy. I will merely indicate to you what I mean by a rational morality of self-interest, what I mean by the opposite of altruism. what kind of morality is possible to man and why. I will preface it by reminding you that most philosophers—especially most of them today—have always claimed that morality is outside the province of reason, that no rational morality can be defined, and that man has no *practical* need of morality. Morality, they claim, is not a necessity of man's existence, but only some sort of mystical luxury or arbitrary social whim; in fact, they claim, nobody can prove why we should be moral at all; in reason, they claim, there's no reason to be moral.

I cannot summarize for you the essence and the base of my morality any better than I did it in *Atlas Shrugged*. So, rather than attempt to paraphrase it, I will read to you the passages from *Atlas Shrugged* which pertain to the nature, the base and the proof of my morality.

"Man's mind is his basic tool of survival. Life is given to him, survival is not. His body is given to him, its sustenance is not. His mind is given to him, its content is not. To remain alive, he must act, and before he can act he must know the nature and purpose of his action. He cannot obtain his food without a knowledge of food and of the way to obtain it. He cannot dig a ditch—or build a cyclotron—without a knowledge of his aim and of the means to achieve it. To remain alive, he must think.

"But to think is an act of choice. The key to what you so recklessly call 'human nature,' the open secret you live with, yet dread to name, is the fact that *man is a being of volitional consciousness*. Reason does not work automatically; thinking is not a mechanical process; the connections of logic are not made by instinct. The function of your stomach, lungs or heart is automatic; the function of your mind is not. In any hour and issue of your life, you are free to think or to evade that effort. But you are not free to escape from your nature, from the fact that *reason* is your means of survival—so that for *you*, who are a human being, the question 'to be or not to be' is the question 'to think or not to think.'

"A being of volitional consciousness has no automatic course of behavior. He needs a code of values to guide his actions. 'Value' is that which one acts to gain and keep, 'virtue' is the action by which one gains and keeps it. 'Value' presupposes an answer to the question: of value to whom and for what? 'Value' presupposes a standard, a purpose and the necessity of action in the face of an alternative. Where there are no alternatives, no values are possible.

"There is only one fundamental alternative in the universe: existence or non-existence—and it pertains to a single class of entities: to living organisms. The existence of inanimate matter is unconditional, the existence of life is not: it depends on a specific course of action. Matter is indestructible, it changes its forms, but it cannot cease to exist. It is only a living organism that faces a constant alternative: the issue of life or death. Life is a process of self-sustaining and self-generated action. If an organism fails in that action, it dies; its chemical elements remain, but its life goes out of existence. It is only the concept of 'Life' that makes the concept of 'Value' possible. It is only to a living entity that things can be good or evil.

"A plant must feed itself in order to live; the sunlight, the water, the chemicals it needs are the values its nature has set it to pursue; its life is the standard of value directing its actions. But a plant has no choice of action; there are alternatives in the conditions it encounters, but there is no alternative in its function: it acts automatically to further its life, it cannot act for its own destruction.

"An animal is equipped for sustaining its life; its senses provide it with an automatic code of action, an automatic knowledge of what is good for it or evil. It has no power to extend its knowledge or to evade it. In conditions where its knowledge proves inadequate, it dies. But so long as it lives, it acts on its knowledge, with automatic safety and no power of choice, it is unable to ignore its own good, unable to decide to choose the evil and act as its own destroyer.

"Man has no automatic code of survival. His particular distinction from all other living species is the necessity to act in the face of alternatives by means of *volitional choice*. He has no automatic knowledge of what is good for him or evil, what values his life depends on, what course of action it requires. Are you prattling about an instinct of self-preservation? An *instinct* of self-preservation is precisely what man does not possess. An 'instinct' is an unerring and automatic form of knowledge. A desire is not an instinct. A desire to live does not give you the knowledge required for living. And even man's desire to live is not automatic: your secret evil today is that *that* is the desire you do not hold. Your fear of death is not a love for life and will not give you the knowledge needed to keep it. Man must obtain his knowledge and choose his actions by a process of thinking, which nature will not force him to perform. Man has the power to act as his own destroyer— and that is the way he has acted through most of his history. . . .

"Man has been called a rational being, but rationality is a matter of choice—and the alternative his nature offers him is: rational being or suicidal animal. Man has to be man—by choice; he has to hold his life as a value—by choice; he has to learn to sustain it—by choice; he has to discover the values it requires and practice his virtues—by choice.

"A code of values accepted by choice is a code of morality.

"Whoever you are, you who are hearing me now, I am speaking to whatever living remnant is left uncorrupted within you, to the remnant of the human, to your *mind*, and I say: There *is* a morality of reason, a morality proper to man, and *Man's Life* is its standard of value.

"All that which is proper to the life of a rational being is the good; all that which destroys it is the evil.

"Man's life, as required by his nature, is not the life of a mindless brute, of a looting thug or a mooching mystic, but the life of a thinking being—not life by means of force or fraud, but life by means of achievement—not survival at any price, since there's only one price that pays for man's survival: reason.

"Man's life is the *standard* of morality, but your own life is its *purpose*. If existence on earth is your goal, you must choose your actions and values by the standard of that which is proper to man—for the purpose of preserving, fulfilling and enjoying the irreplaceable value which is your life."

This, ladies and gentlemen, is what Objectivism offers you. And when you make your choice, I would like you to remember that the only alternative to it is communist slavery. The "middle-of-the-road" is like an unstable, radioactive element that can last only so long—and its time is running out. There is no more chance for a middle-of-the-road.

The issue will be decided, not in the middle, but between the two consistent extremes. It's Objectivism or communism. It's a rational morality based on man's right to exist—or altruism, which means: slave labor camps under the rule of such masters as you might have seen on the screens of your TV last year. If that is what you prefer, the choice is yours.

But don't make that choice blindly. You, the young generation, have been betrayed in the most dreadful way by your elders—by those liberals of the thirties who armed Soviet Russia, and destroyed the last remnants of American capitalism. All that they have to offer you now is foxholes, or the kind of attitude expressed in the quotation on "creative suffering" that I read to you. This is all that you will hear on any side: "Give up before you have started. Give up before you have tried." And to make sure that you give up, they do not even let you know what the nineteenth century was. I hope this may not be fully true here, but I have met too many young people in universities, who have no clear idea, not even in the most primitive terms, of what capitalism really is. They do not let you know what the theory of capitalism is, nor how it worked in practice, nor what was its actual history.

Don't give up too easily; don't sell out your life. If you make an effort to inquire on your own, you will find that it is not necessary to give up and that the allegedly powerful monster now threatening us will run like a rat at the first sign of a human step.

It is not physical danger that threatens you, and it is not military considerations that make our so-called intellectual leaders tell you that we are doomed. That is merely their rationalization. The real danger is that communism is an enemy whom they do not dare to fight on moral grounds, and it can be fought only on moral grounds.

This, then, is the choice. Think it over. Consider the subject, check your premises, check past history and find out whether it is true that men can never be free. It isn't true, because they have been. Find out what made it possible. See for yourself. And then if you are convinced—rationally convinced—then let us save the world together. We still have time.

To quote Galt once more, such is the choice before you. Let your mind and your love of existence decide.

8

From the Horse's Mouth
1975

While recovering from [an] illness, I had a chance to catch up
on some reading I had wanted to do for a long time. Opening
one interesting book, I almost leaped out of bed. I read some
statements which shocked me much more profoundly than
any of today's pronouncements in the news magazines or on
the Op-Ed page of *The New York Times*. I had been reporting
on some of those journalistic writings occasionally, as a warning against the kinds of intellectual dangers (and booby traps)
they represented. But they looked like cheap little graffiti
compared to the sweep of wholesale destruction presented in
a few sentences of that book.

Just as, at the end of *Atlas Shrugged*, Francisco saw a
radiant future contained in a few words, so I saw the long,
dismal, slithering disintegration of the twentieth century held
implicitly in a few sentences. I wanted to scream a warning,
but it was too late: that book had been published in 1898.
Written by Friedrich Paulsen, it is entitled *Immanuel
Kant: His Life and Doctrine*.

Professor Paulsen is a devoted Kantian; but, judging by his
style of writing, he is an honest commentator—in the sense
that he does not try to disguise what he is saying: "There are
three attitudes of the mind towards reality which lay claim to
truth—Religion, Philosophy, and Science. . . . In general,

philosophy occupies an intermediate place between science
and religion. . . . The history of philosophy shows that its task
consists simply in mediating between science and religion. It
seeks to unite knowledge and faith, and in this way to restore
the unity of the mental life. . . . As in the case of the individual, it mediates between the head and the heart, so in society
it prevents science and religion from becoming entirely
strange and indifferent to each other, and hinders also the
mental life of the people from being split up into a faith-hating
science and a science-hating faith or superstition." (New
York, Ungar, 1963, pp. 1–2.)

This means that science and mystic fantasies are equally
valid as methods of gaining knowledge; that reason and
feelings—the worst kinds of feelings: fear, cowardice, self-
abnegation—have equal value as tools of cognition; and that
philosophy, "the love of wisdom," is a contemptible middle-
of-the-roader whose task is to seek a compromise—a
détente—between truth and falsehood.

Professor Paulsen's statement is an accurate presentation
of Kant's attitude, but it is not Kant that shocked me, it is
Paulsen. Philosophic system-builders, such as Kant, set the
trends of a nation's culture (for good or evil), but it is the
average practitioners who serve as a barometer of a trend's
success or failure. What shocked me was the fact that a modest commentator would start his book with a statement of that
kind. I thought (no, *hoped*) that in the nineteenth century a
man upholding the cognitive pretensions of religion to an
equal footing with science, would have been laughed off any
serious lectern. I was mistaken. Here was Professor Paulsen
casually proclaiming—in the nineteenth century—that philosophy is the handmaiden of theology.

Existentially (i.e., in regard to conditions of living, scale of
achievement, and rapidity of progress), the nineteenth century was the best in Western history. Philosophically, it was
one of the worst. People thought they had entered an era of
inexhaustible radiance; but it was merely the sunset of Aris-

totle's influence, which the philosophers were extinguishing. If you have felt an occasional touch of wistful envy at the thought that there was a time when men went to the opening of a new play, and what they saw was not *Hair* or *Grease*, but *Cyrano de Bergerac*, which opened in 1897—take a wider look. I wish that, borrowing from Victor Hugo's *Notre Dame de Paris*, someone had pointed to the Paulsen book, then to the play, and said: "*This* will kill *that*." But there was no such person.

I do not mean to imply that the Paulsen book had so fateful an influence; I am citing the book as a symptom, not a cause. The cause and the influence were Kant's. Paulsen merely demonstrates how thoroughly that malignancy had spread through Western culture at the dawn of the twentieth century.

The conflict between knowledge and faith, Paulsen explains, "has extended through the entire history of human thought" (p. 4) and Kant's great achievement, he claims, consisted in reconciling them. " . . . the critical [Kantian] philosophy solves the old problem of the relation of knowledge and faith. Kant is convinced that by properly fixing the limits of each he has succeeded in furnishing a basis for an honorable and enduring peace between them. Indeed, the significance and vitality of his philosophy will rest principally upon this. . . . it is [his philosophy's] enduring merit to have drawn for the first time, with a firm hand and in clear outline, the dividing line between knowledge and faith. This gives to knowledge what belongs to it—the entire world of phenomena for free investigation; it conserves, on the other hand, to faith its eternal right to the interpretation of life and of the world from the standpoint of value." (P. 6.)

This means that the ancient mind-body dichotomy—which the rise of science had been healing slowly, as men were learning how to live on earth—was revived by Kant, and man was split in two, not with old daggers, but with a meat-ax. It means that Kant gave to science the entire material world (which, however, was to be regarded as unreal), and left ("conserved") one thing to faith: *morality*. If you are not entirely sure of which side would win in a division of that kind, look around you today.

Material objects as such have neither value nor disvalue; they acquire value-significance only in regard to a living being—particularly, in regard to serving or hindering man's goals. Man's goals and values are determined by his moral code. The Kantian division allows man's reason to conquer the material world, but eliminates reason from the choice of the goals for which material achievements are to be used. Man's goals, actions, choices and values—according to Kant—are to be determined irrationally, i.e., by faith.

In fact, man needs morality in order to discover the right way to live on earth. In Kant's system, morality is severed from any concern with man's existence. In fact, man's every problem, goal or desire involves the material world. In Kant's system, morality has nothing to do with this world, nor with reason, nor with science, but comes—via feelings—from another, unknowable, "noumenal" dimension.

If you share the error prevalent among modern businessmen, and tend to believe that nonsense such as Kant's is merely a verbal pastime for mentally unemployed academicians, that it is too preposterous to be of any practical consequence—look again at the opening quotation from Professor Paulsen's book. Yes, it is nonsense and vicious nonsense—but, by grace of the above attitude, it has conquered the world.

There is more than one way of accepting and spreading a philosophic theory. The guiltiest group, which has contributed the most to the victory of Kantianism, is the group that professes to despise it: the scientists. Adopting one variant or another of Logical Positivism (a Kantian offshoot), they rejected Kant's noumenal dimension, but agreed that the material world is unreal, that reality is unknowable, and that science does not deal with facts, but with constructs. They rejected any concern with morality, agreeing that morality is beyond the power of reason or science and must be surrendered to subjective whims.

Now observe the breach between the physical sciences and the humanities. Although the progress of theoretical science is slowing down (by reason of a flawed epistemology, among other things), the momentum of the Aristotelian past is so great that science is still moving forward, while the humanities are bankrupt. Spatially, science is reaching beyond the solar system—while, temporally, the humanities are sliding back into the primeval ooze. Science is landing men on the moon and monitoring radio emissions from other galaxies— while astrology is the growing fashion here on earth; while courses in astrology and black magic are given in colleges; while horoscopes are sent galloping over the airwaves of a great scientific achievement, television.

Scientists are willing to produce nuclear weapons for the thugs who rule Soviet Russia—just as they were willing to produce military rockets for the thugs who ruled Nazi Germany. There was a story in the press that during the first test of an atom bomb in New Mexico, Robert Oppenheimer, head of the Los Alamos group who had produced the bomb, carried a four-leaf clover in his pocket. More recently, there was the story of Edgar Mitchell, an astronaut who conducted ESP experiments on his way to the moon. There was the story of a space scientist who is a believer in occultism and black magic.

Such is the "honorable and enduring peace" between knowledge and faith, achieved by the Kantian philosophy.

Now what if one of those men gained political power and had to consider the question of whether to unleash a nuclear war? As a Kantian, he would have to make his decision, not on the grounds of reason, knowledge and facts, but on the urgings of faith, i.e., of feelings, i.e., on whim.

There are many examples of Kantianism ravaging the field of today's politics in slower, but equally lethal, ways. Observe the farce of inflation versus "compassion." The policies of welfare statism have brought this country (and the whole civilized world) to the edge of economic bankruptcy, the forerunner of which is inflation—yet pressure groups are demanding larger and larger handouts to the nonproductive, and screaming that their opponents lack "compassion." Compassion as such cannot grow a blade of grass, let alone of wheat. Of what use is the "compassion" of a man (or a country) who is broke—i.e., who has consumed his resources, is unable to produce, and has nothing to give away?

If you cannot understand how anyone can evade reality to such an extent, you have not understood Kantianism. "Compassion" is a moral term, and moral issues—to the thoroughly Kantianized intellectuals—are independent of material reality. The task of morality—they believe—is to make demands, with which the world of material "phenomena" has to comply; and, since that material world is unreal, its problems or shortages cannot affect the success of moral goals, which are dictated by the "noumenal" real reality.

Dear businessmen, why do you worry about a half-percent of interest on a loan or investment—when *your* money supports the schools where those notions are taught to your children?

No, most people do not know Kant's theories, nor care. What they do know is that their teachers and intellectual leaders have some deep, tricky justification—the trickier, the better—for the net result of all such theories, which the average person welcomes: "Be rational, except when you don't feel like it."

Note the motivation of those who accepted the grotesque irrationality of Kant's system in the first place—as declared by his admirer, Professor Paulsen: "There is indeed no doubt that the great influence which Kant exerted upon his age was due just to the fact that he appeared as a deliverer from unendurable suspense. The old view regarding the claims of the feelings and the understanding on reality had been more and more called in question during the second half of the

eighteenth century. . . . Science seemed to demand the renunciation of the old faith. *On the other hand, the heart still
clung to it.* . . . Kant showed a way of escape from the dilemma. His philosophy made it possible to be at once a can-
did thinker and an honest man of faith. For that, thousands of
hearts have thanked him with passionate devotion." (Pp. 6–7;
emphasis added—no other comment is necessary.)

Philosophy is a necessity for a rational being: philosophy is
the foundation of science, the organizer of man's mind, the
integrator of his knowledge, the programmer of his subconscious, the selector of his values. To set philosophy against
reason, i.e., against man's power of cognition, to turn philosophy into an apologist for and a protector of superstition—is
such a crime against humanity that no modern atrocities can
equal it: it is the cause of modern atrocities.

If Paulsen is representative of the nineteenth century, the
twentieth never had a chance. But if men grasp the source of
their destruction—if they dedicate themselves to the greatest
of all crusades: a crusade for the absolutism of reason—the
twenty-first century will have a chance once more.

9

Kant Versus Sullivan
1970

In the title essay of *For the New Intellectual,* discussing modern philosophy's concerted attack on man's mind, I referred to the philosophers' division into two camps, "those who claimed that man obtains his knowledge of the world by deducing it exclusively from concepts, which come from inside his head and are not derived from the perception of physical facts (the Rationalists)—and those who claimed that man obtains his knowledge from experience, which was held to mean: by direct perception of immediate facts, with no recourse to concepts (the Empiricists). To put it more simply: those who joined the Witch Doctor, by abandoning reality— and those who clung to reality, by abandoning their mind."

For the past several decades, the dominant fashion among academic philosophers was empiricism—a militant kind of empiricism. Its exponents dismissed philosophical problems by declaring that fundamental concepts—such as existence, entity, identity, reality—are meaningless; they declared that concepts are arbitrary social conventions and that only sense data, "unprocessed" by conceptualization, represent a valid or "scientific" form of knowledge; and they debated such issues as whether man may claim with certainty that he perceives a tomato or only a patch of red.

Sooner or later, it had to become apparent that cooks, let

100

alone scientists, do something with that patch of red by some means which is not direct and immediate sensory perception. And—as in any field of activity ruled by fashion, not facts—the philosophical pendulum began to swing to the other side of the same coin.

Accepting the empiricists' basic premise that concepts have no necessary relation to sense data, a new breed of rationalists is floating up to the surface of the academic mainstream, declaring that *scientific* knowledge does not require any sense data at all (which means: that man does not need his sense organs).

If the empiricist trend—with its glib, glossy, up-to-the-minute modernism of quasi-technological jargon and pseudo-mathematical equations—may be regarded as the miniskirt period of philosophical fashion, then the rationalist revival brings in the maxiskirt period, an old, bedraggled, pavement-sweeping, unsanitary maxiskirt, as unsuited for climbing into a modern car or airplane (or for any kind of climbing) as its equivalent in the field of ladies' garments.

How low this new fashion can fall and what its hemline can pick up may be observed in the November 20, 1969 issue of *The Journal of Philosophy*—a magazine regarded as the most "prestigious" of the American journals of the philosophic profession, published at Columbia University.

The lead article is entitled "Science Without Experience" by Paul K. Feyerabend of the University of California and London University. (Remember that what is meant here by "experience" is the evidence of man's senses.) The article declares: "It must be possible to imagine a natural science without sensory elements, and it should perhaps also be possible to indicate how such a science is going to work.

"Now experience is said to enter science at three points: testing; assimilation of the results of test; understanding of theories."

Whoever is said to have said this, did not include *observation* among his three points, implying that science begins with "testing." If so, what does one "test"? No answer is given.

"It is easily seen that experience is needed at none of the three points just mentioned.

"To start with, it does not need to enter the process of *test:* we can put a theory into a computer, provide the computer with suitable instruments directed by him (her, it) so that relevant measurements are made which return to the computer, leading there to an evaluation of the theory. The computer can give a simple yes-no response from which a scientist may *learn* whether or not a theory has been confirmed without having in any way *participated* in the test (i.e., without having been subjected to some relevant *experience*)." (All italics in original.)

One might feel, at this point, that one's brain is being paralyzed by too many questions. Just to name a few of them: Who built the computer, and was he able to do it without sensory experience? Who programs the computer and by what means? Who provides the computer with "suitable instruments" and how does he know what is suitable? How does the scientist know that the object he is dealing with is a computer?

But such questions become unnecessary if one remembers two fallacies identified in Objectivist epistemology, which can help, not to elucidate, but to account for that paragraph: the fallacies of context-dropping and of "concept-stealing"—which the article seems to flaunt as valid epistemological methods, proceeding, as it does, from the basic premise that the computers are here.

This still leaves the question: by what means does the scientist learn the computer's verdict? To this one, the article's author provides an answer—which is point 2 of his theory of knowledge.

"*Usually* such information travels via the senses, giving rise to distinct sensations. But this is not always the case. Subliminal perception [of what?] leads to reactions directly, and without sensory data. Latent learning leads to memory traces [of what?] directly, and without sensory data. Posthypnotic suggestion [by whom and by what means?] leads to (belated) reactions directly, and without sensory data. In addition there is the whole unexplored field of telepathic phenomena."

Apparently in order not to let this sink in fully, the article's next sentence continues the paragraph uninterrupted. But I have interrupted it precisely to let this sink in fully.

The paragraph's next sentence is: "I am not asserting that the natural sciences as we know them today could be built on these phenomena alone and could be freed from sensations entirely. Considering the peripheral nature of the phenomena and considering also how little attention is given to them in our education (we are not trained to use effectively our ability for latent learning) this would be both unwise and impractical. But the point is made that sensations are not *necessary* for the business of science and that they occur for practical reasons only."

What would be the meaning or value of an *impractical* process of consciousness? Since the practice of the faculty of consciousness is to give us information about reality, an impractical process would be one that fails in this function. Yet it is some such process that the author advocates as superior or, at least, as equal to the processes of sensory experience—and urges our educators to develop in us.

Turning now to point 3 of his theory of knowledge—the relationship of experience to the understanding of theories—the author announces that "experience arises *together with* theoretical assumptions, *not* before them . . ." He proves it as follows: "eliminate part of the theoretical knowledge of a sensing subject and you have a person who is completely disoriented, incapable of carrying out the simplest action."

A disoriented person is an adult who, losing part of his *acquired* conceptual knowledge, is unable to function on a purely sensory-perceptual level, i.e., unable to revert to the stage of infancy. Normally developing infants and children are not *disoriented*. It is the *abnormal* state of an adult that the article offers as a demonstration of the cognitive impotence of sense data.

Then the article's author plunges rapidly into *his* theory of a child's cognitive development, as follows: the development "gets started only because the child reacts correctly toward signals, *interprets them correctly,* because he possesses means of interpretation even before he has experienced his first clear sensation."

The possession of *means* and their *use* are not the same thing: e.g., a child possesses the means of digesting food, but would you accept the notion that he performs the process of digestion *before* he has taken in any food? In the same way, a child possesses the means of "interpreting" sense data, i.e., a conceptual faculty, but this faculty cannot interpret anything, let alone interpret it "correctly," before he has experienced his first clear sensation. What would it be interpreting?

"Again we can imagine that this interpretative apparatus acts without being accompanied by sensations (as do all reflexes and all well-learned movements such as typing). The theoretical knowledge it contains certainly can be *applied* correctly, though it is perhaps not *understood.* But what do sensations contribute to our understanding? Taken by themselves, i.e., taken as they would appear to a completely disoriented person, they are of no use, either for understanding, or for action."

After a few more sentences of the same kind, the paragraph concludes: "Understanding in the sense demanded here thus turns out to be ineffective and superfluous. Result: sensations can be eliminated from the process of understanding also (though they may of course continue to *accompany* it, just as a headache accompanies deep thought)."

Let me now summarize the preceding, i.e., that article's theory of man and of knowledge: a zombie whose mental apparatus produces theoretical knowledge which he does not understand, but which "interprets" signals "correctly" and enables him to "apply" it correctly, i.e., to act without any understanding—directed by his ultimate cognitive authority, the scientist, a blind-deaf-mute who engages in mental telepathy with a computer.

Now for the article's payoff or cashing-in: "Why is it preferable to interpret theories on the basis of an *observational* language rather than on the basis of a language of intuitively evident statements (as was done only a few centuries ago and as must be done anyway, for observation does not help a disoriented person), or on the basis of a language containing short sentences (as is done in every elementary physics course)? . . . Knowledge can *enter* our brain without touching our senses. And some knowledge *resides* in the individual brain without ever having entered it. Nor is observational knowledge the most reliable knowledge we possess. Science took a big step forward when the Aristotelian idea of the reliability of our everyday experience was given up and was replaced by an empiricism of a more subtle kind. . . Empiricism . . . is therefore an unreasonable doctrine, not in agreement with scientific practice."

Summing up his procedure, the article's author concludes with: "Proceeding in this way of course means leaving the confines of empiricism and moving on to a more comprehensive and more satisfactory kind of philosophy." The "confines of empiricism," in this context, means: the confines of reality.

Before we return to the morgue for the task of dissection, let us pause for a breath of fresh air—for a moment's tribute to the lonely giant whom, two-thousand three hundred years after his death, the enemies of man's mind still have to try to attack before they can destroy the rest of us.

A graphic description of what a non-observational, non-Aristotelian language would be like is given in an academically less prestigious journal—*Look* magazine, January 13, 1970. An article entitled "Growl to Me Softly and I'll Understand" declares: "On a personal level, there'll be no need to cling to formal grammar to convey meaning. Speech doesn't have to be linear; it can come out as a compressed overlay of facts and sensations and moods and ideas and images. Words can serve as signals, and others will understand. The way a man feels can be unashamedly expressed in sheer sound, such as a low, glottal hum, like the purring of a cat, to indicate contentment. . . . Feelings have meaning. Sounds have meaning. Open language can be a joy—a language we can grow with, growl with. Words can cramp your style."

Suppose that you are on trial for a crime you did not commit; you need the clearest focus, the fullest concentration on facts, the strictest justice in the minds of those you face, in order to prove your innocence; but what "comes out" of the judge and jury is "a compressed overlay of facts and sensations and moods and ideas and images."

Suppose that the government issues a decree which expropriates everything you own, sends your children to a concentration camp, your wife to a firing squad, yourself to forced labor, and your country into a nuclear war; you struggle frantically to understand why; but what "comes out" of your country's leaders is "a compressed overlay of facts and sensations and moods and ideas and images."

These examples are not exaggerations; they are precisely what the two articles quoted mean, and the *only* things they can mean—in that factual, existential reality where your sole tool of protection and survival is *concepts*, i.e., language.

The *Look* article wears a thin fig leaf, in the form of restricting the growls to the "personal level" (which cannot be done, since the human mind is unable to carry for long that kind of double psycho-epistemology). But *The Journal of Philosophy* article advocates the method of the "compressed overlay"—a non-observational language—for the mental activities of scientists.

"Science Without Experience" heralds the retrogression of philosophy to the primordial, pre-philosophical rationalism of the jungle ("as was done only a few centuries ago," states the author, in support of a non-observational language). But what is innocent and explicable in an infant or a savage becomes senile corruption when the snake oil, totem poles and magic potions are replaced by a computer. This is the sort of rationalism that Plato, Descartes and all the others of that school would be ashamed of; but not Kant. This is *his* baby and *his* ultimate triumph, since he is the most fertile father of the doctrine equating the *means* of consciousness with its *content*—I refer you to his notion that the machinery of consciousness produces its own (categorial) content.

"Science Without Experience" is an article without significance and would not be worth considering or discussing if it were not for the shocking fact that it was published in the leading American journal of the philosophic profession. If *this* is the view of man, of reason, of knowledge, of science, of existence sanctioned and propagated by the philosophic authorities of our time, can you blame the hippies and yippies who are their products? Can you blame an average youth who is thrown out into the world with *this* kind of mental equipment? Do you need any committees, commissions or multi-million-dollar studies to tell you the causes of campus violence and drug addiction?

A brilliant young professor of philosophy gave me the following explanation of the appearance of that article: "They [the academic philosophers] would enjoy it because it attacks philosophy, in a hooligan manner, including some of their own most cherished beliefs, such as empiricism. They get a kick out of it. They will read and publish anything, so long as it does not imply or advocate a broad, consistent, integrated *system* of ideas."

For a long time, the academic philosophers have been able to do nothing but attack and refute one another (which is not difficult) without being able to offer any theory of a constructive or positive nature. Every new attack confirms their notion that nothing else is possible to their profession and nothing else can be demanded of them. If the style of the attack is hooligan, it reassures them: they don't have to take it (or philosophy) seriously. They will tolerate anything, so long as it does not require that they check the validity of their own premises—i.e., so long as it does not threaten the belief that one set of (arbitrary) assumptions is as good as another.

In *For the New Intellectual*, I mentioned the central cause

of the post-Renaissance philosophy's disaster, the issue that
brought its eventual collapse. "They [the philosophers] were
unable to offer a solution to the 'problem of universals,' that
is: to define the nature and source of abstractions, to determine the relationship of concepts to perceptual data—and to
prove the validity of scientific induction. . . . [They] were unable to refute the Witch Doctor's claim that their concepts
were as arbitrary as his whims and that their scientific knowledge had no greater metaphysical validity than his revelations."

(Observe that the demand for this sort of epistemological
equality is still the irrationalists' policy, strategy and goal.
"Why is it preferable to interpret theories on the basis of an
observational language rather than on the basis of a language
of intuitively evident statements . . . ?" asks the author of
"Science Without Experience." This is the perverse form in
which mystics are compelled to acknowledge the supremacy
of reason and to confess their motive, their envy and their
fear; an advocate of reason does not ask that his knowledge
be granted equality with the intuitions and revelations of
mystics.)

Concepts are the products of a mental process that integrates and organizes the evidence provided by man's senses.
(See my *Introduction to Objectivist Epistemology.*) Man's
senses are his only direct cognitive contact with reality and,
therefore, his only *source* of information. Without sensory
evidence, there can be no concepts; without concepts, there
can be no language; without language, there can be no knowledge and no science.

The answer to the question of the relationship of concepts
to perceptual data determines man's evaluation of the cognitive efficacy of his mind; it determines the course of every
individual life and the fate of nations, of empires, of science,
of art, of civilization. There are not many men who would die
for the sake of protecting the right answer to that question,
yet countless millions have died because of the wrong answers.

Through all the ages, a major attack on man's conceptual faculty was directed at its foundation, i.e., at his senses—in the form of the allegation that man's senses are "unreliable." It remained for the brazenness of the twentieth century to declare that man's senses are superfluous.

If you want to grasp fully the abysmal nature of that claim and, simultaneously, to grasp the origin of concepts and their dependence on sensory evidence, I will refer you to a famous play. One might think that such a subject cannot be dramatized, but it has been—simply, eloquently, heartbreakingly—and it is not a work of fiction, but a dramatization of historical facts. It is *The Miracle Worker* by William Gibson and it tells the story of how Annie Sullivan brought Helen Keller to grasp the nature of *language*.

If you have seen the superlative performance of Patty Duke in the role of Helen Keller, in the stage or screen version of the play, you have seen the image of man projected by "Science Without Experience"—or as near to it as a living human being can come. Helen Keller was not that article's ideal—a creature devoid of all sensory contact with reality—but she came close to it: blind and deaf since infancy, i.e., deprived of sight and hearing, she was left with nothing but the sense of touch to guide her (she retained also the senses of smell and taste, which are not of great cognitive value to a human being).

Try to remember the incommunicable horror of that child's state, communicated by Patty Duke: a creature who is neither human nor animal, with all the power of a human potential, but reduced to a sub-animal helplessness; a savage, violent, hostile creature fighting desperately for self-preservation in an unknowable world, fighting to live somehow with a chronic state of terror and hopeless bewilderment; a human mind (proved later to be an unusually intelligent mind) struggling frantically, in total darkness and silence, to perceive, to grasp, to *understand*, but unable to understand its own need, goal or struggle.

"Without being accompanied by sensations," her "interpretative apparatus" did not act; it did not act "as do all reflexes"; it did not produce any knowledge at all, let alone any "theoretical knowledge." "Knowledge," that article declares, "can *enter* our brain without touching our senses." None entered hers. Would she have been able to operate a computer? She was not able to learn to use a fork or to fold her napkin.

Annie Sullivan, her young teacher (superlatively portrayed by Anne Bancroft), is fiercely determined to transform this creature into a human being, and she knows the only means that can do it: *language*, i.e., the development of the conceptual faculty. But how does one communicate the nature and function of language to a blind-deaf-mute? The entire action of the play is concerned with this single central issue: Annie's struggle to make Helen's mind grasp a *word*—not a signal, but a word.

The form of the language is a code of tactile symbols, a touch alphabet by means of which Annie keeps spelling words into Helen's palm, always making her other hand touch the objects involved. Helen catches on, in part, very rapidly: she learns to repeat the signals into Annie's palm, *but* with no relation to the objects, she learns to spell many words, *but* she does not grasp the connection of the signals to their *referents*, she thinks it is a game, she is merely mimicking motions at random, without any understanding. (At this stage, she is learning "language" as most of today's college students are taught to use it—as a totally *non-observational* set of motions denoting nothing.)

When Helen's father compliments Annie on the fact that she has taught Helen the rudiments of discipline, Annie, discouraged, answers: ". . . to do nothing but obey is—no gift, obedience without understanding is a —blindness, too."

Annie's determination leads her through as heroic a struggle as has ever been portrayed on the stage. She has to fight the doubts, the weary resignation, of Helen's parents; she has to fight their love and pity for the child, their accusations that she is treating Helen too severely; she has to fight Helen's stubborn resistance and uncomprehending fear, which grows into obvious hatred for the teacher; she has to fight her own doubts, the moments of discouragement when she wonders whether the achievement of the goal she has set herself is possible: she does not know what to do, in the face of one disappointment after another, she does not know whether an arrested human mind can be reached and awakened—it has never been done before. Her only weapon is to go on, hour after hour, day after day, endlessly pulling Helen's hand to touch the objects they encounter (to gain *sensory* evidence) and spelling into her palm: "C-A-K-E . . . M-I-L-K . . . W-A-T-E-R . . ." over and over again, without any results.

Helen's older half-brother, James, skeptical of Annie's efforts, remarks that Helen might not want to learn, that maybe "there's such a thing as—dullness of heart. Acceptance. And letting go. Sooner or later we all give up, don't we?

"Annie. Maybe you all do. It's my idea of the original sin.

"James. What is?

"Annie. Giving up.

"James. You won't open her. Why can't you let her be? Have some—pity on her, for being what she is—

"Annie. If I'd ever once thought like that, I'd be dead!"

In today's world, many physically healthy but intellectually crippled people (particularly college students) need Annie Sullivan's help, which they can use if they have retained the capacity to grasp (not merely look at and repeat, but *grasp*) the full meaning of two statements of Annie Sullivan:

Addressed to Helen's father: ". . . words can be her *eyes*, to everything in the world outside her, and inside too, what is she without words? With them she can think, have ideas, be reached, there's not a thought or fact in the world that can't be hers. . . . And she has them already . . . eighteen nouns and three verbs, they're in her fingers now, I need only time to push *one* of them into her mind! One, and everything under the sun will follow."

Addressed to Helen, who cannot hear her: "I wanted to teach you—oh, everything the earth is full of, Helen, everything on it that's ours for a wink and it's gone, and what we are on it, the—light we bring to it and leave behind in—words, why, you can see five thousand years back in a light of words, everything we feel, think, know—and share, in words, so not a soul is in darkness, or done with, even in the grave. And I know, I *know*, one word and I can—put the world in your hand—and whatever it is to me, I won't take less!"

("Words can cramp your style," answers *Look* magazine.)

To my knowledge, *The Miracle Worker* is the only *epistemological* play ever written. It holds the viewer in tensely mounting suspense, not over a chase or a bank robbery, but over the question of whether a human mind will come to life. Its climax is magnificent: after Annie's crushing disappointment at Helen's seeming retrogression, water from a pump spills over Helen's hand, while Annie is automatically spelling "W-A-T-E-R" into her palm, and suddenly Helen *understands*. The two great moments of that climax are incommunicable except through the art of acting: one is the look on Patty Duke's face when she grasps that the signals mean the liquid—the other is the sound of Anne Bancroft's voice when she calls Helen's mother and cries: "She *knows!*"

The quietly sublime intensity of that word—with everything it involves, connotes and makes possible—is what modern philosophy is out to destroy.

I suggest that you read *The Miracle Worker* and study its implications. I am not acquainted with William Gibson's other works; I believe that I would disagree with many aspects of his philosophy (as I disagree with much of Helen Keller's adult philosophy), but this particular play is an invaluable lesson in the fundamentals of a rational epistemology.

I suggest that you consider Annie Sullivan's titanic struggle to arouse a child's conceptual faculty by means of a single sense, the sense of touch, then evaluate the meaning, motive and moral status of the notion that man's conceptual faculty does not require any sensory experience.

I suggest that you consider what an enormous intellectual feat Helen Keller had to perform in order to develop a full conceptual range (including a college education, which required more in her day than it does now), then judge those normal people who learn their first, perceptual-level abstractions without any difficulty and freeze on that level, and keep the higher ranges of their conceptual development in a chaotic fog of swimming, indeterminate approximations, playing a game of signals without referents, as Helen Keller did at first, but without her excuse. Then check on whether *you* respect and how carefully *you* employ your priceless possession: language.

And, lastly, I suggest that you try to project what would have happened if, instead of Annie Sullivan, a sadist had taken charge of Helen Keller's education. A sadist would spell "water" into Helen's palm, while making her touch water, stones, flowers and dogs interchangeably; he would teach her that water is called "water" today, but "milk" tomorrow; he would endeavor to convey to her that there is no necessary connection between names and things, that the signals in her palm are a game of arbitrary conventions and that she'd better obey him without trying to understand.

If this projection is too monstrous to hold in one's mind for long, remember that *this* is what today's academic philosophers are doing to the young—to minds as confused, as plastic and almost as helpless (on the higher conceptual levels) as Helen Keller's mind was at her start.

10

Causality Versus Duty
1970

One of the most destructive anti-concepts in the history of moral philosophy is the term "duty."

An anti-concept is an artificial, unnecessary and rationally unusable term designed to replace and obliterate some legitimate concept. The term "duty" obliterates more than single concepts; it is a metaphysical and psychological killer: it negates all the essentials of a rational view of life and makes them inapplicable to man's actions.

The legitimate concept nearest in meaning to the word "duty" is "obligation." The two are often used interchangeably, but there is a profound difference between them which people sense, yet seldom identify.

The Random House Dictionary of the English Language (Unabridged Edition, 1966) describes the difference as follows: "*Duty, obligation* refer to what one feels bound to do. *Duty* is what one performs, or avoids doing, in fulfillment of the permanent dictates of conscience, piety, right, or law: *duty to one's country; one's duty to tell the truth, to raise children properly. An obligation* is what one is bound to do to fulfill the dictates of usage, custom, or propriety, and to carry out a particular, specific, and often personal promise or agreement: *financial or social obligations.*"

From the same dictionary: "*Dutiful*—Syn. 1. respectful, docile, submissive . . ."

An older dictionary is somewhat more open about it: "*Duty*—1. Conduct due to parents and superiors, as shown in obedience or submission . . ." "*Dutiful*—1. Performing, or ready to perform, the duties required by one who has the right to claim submission, obedience, or deference . . ." (*Webster's International Dictionary*, Second Edition, 1944.)

The meaning of the term "duty" is: the moral necessity to perform certain actions for no reason other than obedience to some higher authority, without regard to any personal goal, motive, desire or interest.

It is obvious that that anti-concept is a product of mysticism, not an abstraction derived from reality. In a mystic theory of ethics, "duty" stands for the notion that man *must* obey the dictates of a supernatural authority. Even though the anti-concept has been secularized, and the authority of God's will has been ascribed to earthly entities, such as parents, country, State, mankind, etc., their alleged supremacy still rests on nothing but a mystic edict. Who in hell can have the right to claim that sort of submission or obedience? This is the only proper form—and locality—for the question, because nothing and no one can have such a right or claim here on earth.

The arch-advocate of "duty" is Immanuel Kant; he went so much farther than other theorists that they seem innocently benevolent by comparison. "Duty," he holds, is the only standard of virtue; but virtue is not its own reward: if a reward is involved, it is no longer virtue. The only moral motivation, he holds, is devotion to duty for duty's sake; only an action motivated exclusively by such devotion is a moral action (i.e., an action performed without any concern for "inclination" [desire] or self-interest).

"It is a duty to preserve one's life, and moreover everyone has a direct inclination to do so. But for that reason the often anxious care which most men take of it has no intrinsic worth, and the maxim of doing so has no moral import. They preserve their lives according to duty, but not from duty. But if adversities and hopeless sorrow completely take away the relish for life, if an unfortunate man, strong in soul, is indignant rather than despondent or dejected over his fate and wishes for death, and yet preserves his life without loving it and from neither inclination nor fear but from duty—then his maxim has a moral import." (Immanuel Kant, *Foundations of the Metaphysics of Morals*, ed. R. P. Wolff, New York, Bobbs-Merrill, 1969, pp. 16–17.)

And: "It is in this way, undoubtedly, that we should understand those passages of Scripture which command us to love our neighbor and even our enemy, for love as an inclination cannot be commanded. But beneficence from duty, when no inclination impels it and even when it is opposed by a natural and unconquerable aversion, is practical love, not pathological love; it resides in the will and not in the propensities of feeling, in principles of action and not in tender sympathy; and it alone can be commanded.

"[Thus the first proposition of morality is that to have moral worth an action must be done from duty.]" (*Ibid.*, pp. 18–19; the sentence in brackets is Wolff's.)

If one were to accept it, the anti-concept "duty" destroys the concept of reality: an unaccountable, supernatural power takes precedence over facts and dictates one's actions regardless of context or consequences.

"Duty" destroys reason: it supersedes one's knowledge and judgment, making the process of thinking and judging irrelevant to one's actions.

"Duty" destroys values: it demands that one betray or sacrifice one's highest values for the sake of an inexplicable command—and it transforms values into a threat to one's moral worth, since the experience of pleasure or desire casts doubt on the moral purity of one's motives.

"Duty" destroys love: who could want to be loved not from "inclination," but from "duty"?

"Duty" destroys self-esteem: it leaves no self to be esteemed.

If one accepts that nightmare in the name of morality, the infernal irony is that "duty" destroys morality. A deontological (duty-centered) theory of ethics confines moral principles to a list of prescribed "duties" and leaves the rest of man's life without any moral guidance, cutting morality off from any application to the actual problems and concerns of man's existence. Such matters as work, career, ambition, love, friendship, pleasure, happiness, values (insofar as they are not pursued as duties) are regarded by these theories as *amoral*, i.e., outside the province of morality. If so, then by what standard is a man to make his daily choices, or direct the course of his life?

In a deontological theory, all personal desires are banished from the realm of morality; a personal desire has no moral significance, be it a desire to create or a desire to kill. For example, if a man is not supporting his life from duty, such a morality makes no distinction between supporting it by honest labor or by robbery. If a man *wants* to be honest, he deserves no moral credit; as Kant would put it, such honesty is "praiseworthy," but without "moral import." Only a vicious represser, who feels a profound desire to lie, cheat and steal, but forces himself to act honestly for the sake of "duty," would receive a recognition of moral worth from Kant and his ilk.

This is the sort of theory that gives morality a bad name.

The widespread fear and/or resentment of morality—the feeling that morality is an enemy, a musty realm of suffering and senseless boredom—is not the product of mystic, ascetic or Christian codes as such, but a monument to the ugliest repository of hatred for life, man and reason: the soul of Immanuel Kant.

(Kant's theories are, of course, mysticism of the lowest order [of the "noumenal" order], but he offered them in the name of reason. The primitive level of men's intellectual development is best demonstrated by the fact that he got away with it.)

If "genius" denotes extraordinary ability, then Kant may be

called a genius in his capacity to sense, play on and perpetuate human fears, irrationalities and, above all, ignorance.
His influence rests not on philosophical but on *psychological*
factors. His view of morality is propagated by men who have
never heard of him—he merely gave them a formal, academic
status. A Kantian sense of "duty" is inculcated by parents
whenever they declare that a child *must* do something because he *must*. A child brought up under the constant batter-
ing of causeless, arbitrary, contradictory, inexplicable
"musts" loses (or never acquires) the ability to grasp the distinction between realistic necessity and human whims—and
spends his life abjectly, dutifully obeying the second and defying the first. In the full meaning of the term, he grows up
without a clear grasp of reality.

As an adult, such a man may reject all forms of mysticism,
but his Kantian psycho-epistemology remains (unless he cor-
rects it). He continues to regard any difficult or unpleasant
task as some inexplicable imposition upon him, as a duty
which he performs, but resents; he believes that it is his
"duty" to earn a living, that it is his "duty" to be moral, and,
in extreme cases, even that it is his "duty" to be rational.

In reality and in the Objectivist ethics, there is no such
thing as "duty." There is only choice and the full, clear
recognition of a principle obscured by the notion of "duty":
the Law of Causality.

The proper approach to ethics, the start from a metaphysically clean slate, untainted by any touch of Kantianism, can
best be illustrated by the following story. In answer to a man
who was telling her that she's *got to* do something or other, a
wise old Negro woman said: "Mister, there's nothing I've *got
to* do except die."

Life or death is man's only fundamental alternative. To live
is his basic act of choice. If he chooses to live, a rational
ethics will tell him what principles of action are required to
implement his choice. If he does not choose to live, nature
will take its course.

Reality confronts man with a great many "musts," but all of

them are conditional; the formula of realistic necessity is: "You must, if—" and the "if" stands for man's choice: "—if you want to achieve a certain goal." You must eat, if you want to survive. You must work, if you want to eat. You must think, if you want to work. You must look at reality, if you want to think—if you want to know what to do—if you want to know what goals to choose—if you want to know how to achieve them.

In order to make the choices required to achieve his goals, a man needs the constant, automatized awareness of the principle which the anti-concept "duty" has all but obliterated in his mind: the principle of causality—specifically, of Aristotelian *final causation* (which, in fact, applies only to a conscious being), i.e., the process by which an end determines the means, i.e., the process of choosing a goal and taking the actions necessary to achieve it.

In a rational ethics, it is causality—not "duty"—that serves as the guiding principle in considering, evaluating and choosing one's actions, particularly those necessary to achieve a long-range goal. Following this principle, a man does not act without knowing the purpose of his action. In choosing a goal, he considers the means required to achieve it, he weighs the value of the goal against the difficulties of the means and against the full, hierarchical context of all his other values and goals. He does not demand the impossible of himself, and he does not decide too easily which things are impossible. He never drops the context of the knowledge available to him, and never evades reality, realizing fully that his goal will not be granted to him by any power other than his own action, and, should he evade, it is not some Kantian authority that he would be cheating, but himself.

If he becomes discouraged by difficulties, he reminds himself of the goal that requires them, knowing that he is fully free to reconsider—to ask: "Is it worth it?"—and that no punishment is involved except the renunciation of the value he desires. (One seldom gives up in such cases, unless one finds that it is rationally necessary.)

In similar circumstances, a Kantian does not focus on his goal, but on his own *moral character*. His automatic reaction is guilt and fear—fear of failing his "duty," fear of some weakness which "duty" forbids, fear of proving himself morally "unworthy." The value of his goal vanishes from his mind, drowned in a flood of self-doubt. He might drive himself on in this cheerless fashion for a while, but not for long. A Kantian seldom carries out or undertakes important goals: they are a threat to his self-esteem.

This is one of the crucial psychological differences between the principle of "duty" and the principle of final causation. A disciple of causation looks outward, he is value-oriented and action-oriented, which means: reality-oriented. A disciple of "duty" looks inward, he is self-centered, not in the rational-existential, but in the psychopathological sense of the term, i.e., concerned with a self cut off from reality; "self-centered" in this context means: "self-doubt-centered."

There are many other differences between the two principles. A disciple of causation is profoundly dedicated to his values, knowing that he is able to achieve them. He is incapable of desiring contradictions, of relying on a "somehow," of rebelling against reality. He knows that in all such cases, it is not some Kantian authority that he would be defying and injuring, but himself—and that the penalty would be not some mystic brand of "immorality," but the frustration of his own desires and the destruction of his values.

A Kantian or even a semi-Kantian cannot permit himself to value anything profoundly, since an inexplicable "duty" may demand the sacrifice of his values at any moment, wiping out any long-range plan or struggle he might have undertaken to achieve them. In the absence of personal goals, any task, such as earning a living, becomes a senseless drudgery, but he regards it as a "duty"—and he regards compliance with the requirements of reality as a "duty." Then, in blind rebellion against "duty," it is reality that he begins to resent and, ultimately, to escape, in search of some realm where wishes are granted automatically and ends are achieved without means. This is the subconscious process by which Kant makes recruits for mysticism.

The notion of "duty" is intrinsically anti-causal. In its origin, a "duty" defies the principle of efficient causation— since it is causeless (or supernatural); in its effects, it defies the principle of final causation—since it must be performed regardless of consequences. This is the kind of irresponsibility that a disciple of causation would not permit himself. He does not act without considering—and accepting—all the foreseeable consequences of his actions. Knowing the causal efficacy of his actions, seeing himself as a causal agent (and never seeking to get away with contradictions), he develops a virtue killed by Kantianism: a sense of *responsibility*.

Accepting no mystic "duties" or unchosen obligations, he is the man who honors scrupulously the obligations which *he* chooses. The obligation to keep one's promises is one of the most important elements in proper human relationships, the element that leads to mutual confidence and makes cooperation possible among men. Yet observe Kant's pernicious influence: in the dictionary description quoted earlier, personal obligation is thrown in almost as a contemptuous footnote; the source of "duty" is defined as "the permanent dictates of conscience, piety, right, or law"; the source of "obligation," as "the dictates of usage, custom, or propriety"— then, as an afterthought: "and to carry out a particular, specific, and *often personal* promise or agreement." (Italics mine.) A personal promise or agreement is the only valid, binding obligation, without which none of the others can or do stand.

The acceptance of full responsibility for one's own choices and actions (and their consequences) is such a demanding moral discipline that many men seek to escape it by surrendering to what they believe is the easy, automatic, unthinking safety of a morality of "duty." They learn better, often when it is too late.

The disciple of causation faces life without inexplicable

chains, unchosen burdens, impossible demands or supernatural threats. His metaphysical attitude and guiding moral
principle can best be summed up by an old Spanish proverb:
"God said: 'Take what you want and pay for it.'" But to know
one's own desires, their meaning and their costs requires the
highest human virtue: rationality.

11

An Untitled Letter
1973

The most appropriate title for this discussion would be "I told you so." But since that would be in somewhat dubious taste, I shall leave this [issue of *The Ayn Rand Letter*] untitled.

In *Atlas Shrugged*, and in many subsequent articles, I said that the advocates of mysticism are motivated not by a quest for truth, but by hatred for man's mind; that the advocates of altruism are motivated not by compassion for suffering, but by hatred for man's life; that the advocates of collectivism are motivated not by a desire for men's happiness, but by hatred for man; that their three doctrines come from the same root and blend into a single passion: hatred of the good for being the good; and that the focus of that hatred, the target of its passionate fury, is the man of ability.

Those who thought that I was exaggerating have seen event after event confirm my diagnosis. Reality has been providing me with references and footnotes, including explicit admissions by the advocates of those doctrines. The admissions are becoming progressively louder and clearer.

The major ideological campaigns of the mystic-altruist-collectivist axis are usually preceded by trial balloons that test the public reaction to an attack on certain fundamental principles. Today, a new kind of intellectual balloon is beginning to bubble in the popular press—testing the climate for a large-scale attack intended to obliterate the concept of *justice*.

The new balloons acquire the mark of a campaign by carrying, like little identification tags, the code words: "A New Justice." This does not mean that the campaign is consciously directed by some mysterious powers. It is a conspiracy, not of men, but of basic premises—and the power directing it is logic: if, at the desperate stage of a losing battle, some men point to a road logically necessitated by their basic premises, those who share the premises will rush to follow.

Since my capacity for intellectual slumming is limited, I do not know who originated this campaign at this particular time (its philosophical roots are ancient). The first instance that came to my attention was a brief news item over a year ago. Dr. Jan Tinbergen from the Netherlands, who had received a Nobel Prize in Economic Science, spoke at an international conference in New York City and suggested "that there be a tax on personal capabilities. 'A modest first step might be a special tax on persons with high academic scores,' he said." We reprinted this item in the "Horror File" of *The Objectivist* (June 1971). The reaction of my friends, when they read it, was an incredulously indignant amusement, with remarks such as: "He's crazy!"

But it is not amusing any longer when a news item in *The New York Times* (January 2, 1973) announces that Pope Paul VI "issued a call today for a 'new justice.' True justice recognizes that all men are in substance equal, the Pontiff said. . . . 'The littler, the poorer, the more suffering, the more defenseless, even the lower a man has fallen, the more he deserves to be assisted, raised up, cared for, and honored. We learn this from the Gospel.'"

Observe the package-deal: to be "little," "poor," "suffering," "defenseless" is not necessarily to be immoral (it depends on the cause of these conditions). But "*even* the lower a man has fallen" implies, in this context, not misfortune but immorality. Are we asked to absorb the notion that the lower a man's vices, the more concern he deserves—and the more *honor?* Another package-deal: to be "assisted," "raised up," "cared for" obviously does not apply to those who are great, rich, happy or strong; they do not need it. But—*"to be honored"?* They are the men who would have to do the assisting, the raising up, the caring for—but they do *not* deserve to be honored? *They* deserve less honor than the man who is saved by *their* virtues and values?

In *Atlas Shrugged*, exposing the meaning of altruism, John Galt says: "What passkey admits you to the moral elite? The passkey is *lack of value*. Whatever the value involved, it is your lack of it that gives you a claim upon those who don't lack it. . . . To demand rewards for your virtue is selfish and immoral; it is your *lack of virtue* that transforms your demand into a moral right."

What is an abstract ethical suggestion in the Pope's message, becomes specific and political in a brief piece that appeared in the *Times* on January 20, 1973—"The New Inequality" by Peregrine Worsthorne, a columnist for *The Sunday Telegraph* of London. In addition to altruism, which is its base, this piece was made possible by two premises: 1. the refusal to recognize the difference between mind and force (i.e., between economic and political power); and 2. the refusal to recognize the difference between existence and consciousness (i.e., between the metaphysical and the man-made). Those who ignore or evade the crucial importance of these distinctions will find Mr. Peregrine Worsthorne ready to welcome them at the end of their road.

There was a time, Mr. Worsthorne begins, when "gross hereditary inequalities of wealth, status and power were universally accepted as a divinely ordained fact of life." He is speaking of feudalism and of the British caste system. But modern man, he says, "finds this awfully difficult to understand. To him it seems absolutely axiomatic that each individual ought to be allowed to make his grade according to merit, regardless of the accident of birth. All positions of power, wealth and status should be open to talent. To the extent that this ideal is achieved a society is deemed to be just."

If you think that this is a proclamation of individualism,

think twice. Modern liberals, Mr. Worsthorne continues, "have tended to believe it to be fair enough that the man of merit should be on top and the man without merit should be underneath." On top—of what? Underneath—what? Mr. Worsthorne doesn't say. Judging by the rest of the piece, his answer would be: on top of anything—political power, self-made wealth, scientific achievement, artistic genius, the status of earned respect or of a government-granted title of nobility—anything anyone may ever want or envy.

The current social "malaise," he explains, is caused by "the increasing evidence that this assumption [about a just society] should be challenged. The ideal of a meritocracy no longer commands such universal assent."

"Meritocracy" is an old anti-concept and one of the most contemptible package-deals. By means of nothing more than its last five letters, that word obliterates the difference between mind and force: it equates the men of ability with *political* rulers, and the power of their creative achievements with *political* power. There is no difference, the word suggests, between freedom and tyranny: an "aristocracy" is tyranny by a politically established elite, a "democracy" is tyranny by the majority—and when a government protects individual rights, the result is tyranny by talent or "merit" (and since "to merit" means "to deserve," a free society is ruled by the tyranny of justice).

Mr. Worsthorne makes the most of it. His further package-dealing becomes easier and cruder. "It used to be considered manifestly unjust that a child should be given an enormous head-start in life simply because he was the son of an earl, or a member of the landed gentry. But what about a child today born of affluent, educated parents whose family life gets him off to a head-start in the educational ladder? Is he not the beneficiary of a form of hereditary privilege no less unjust than that enjoyed by the aristocracy?"

What about Thomas Edison, the Wright brothers, Commodore Vanderbilt, Henry Ford, Sr. or, in politics, Abraham

Lincoln, and *their* "enormous head-start in life"? On the other hand, what about the Park Avenue hippies or the drug-eaten children of college-bred intellectuals and multi-millionaires?

Mr. Worsthorne, it seems, had counted on "universal public education" to level things down, but it has disappointed him. "Family life," he declares, "is more important than school life in determining brain power. . . . Educational qualifications are today what armorial quarterings were in feudal times. Yet access to them is almost as unfairly determined by accidents of birth as was access to the nobility." This, he says, defeats "any genuine faith in equality of opportunity" —and "accounts for the current populist clamor to do away with educational distinctions such as exams and diplomas, since they are seen as the latest form of privilege which, in a sense, they are."

This means that if a young student (named, say, Thomas Hendricks), after days and nights of conscientious study, proves that he knows the subject of medicine, and passes an exam, he is given an arbitrary privilege, an unfair advantage over a young student (named Lee Hunsacker) who spent his time in a drugged daze, listening to rock music. And if Hendricks gets a diploma and a job in a hospital, while Hunsacker does not, Hunsacker will scream that he could not help it and that he never had a chance. Volitional effort? There is no such thing. Brain power? It's determined by family life—and he couldn't help it if Mom and Pop did not condition him to be willing to study. He is *entitled* to a job in a hospital, and a *just* society would guarantee it to him. The fate of the patients? He's as good as any other fellow—"all men are in substance equal"—and the only difference between him and the privileged bastards is a diploma granted as unfairly as armorial quarterings! Equal opportunity? Don't make him laugh!

Socialists, Mr. Worsthorne remarks, have used "the ideal of equality of opportunity" as "a way of moving in the right, that is to say the Left, direction." They regarded it as "the thin end of the egalitarian wedge."

Then, suddenly, Mr. Worsthorne starts dispensing advice to
the Right—which the Left has always insisted on doing (and
with good reason: any "rightist" who accepts it, deserves it).
His advice, as usual, involves a threat and counts on fear.
"But there is a problem here for the Right quite as much as
for the Left. It seems to me certain that there will be a growing awareness in the coming decades of the unfairness of
existing society, of the new forms of arbitrary allocation of
power, status and privilege. Resentment will build up against
the new meritocracy just as it built up against the old aristocracy and plutocracy."

The Right, he claims, must "devise new ways of disarming
this resentment, without so curbing the high-flyers, so
penalizing excellence, or so imposing uniformity as to destroy
the spirit of a free and dynamic society." Observe that he
permits himself to grasp and cynically to admit that such an
issue as *the penalizing of excellence* is involved, but he regards it as the Right's concern, not his own—and he does not
object to penalizing virtue for being virtue, provided the
penalties do not go to extremes. This—in an article written as
an appeal for justice.

Mr. Worsthorne has a solution to offer to the Right—and
here comes the full flowering of altruism's essence and purpose, spreading out its petals like a hideous jungle plant, the
kind that traps insects and eats them. The purpose is not to
burn sacrificial victims, but to have them leap into the furnaces of their own free will: "What will be required of the
new meritocracy is a formidably revived and reanimated spirit
of *noblesse oblige*, rooted in the recognition that they *are* im-
mensely privileged and must, as a class, behave accordingly,
being prepared to pay a far higher social price, in terms of
taxation, in terms of service, for the privilege of exercising
their talents."

Who granted them "the privilege of exercising their talents"? Those who have no talent. To *whom* must they "pay a
higher social price"? To those who have no social value to
offer. *Who* will impose taxation on their productive work?

Those who have produced nothing. *Whom* do they have to serve? Those who would be unable to survive without them.

"Did you want to know who is John Galt? I am the first man of ability who refused to regard it as guilt. I am the first man who would not do penance for my virtues or let them be used as the tools of my destruction. I am the first man who would not suffer martyrdom at the hands of those who wished me to perish for the privilege of keeping them alive." (*Atlas Shrugged*.)

"This [the 'social price'] is not an easy idea for a meritocracy to accept," Mr. Worsthorne concludes. "They like to think that they deserve their privileges, having won them by their own efforts. But this is an illusion, or at any rate a half truth. The other half of the truth is that they are terribly lucky and if their luck is not to run out they must be prepared to pay much more for their good fortune than they had hoped or even feared."

I submit that any man who ascribes success to "luck" has never achieved anything and has no inkling of the relentless effort which achievement requires. I submit that a successful man who ascribes his own (legitimate) success in part to luck is either a modest, concrete-bound represser who does not understand the issue—or an appeaser who tries to mollify the resentment of envious mediocrities. (For the nature of such resentment, see my article "The Age of Envy" in [*The New Left: The Anti-Industrial Revolution*].)

Envy is a widespread sentiment in Europe, not in America. Most Americans admire success: they know what it takes. They believe that one must pay for one's sins, not for one's virtues—and the monstrous notion of paying ransoms for good fortune would not occur to them, nor would they take it seriously.

Resentment against "meritocracy"? Our last Presidential election [the landslide against McGovern] was a spectacular demonstration of America's loyalty to achievement (on any level)—and of resentment against those egalitarian intellectuals who are trying to smuggle this country into a new caste system proposed by their British mentors: a *mediocracy*.

Politically, statism breeds a swarm of "little Caesars," who are motivated by power-lust. Culturally, statism breeds still lower a species: a swarm of "little Neros," who sing odes to depravity while the lives of their forced audiences go up in smoke.

I have said repeatedly that American intellectuals, with rare exceptions, are the slavish dependents and followers of Europe's intellectual trends. The notion of a cultural aristocracy established and financed by the government is so grotesque in this country that one wonders how an article such as Mr. Peregrine Worsthorne's got published here. Can you see any group or class in America posturing about in the "spirit of *noblesse oblige"?* Can you see Americans bowing to, say, Sir Burrhus Frederic (Skinner) or Dame Jane (Fonda), thanking them for their charitable contributions? Yet this is the goal of Britain's little Neros—and of their American followers. I refer you to [*The Ayn Rand Letter*] of January 1, 1973, "To Dream the Non-Commercial Dream," for a discussion of why such "aristocrats" would have a vested interest in altruism and why they would be eager to pay a social price "for the privilege of exercising their talents."

If, by "meritocracy," Mr. Worsthorne means a government-picked elite (for instance, the B.B.C.), then it is true that such an elite owes its privileges to luck (and pull) more than to merit. If he means the men of ability who demonstrate their merit in the free marketplace (of ideas or of material goods), then his notions are worse than false. Package-dealing is essential to the selling of such notions. Mr. Worsthorne's technique consists in making no distinction between these two kinds of "merit"—which means: in seeing no difference between Homer and Nero.

An article such as Mr. Worsthorne's (and its various equivalents) would not appear in a newspaper, without some heavy academic-philosophical base. Newspapers are not published by or for theoretical innovators. Journalists do not venture to propagate an outrageous theory unless they know that they can refer to some "reputable" source able, they hope, to explain the inexplicable and defend the indefensible. An enormous amount of unconscionable nonsense comes out of the academic world each year; most of it is stillborn. But when echoes of a specific work begin to spurt in the popular press, they acquire significance as an advance warning—as an indication of the fact that some group(s) has a practical interest in shooting these particular bubbles into the country's cultural arteries.

In the case of the new egalitarianism, an academic source does exist. It may not be the first book of that kind, but it is the one noticeably touted at present. It is *A Theory of Justice* by John Rawls, professor of philosophy at Harvard University.

The New York Times Book Review (December 3, 1972) lists it among "Five Significant Books of 1972" and explains: "Although it was published in 1971, it was not widely reviewed until 1972, because critics needed time to get a grip on its complexities. In fact, it may not be properly understood until it has been studied for years. . . ." The *Book Review* itself did not review it until July 16, 1972, at which time it published a front-page review written by Marshall Cohen, professor of philosophy at the City University of New York. The fact that the timing of that review coincided with the period of George McGovern's campaign may or may not be purely coincidental.

Let me say that I have not read and do not intend to read that book. But since one cannot judge a book by its reviews, please regard the following discussion as the review of a review. Mr. Cohen's remarks deserve attention in their own right.

According to the review, Rawls "is not an equalitarian, for he allows that inequalities of wealth, power and authority may be just. He argues, however, that these inequalities are just only when they can reasonably be expected to work out to the advantage of those who are worst off. The expenses incurred [by whom?] in training a doctor, like the rewards that encourage better performance from an entrepreneur, are permissible only if eliminating them, or reducing them further, would leave the worst off worse off still. If, however, permitting such inequalities contributes to improving the health or raising the material standards of those who are least advantaged, the inequalities are justified. But they are justified only to that extent—never as rewards for 'merit,' never as the just deserts of those who are born with greater natural advantages or into more favorable social circumstances."

I assume that this is an accurate summary of Mr. Rawls's thesis. The *Book Review*'s plug of December 3 offers corroboration: "The talented or socially advantaged person hasn't *earned* anything: 'Those who have been favored by nature, whoever they are,' he [Rawls] writes, 'may gain from their good fortune only on terms that improve the situation of those who have lost out.'"

(" . . . it is the parasites who are the moral justification for the existence of the producers, but the existence of the parasites is an end in itself. . . ." John Galt, analyzing altruism, in *Atlas Shrugged.*)

Certain evils are protected by their own magnitude: there are people who, reading that quotation from Rawls, would not believe that it means what it says, but it does. It is not against social institutions that Mr. Rawls (and Mr. Cohen) rebels, but against the existence of human *talent*—not against political privileges, but against *reality*—not against governmental favors, but against *nature* (against "those who have been *favored by nature*," as if such a term as "favor" were applicable here)—not against social injustice, but against *metaphysical* "injustice," against the fact that some men are born with better brains and make better use of them than others are and do.

The new "theory of justice" demands that men counteract the "injustice" of nature by instituting the most obscenely unthinkable injustice among men: deprive "those favored by nature" (i.e., the talented, the intelligent, the creative) of the right to the rewards they produce (i.e., the right to life)—and grant to the incompetent, the stupid, the slothful a right to the effortless enjoyment of the rewards they could not produce, could not imagine, and would not know what to do with.

Mr. Cohen would object to my formulation. "It is important to understand," he writes, "that according to Rawls it is neither just nor unjust that men are born with differing natural abilities into different social positions. These are simply natural facts. [True, but if so, what is the purpose of the next sentence?] To be sure, no one deserves his greater natural capacity or merits a more favorable starting point in society. The natural and social 'lottery' is arbitrary from a moral point of view. But it does not follow, as the equalitarian supposes, that we should eliminate these differences. There is another way to deal with them. As we have seen, they can be put to work for the benefit of all and, in particular, for the benefit of those who are worst off." If a natural fact is neither just nor unjust, by what mental leap does it become a *moral* problem and an issue of *justice?* Why should those "favored by nature" be made to atone for what is *not* an injustice and is not of their making?

Mr. Cohen does not explain. He continues: "What justice requires, then, is that natural chance and social fortune be treated as a collective resource and put to work for the common good. Justice does not require equality, but it does require that men share one another's fate." This is the conclusion that required reading a 607-page book and taking a year "to get a grip on its complexities." That this is regarded as a *new* theory, raises the question of where Mr. Rawls's readers and admirers have been for the last two thousand years. There is more than this to the book, but let us pause at this point for a moment.

Observe that Mr. Cohen's (and the egalitarians') view of man is literally the view of a children's fairy tale—the notion that man, before birth, is some sort of indeterminate thing, an entity without identity, something like a shapeless chunk of human clay, and that fairy godmothers proceed to grant or deny him various attributes ("favors"): intelligence, talent, beauty, rich parents, etc. These attributes are handed out "arbitrarily" (this word is preposterously inapplicable to the processes of nature), it is a "lottery" among pre-embryonic non-entities, and—the supposedly adult mentalities conclude—since a winner could not possibly have "deserved" his "good fortune," a man does not deserve or earn anything after birth, as a human being, because he acts by means of "undeserved," "unmerited," "unearned" attributes. Implication: to earn something means to choose and earn your personal attributes *before* you exist.

Stuff of that kind has a certain value: it is a psychological confession projecting the enormity of that envy and hatred for the man of ability which are the root of all altruistic theories. By preaching the basest variant of the old altruist tripe, Mr. Rawls's book reveals altruism's ultimate meaning—which may be regarded as an ethical innovation. But *A Theory of Justice* is not primarily a book on ethics: it is a treatise on politics. And, believe it or not, it might be taken by some people as a way to save capitalism—since Mr. Rawls allegedly offers a "new" moral justification for the existence of social inequalities. It is fascinating to observe against whom Mr. Rawls's polemic is directed: against the utilitarians.

Virtually all the defenders of capitalism, from the nineteenth century to the present, accept the ethics of utilitarianism (with its slogan "The greatest happiness of the greatest number") as their moral base and justification—evading the appalling contradiction between capitalism and the altruist-collectivist nature of the utilitarian ethics. Mr. Cohen points out that utilitarianism is incompatible with justice, because it endorses the sacrifice of minorities to the interests of the majority. (I said this in 1946—see my old pamphlet *Textbook of Americanism*.) If the alleged defenders of capitalism insist on clinging to altruism, Mr. Rawls is the retribution they have long since deserved: with far greater consistency than theirs, he substitutes a new standard of ethics for their old, utilitarian one: "The greatest happiness for the least deserving."

His main purpose, however, is to revive, as a moral-political base, the theory of social contract, which utilitarianism had replaced. In the opinion of John Rawls, writes Mr. Cohen, "the social contract theory of Rousseau and Kant" (wouldn't you know it?) provides an alternative to utilitarianism.

Mr. Cohen proceeds to offer a summary of the way Mr. Rawls would proceed to establish a "social contract." Men would be placed in what he calls the "original position"—which is not a state of nature, but "a hypothetical situation that can be entered into at any time." Justice would be ensured "by requiring that the principles which are to govern society be chosen behind a 'veil of ignorance.' This veil prevents those who occupy the 'original position' from knowing their own natural abilities or their own positions in the social order. What they do not know they cannot turn to their own advantage; this ignorance guarantees that their choice will be fair. And since everyone in the 'original position' is assumed to be rational [?!], everyone will be convinced by the same arguments [??!!]. In the social contract tradition the choice of political principles is unanimous." No, Mr. Cohen does not explain or define what that "original position" is—probably, with good reason. As he goes on, he seems to hint that that "hypothetical situation" is the state of the pre-embryonic human clay.

"Rawls argues that given the uncertainties that characterize the 'original position' (men do not know whether they are well- or ill-endowed, rich or poor) and given the fateful nature of the choice to be made (these are the principles by which they will live) rational men would choose according to the 'maximin' rule of game theory. This rule defines a conservative strategy—in making a choice among alternatives, we should choose that alternative whose worst possible outcome is superior to the worst possible outcome of the others." And thus, men would "rationally" choose to accept Mr. Rawls's ethical-political principles.

Regardless of any Rube Goldberg complexities erected to arrive at that conclusion, I submit that it is impossible for men to make any choice on the basis of ignorance, i.e., using ignorance as a criterion: if men do not know their own identities, they will not be able to grasp such things as "principles to live by," "alternatives" or what is a good, bad or worst "possible outcome." Since in order to be "fair" they must not know what is to their own advantage, how would they be able to know which is the least advantageous (the "worst possible") outcome?

As to the "maximin" rule of choice, I can annul Mr. Rawls's social contract, which requires *unanimity*, by saying that in long-range issues I choose that alternative whose *best* possible outcome is superior to the *best* possible outcome of the others. "You seek escape from pain. We seek the achievement of happiness. You exist for the sake of avoiding punishment. We exist for the sake of earning rewards. Threats will not make us function; fear is not our incentive. It is not death that we wish to avoid, but life that we wish to live." *(Atlas Shrugged.)*

Mr. Cohen is not in full agreement with Mr. Rawls. He seems to think that Mr. Rawls is not egalitarian enough: " . . . one would like to be clearer about the sorts of inequalities that are in fact justified in order to 'encourage' better performance. And is it in fact legitimate for Rawls to exclude considerations of what he calls envy from the calculations that are made in the 'original position'? It is arguable that including them would lead to the choice of more equalitarian principles." Does this mean that pre-embryos without attributes are able to experience envy of other pre-embryos without attributes? Does this mean that a just society must grind its best members down to the level of its worst, in order to pander to *envy?*

I am inclined to guess that the answer is affirmative, because Mr. Cohen continues as follows: "However that may be, I, for one, am inclined to argue that once an adequate social minimum has been reached, justice requires the elimination of many economic and social inequalities, even if their elimination inhibits a further raising of the minimum." Is *this* motivated by the desire to uplift the weak or to degrade the strong—to help the incompetent or to destroy the able? Is this the voice of love or of hatred—of compassion or of envy?

What value would be gained by such a cerebrocidal atrocity? "I ought to forgo some economic benefits," says Mr. Cohen, "if doing so will reduce the evils of social distance, strengthen communal ties, and enhance the possibilities for a fuller participation in the common life." *Whose* life? In common with *whom?* On whose standard of value: the folks' next door?—the corner louts'?—the hippies'?—the drug addicts'?

"Dagny . . . I had seen . . . what it was that I had to fight for . . . I had to save you . . . not to let you stumble the years of your life away, struggling on through a poisoned fog . . . struggling to find, at the end of your road, not the towers of a city, but a fat, soggy, mindless cripple performing his enjoyment of life by means of swallowing the gin *your* life had gone to pay for!" *(Atlas Shrugged.)*

Mr. Cohen mentions that Mr. Rawls rejects "the perfectionistic doctrines of Aristotle." (Wouldn't you know *that?*) Mr. Rawls, by the way, is an American, educated in American universities, but he completed his education in Great Britain, at Oxford, on a Fulbright Fellowship.

What is the cause of today's egalitarian trend? For over two hundred years, Europe's predominantly altruist-collectivist intellectuals had claimed to be the voice of the people—the champions of the downtrodden, disinherited masses and of unlimited majority rule. "Majority" was the omnipotent word of the intellectuals' theology. "Majority will" and "majority welfare" were their moral base and political goal which—they claimed—permitted, vindicated and justified anything. With varying degrees of consistency, this belief was shared by most of Europe's social thinkers, from Marx to Bentham to John Stuart Mill (whose *On Liberty* is the most pernicious piece of collectivism ever adopted by suicidal defenders of liberty).

In mid-twentieth century, the intellectuals were traumatized by seeing their axiomatic bedrock disintegrate into thin ice. The concept of "majority will" collapsed when they saw that the majority was not with them and did not share their "ideals." The concept of "majority welfare" collapsed when they discovered—through the experiences of communist Russia, Nazi Germany, welfare-state England, and sundry lesser socialist regimes—that only their hated adversary, the free, selfish, individualistic system of capitalism, is able to benefit the majority of the people (in fact, *all* of the people).

Some intellectuals began to stumble toward the Right—a bankrupt Right, which had nothing to offer. Some gave up, turning to drugs and astrology. The vanguard—stripped of cover, of respect, of credibility, and of safely popular bromides—began to reveal their hidden motives in the open glare of verbalized theory.

The cult of the "majority" has come to an end among the atruist-collectivists. They are not declaring any longer: "Why shouldn't a minuscule elite of geniuses and millionaires be sacrificed to the broad masses of mankind?"—they are declaring that the broad masses of mankind should be sacrificed to a minuscule elite, not of gods, kings or heroes, but of congenital incompetents. They are not declaring that greedy capitalists are exploiting and stifling men of talent—they are declaring that men of talent should not be permitted to function. They are not declaring that capitalism is impeding technological progress—they are declaring that technological progress should be retarded or abolished. They are not deriding the promise of "pie in the sky"—they are demanding that pie on earth be forbidden. They are not promising to raise men's standard of living—they are proclaiming that it should be lowered. They are not seeking to redistribute wealth—they are seeking to wipe it out. What, then, remains of their former creed? Only one constant: *sacrifice*—which they are now preaching openly in the form they had always endorsed secretly: sacrifice for the sake of sacrifice.

"It is not your wealth that they're after. Theirs is a conspiracy against the mind, which means: against life and man." *(Atlas Shrugged.)*

Anyone who proposes to reduce mankind to the level of its lowest specimens, cannot claim benevolence as his motive. Anyone who proposes to deprive men of aspiration, ambition or hope, and sentence them to stagnation for life, cannot claim compassion as his motive. Anyone who proposes to forbid men's progress beyond the limit accessible to a cripple, cannot claim love for men as his motive. Anyone who proposes to forbid to a genius any achievement which is not of value to a moron, cannot claim *any* motive but envy and hatred.

Observe that it has never been possible to preach an evil notion on the basis of reason, of facts, of this earth. The advocates of man-destroying theories have always had to step outside reality, to seek a mystic base or sanction. Just as religionists had to invoke the myth of Adam's sin in order to propagate the notion of man's prenatal guilt—just as Kant had to rely on a noumenal world in order to destroy the world that exists—just as Hegel had to call on the Absolute Idea, and Marx had to call on Hegel—so today, on the grubby scale of our shrinking culture, those who want to deprive man of his right to life are proclaiming the rights of the fetus, and those who want to deny all rights to the man of ability, are demanding that he atone for what he did not earn before he was a fetus and for nature's prenatal unfairness to the Mongolian idiot next door.

Observe also that an honest theoretician does not try to present his ideas in the guise of their opposites. But Kant's philosophy is presented as "pure reason"—altruism is presented as a doctrine of "love"—communism is presented as "liberation"—and egalitarianism is presented as "justice."

"Justice is the recognition of the fact that you cannot fake the character of men as you cannot fake the character of nature . . . that every man must be judged for what he *is* and treated accordingly . . . that to place any other concern higher than justice is to devaluate your moral currency and defraud the good in favor of the evil . . . and that the bottom of the pit at the end of that road, the act of moral bankruptcy, is to punish men for their virtues and reward them for their vices. . . ." *(Atlas Shrugged.)*

Mr. Rawls's book is entitled *A Theory of Justice*, and yet, curiously enough, Mr. Cohen never mentions Mr. Rawls's definition of "justice"—which, I suspect, may not be Mr. Cohen's fault.

In *Atlas Shrugged*, in the sequence dealing with the tunnel catastrophe, I list the train passengers who were philosophically responsible for it, in hierarchical order, from the less guilty to the guiltiest. The last one on the list is a humanitarian who had said: "The men of ability? I do not care what or if they are made to suffer. They must be penalized in order to support the incompetent. Frankly, I do not care whether this is just or not. I take pride in not caring to grant any justice to the able, where mercy to the needy is concerned." Today, a "scientific" volume of 607 pages is devoted to claiming that *this* constitutes justice.

In *Capitalism: The Unkown Ideal*, I wrote: "The moral justification of capitalism lies in the fact that it is the only system consonant with man's rational nature, that it protects man's survival *qua* man, and that its ruling principle is: *justice.*" If capitalism and its moral-metaphysical base, man's rational nature, are to be destroyed, then it is the concept of justice that has to be destroyed. Apparently, the egalitarians understand this; the utilitarian defenders of capitalism do not.

Is *A Theory of Justice* likely to be widely read? No. Is it likely to be influential? Yes—precisely for that reason.

If you wonder how so grotesquely irrational a philosophy as

Kant's came to dominate Western culture, you are now witnessing an attempt to repeat that process. Mr. Rawls is a disciple of Kant—philosophically and psycho-epistemologically. Kant originated the technique required to sell irrational notions to the men of a skeptical, cynical age who have formally rejected mysticism without grasping the rudiments of rationality. The technique is as follows: if you want to propagate an outrageously evil idea (based on traditionally accepted doctrines), your conclusion must be brazenly clear, but your proof unintelligible. Your proof must be so tangled a mess that it will paralyze a reader's critical faculty—a mess of evasions, equivocations, obfuscations, circumlocutions, non sequiturs, endless sentences leading nowhere, irrelevant side issues, clauses, sub-clauses and sub-sub-clauses, a meticulously lengthy proving of the obvious, and big chunks of the arbitrary thrown in as self-evident, erudite references to sciences, to pseudo-sciences, to the never-to-be-sciences, to the untraceable and the unprovable—all of it resting on a zero: the *absence* of definitions. I offer in evidence the *Critique of Pure Reason.*

Mr. Cohen gives some indications that such is the style of Mr. Rawls's book. E.g.: " . . . the boldness and simplicity of Rawls's formulations depend on a *considered,* but questionable, looseness in his understanding of some fundamental political concepts." (Emphasis added.) "Considered" means "deliberate."

Like any overt school of mysticism, a movement seeking to achieve a vicious goal has to invoke the higher mysteries of an incomprehensible authority. An unread and unreadable book serves this purpose. It does not count on men's intelligence, but on their weaknesses, pretensions and fears. It is not a tool of enlightenment, but of intellectual intimidation. It is not aimed at the reader's understanding, but at his inferiority complex.

An intelligent man will reject such a book with contemptuous indignation, refusing to waste his time on untangling what

he perceives to be gibberish—which is part of the book's
technique: the man able to refute its arguments will not (unless he has the endurance of an elephant and the patience of a
martyr). A young man of average intelligence—particularly a
student of philosophy or of political science—under a barrage
of authoritative pronouncements acclaiming the book as
"scholarly," "significant," "profound," will take the blame for
his failure to understand. More often than not, he will assume
that the book's theory has been scientifically proved and that
he alone is unable to grasp it; anxious, above all, to hide his
inability, he will profess agreement, and the less his understanding, the louder his agreement—while the rest of the
class are going through the same mental process. Most of
them will accept the book's doctrine, reluctantly and uneas-
ily, and lose their intellectual integrity, condemning themselves to a chronic fog of approximation, uncertainty, self-
doubt. Some will give up the intellect (particularly philosophy)
and turn belligerently into "pragmatic," anti-intellectual
Babbitts. A few will see through the game and scramble eagerly for the driver's seat on the bandwagon, grasping the
possibilities of a road to the mentally unearned.

Within a few years of the book's publication, commentators
will begin to fill libraries with works analyzing, "clarifying"
and interpreting its mysteries. Their notions will spread all
over the academic map, ranging from the appeasers, who will
try to soften the book's meaning—to the glamorizers, who
will ascribe to it nothing worse than their own pet inanities—
to the compromisers, who will try to reconcile its theory with
its exact opposite—to the avant-garde, who will spell out and
demand the acceptance of its logical consequences. The contradictory, antithetical nature of such interpretations will be
ascribed to the book's profundity—particularly by those who
function on the motto: "If I don't understand it, it's deep."
The students will believe that the professors know the proof
of the book's theory, the professors will belive that the commentators know it, the commentators will believe that the

author knows it—and the author will be alone to know that no proof exists and that none was offered.

Within a generation, the number of commentaries will have grown to such proportions that the original book will be accepted as a subject of philosophical specialization, requiring a lifetime of study—and any refutation of the book's theory will be ignored or rejected, if unaccompanied by a full discussion of the theories of all the commentators, a task which no one will be able to undertake.

This is the process by which Kant and Hegel acquired their dominance. Many professors of philosophy today have no idea of what Kant actually said. And no one has ever read Hegel (even though many have looked at every word on his every page).

This process has already begun in regard to Mr. Rawls's book, in the form of such manifestations as Mr. Peregrine Worsthorne's "The New Inequality." But the process is being forced by P.R. techniques; it is being pushed artificially and in the wrong direction: toward the popular press and the man in the street, who, in this country, is the least likely prospect for the role of sucker. Furthermore, Mr. Rawls is not in Kant's league: he is a politically oriented lightweight, who has scrambled together the worst of the old philosophic traditions, adding nothing new. His two outstanding points of similarity to Kant are: the method—and the motive.

The danger lies in the cultural similarity of Kant's time and ours. An age ruled by skepticism and cynicism can be swayed by anyone, even Mr. Rawls. There is no intellectual opposition to anything today—as there was none to Kant. Kant's opponents were men who shared all his fundamental premises (particularly altruism and mysticism), and merely engaged in nit-picking, thus hastening his victory. Today, the utilitarians, the religionists, and sundry other "conservatives" share all of Mr. Rawls's fundamental premises (particularly altruism). If his book does not make them see the nature of altruism and its logical consequences, if it does not make them realize that altruism is the destroyer of man (and of reason, justice, morality, civilization), then nothing will. When and if they get Mr. Rawls's world, they will have deserved it. So will the "practical" men whose lard-encrusted souls feel that ideas are innocuous playthings to be left to impractical intellectuals, and that any idea can be circumvented by making a deal with the government.

But it is only by default—by intellectual default—that theories such as Kant's or Rawls's can win. An intransigent, *rational* opposition could have stopped Kant in his time. Rawls is easier to defeat—particularly in this country, which is the living monument to a diametrically opposite philosophy (he would have had a better chance in Europe). If there is any spirit of rebellion on American campuses (and elsewhere), *here* is an evil to rebel against, to rebel *intellectually*, righteously, intransigently: any hint, touch, smell, or trial balloon of *A Theory of Justice* and of the egalitarian movement.

If rational men do not rebel, the egalitarians will succeed. Succeed in establishing a world of shoddy equality and brotherly stagnation? No—but this is not their purpose. Just as Kant's purpose was to corrupt and paralyze man's mind, so the egalitarians' purpose is to shackle and paralyze the men of ability (even at the price of destroying the world).

If you wish to know the actual motive behind the egalitarians' theories—behind all their maudlin slogans, mawkish pleas, and ponderous volumes of verbal rat-traps—if you wish to grasp the enormity of the smallness of spirit for the sake of which they seek to immolate mankind, it can be presented in a few lines:

"'When a man thinks he's good—*that's* when he's rotten. Pride is the worst of all sins, no matter what he's done.'

"'But if a man knows that what he's done is good?'

"'Then he ought to apologize for it.'

"'To whom?'

"'To those who haven't done it.'" *(Atlas Shrugged.)*

12

Egalitarianism and Inflation

1974

The classic example of vicious irresponsibility is the story of Emperor Nero who fiddled, or sang poetry, while Rome burned. An example of similar behavior may be seen today in a less dramatic form. There is nothing imperial about the actors, they are not one single bloated monster, but a swarm of undernourished professors, there is nothing resembling poetry, even bad poetry, in the sounds they make, except for pretentiousness—but they are prancing around the fire and, while chanting that they want to help, are pouring paper refuse on the flames. They are those amorphous intellectuals who are preaching *egalitarianism* to a leaderless country on the brink of an unprecedented disaster.

Egalitarianism is so evil—and so silly—a doctrine that it deserves no serious study or discussion. But that doctrine has a certain diagnostic value: it is the open confession of the hidden disease that has been eating away the insides of civilization for two centuries (or longer) under many disguises and cover-ups. Like the half-witted member of a family struggling to preserve a reputable front, egalitarianism has escaped from a dark closet and is screaming to the world that the motive of its compassionate, "humanitarian," altruistic, collectivist brothers is not the desire to help the poor, but to destroy the competent. The motive is hatred of the good for being the good—a hatred focused specifically on the fountainhead of all goods, spiritual or material: the men of ability.

The mental process underlying the egalitarians' hope to achieve their goal consists of three steps: 1. they believe that that which they refuse to identify does not exist; 2. therefore, human ability does not exist; and 3. therefore, they are free to devise social schemes which would obliterate this non-existent. Of special significance to the present discussion is the egalitarians' defiance of the Law of Causality: their demand for equal results from unequal causes—or equal rewards for unequal performance.

As an example, I shall quote from a review by Bennett M. Berger, professor of sociology at the University of California, San Diego (*The New York Times Book Review*, January 6, 1974). The review discusses a book entitled *More Equality* by Herbert Gans. I have not read and do not intend to read that book: it is the reviewer's own notions that are particularly interesting and revealing. "[Herbert Gans] makes it clear from the start," writes Mr. Berger, "that he's not talking about equality of opportunity, which almost nobody seems to be against any more, but about equality of 'results,' what used to be called 'equality of condition.' . . . What he cares most about is reducing inequalities of income, wealth and political power. . . . More equality could be achieved, according to Gans, by income redistribution (mostly through a version of the Credit Income Tax) and by decentralizations of power ranging from more equality in hierarchical organizations (e.g., corporations and universities) to a kind of 'community control' that would provide to those minorities most victimized by inequality some insulation against being consistently outvoted by the relatively affluent majorities of the larger political constituencies."

If being consistently *outvoted* is a social injustice, what about big businessmen, who are the smallest minority and would always be consistently outvoted by other groups? Mr. Berger does not say, but since he consistently equates economic power with political power, and seems to believe that money can buy anything, one can guess what his answer would be. And, in any case, he is not an admirer of "democracy."

Mr. Berger reveals some of his motivation when he describes Herbert Gans as a "policy scientist" who suffers from a certain "malaise." "Part of this malaise is a nightmare in which 'the policy scientist'—not *poorly* prepared, but *in full possession* of the facts, reasons and plans he needs to promote persuasively the changes he advocates . . .—is frustrated, defeated, humiliated by Congressional committees and executive staffs politically beholden to the constituencies and the patrons who keep them in office." In other words: they did not let him have his way.

Lest you think it is only material wealth that Mr. Berger is out to destroy, consider the following: "Decentralization of power, for example, doesn't necessarily produce more equality. . . . Even the direct democracy of the New England town meeting . . . does very little to rid the local political community of the excessive influence exercised by the more educated, the more articulate, the more politically hip." This means that the educated and the ignorant, the articulate and the incoherent, the politically active and the passive or inert should have an equal influence and an equal power over everyone's life. There is only one instrument that can create an equality of this kind: a gun.

Mr. Berger stresses that he agrees with Mr. Gans's egalitarian goal, but he doubts that it can be achieved by the open advocacy of more equality. And, with remarkably open cynicism, Mr. Berger suggests "another strategy": "The advocacy of equality inevitably comes into conflict with other liberal values, such as individualism and achievement. But . . . the advocacy of 'citizenship' does not, and the history of democracy is a history of political struggles to win more and more 'rights' for more and more people to bring ever larger proportions of the population to fully functioning citizenship. . . . in the 20th century there have been struggles to remove racial and sexual impediments . . . to win rights to decent housing, medical care, education—all on the grounds not of 'equality,' but on the grounds that they are necessary conditions for citizens, equal by definition, to exercise their responsibility to govern themselves. Who knows what 'rights' lie over the horizon: a right to orgasm, to feel beautiful? I think these will make people better citizens." In other words, he suggests that egalitarian goals can be achieved by blowing up the term "citizenship" into a totalitarian concept, i.e., a concept embracing all of life.

If Mr. Berger is that open in advising the setting up of an ideological booby trap, who are the boobs he expects to catch? The underendowed? The general public? Or the intellectuals, whom he tempts with such bait as "a right to orgasm" in exchange for forgetting individualism and achievement? I hope your guess is as good as mine.

I will not argue against egalitarian doctrines by defending individualism, achievement, and the men of ability—not after writing *Atlas Shrugged*. I will let reality speak for me—it usually does.

Under the heading of "Allende's Legacy," an article in *The Wall Street Journal* (April 19, 1974) offers some concrete, real-life examples of what happens when income, wealth and power are distributed equally among all men, regardless of their competence, character, knowledge, achievement, or brains.

"By the time the military acted to overthrow the Allende government, prices had soared more than 1000 percent in two years and were climbing at the rate of 3 percent a day at the very end. The national treasury was practically empty." The socialist government had seized a number of American-owned industrial firms. The new military government invited the American managements to come back. Most of them accepted.

Among them was the Dow Chemical Company, which

owned a plastics plant in Chile. Bob G. Caldwell, Dow's di-
rector of operations for South America, came with a technical
team to inspect the remains of their plant. "'What we found
was unbelievable to us,' he recalls. 'The plant was still oper-
able, but in another six months we wouldn't have had any
plant at all. They never checked anything. We found valves
that hadn't been maintained leaking corrosive chemicals that
would have eventually eaten away practically everything.' . . .
Worse yet, the highly inflammable chemicals handled at the
plant were in imminent danger of blowing up. 'Safety went to
pot,' Mr. Caldwell says. 'The fire-sprinkler system was dis-
connected and the valves taken away for some other use outside. Then they were smoking in the most dangerous areas.
They told us, "You didn't have any fires while you were here
before, so it must not be as dangerous as you said."'"

I submit that the mentality represented by this last
sentence, a mentality capable of functioning in this manner,
is the loathsomely evil root of all human evils.

Apparently, some mentalities in the new Chilean government belong to the same category: they have the same range
and scope, but the consequences of *their* actions are not so
immediately perceivable, though not much farther away. In
order to avoid labor disputes, the new government has frozen
all labor contracts in the form and on the terms established
under the Allende regime. For example, the Dow Company's
contract includes a "requirement that all the plant's plastic
scrap be given to the union, which then sells it. 'We hope to
get that one changed,' a company official says, 'because it's a
clear incentive to produce almost nothing but scrap.'"

Then there is the case of a big Santiago textile firm. "Its
contract with 1,300 workers virtually guarantees bankruptcy.
The textile firm's employes get a certain amount of cloth free
as part of their wages and can buy unlimited quantities at a 37
percent discount; at those prices the firm loses money. Under
President Allende the workers sold the cloth on the black
market at huge profits, and it was an important factor in assuring their backing for the Allende government."

How long can a company—or a country, or mankind—
survive under a policy of this sort? Most people today do not
see the answer, but some do. Material shortages are the consequence of another, much more profound shortage, which is
created by egalitarian governments and ignored by the
public—until it is too late. "Chile's experiment with Marxism
has also left the country with a shortage of engineers and
technicians that could reach serious proportions. Thousands
of them left during the Allende regime. Despite incentives offered by the junta, they haven't been coming back, and many
more key people continue to leave for higher-paying jobs
abroad. . . . 'Here in Chile [says a business executive] we
must get used to the fact that good people must be paid
well.'"

But here in the United States, we are told to get used to the
idea that they must not.

There is no such thing as "good people," cries Professor
Berger—or Professor Gans, or Professor Rawls—and if some
are good, it's because they're exploiting those who aren't.
There is no such thing as "key people," says Professor Berger, we're all equal by definition. No, says Professor Rawls,
some were born with unfair advantages, such as intelligence,
and should be made to atone for it to those who weren't. We
want more equality, says Professor Gans, so that those who
devise sprinkler systems and those who smoke around inflammable chemicals would have equal pay, equal influence,
and an equal voice in the community control of science and
production.

The term "brain drain" is known the world over: it names a
problem which various governments are beginning to recognize, and are trying to solve by chaining the men of ability to
their homelands—yet social theoreticians see no connection
between intelligence and production. The best among men
are running—from every corner and slave-pen of the
globe—running in search of freedom. Their refusal to coop-
erate with slave drivers is the noblest moral action they could
take—and, incidentally, the greatest service they could ren-

der mankind—but they don't know it. No voices are raised anywhere in their honor, in acknowledgment of their value, in recognition of their importance. Those whose job it is to know—those who profess concern with the plight of the world—look on and say nothing. The intellectuals turn their eyes away, refusing to know—the practical men do know, but keep silent.

One can't blame the dazed brutes of Chile, who swoop down on an industrial plant and cavort at a black-market fiesta, for not understanding that the plant cannot run at a loss—if their social superiors tell them that they are entitled to more equality. One can't blame savages for not understanding that everything has its price, and what they steal, seize or extort today will be paid for by their own starvation tomorrow—if their social superiors, in management offices, in university classrooms, in newspaper columns, in parliamentary halls, are afraid to tell them.

What are all those people counting on? If a Chilean factory goes bankrupt, the equalizers will find another factory to loot. If that other factory starts crumbling, it will get a loan from the bank. If the bank has no money, it will get a loan from the government. If the government has no money, it will get a loan from a foreign government. If no foreign government has any money, all of them will get a loan from the United States.

What they don't know—and neither does this country—is that the United States is broke.

Justice does exist in the world, whether people choose to practice it or not. The men of ability are being avenged. The avenger is reality. Its weapon is slow, silent, invisible, and men perceive it only by its consequences—by the gutted ruins and the moans of agony it leaves in its wake. The name of the weapon is: *inflation*.

Inflation is a man-made scourge, made possible by the fact that most men do not understand it. It is a crime committed on so large a scale that its size is its protection: the integrating capacity of the victims' minds breaks down before the magnitude—and the seeming complexity—of the crime, which permits it to be committed openly, in public. For centuries, inflation has been wrecking one country after another, yet men learn nothing, offer no resistance, and perish—not like animals driven to slaughter, but worse: like animals stampeding in search of a butcher.

If I told you that the *precondition* of inflation is psycho-epistemological—that inflation is hidden under perceptual illusions created by broken conceptual links—you would not understand me. *That* is what I propose to explain and to prove.

Let us start at the beginning. Observe the fact that, as a human being, you are compelled by nature to eat at least once a day. In a modern American city, this is not a major problem. You can carry your sustenance in your pocket—in the form of a few coins. You can give it no thought, you can skip meals, and, when you're hungry, you can grab a sandwich or open a can of food—which, you believe, will always be there.

But project what the necessity to eat would mean in nature, i.e., if you were alone in a primeval wilderness. Hunger, nature's ultimatum, would make demands on you daily, but the satisfaction of the demands would not be available immediately: the satisfaction takes time—and tools. It takes time to hunt and to make your weapons. You have other needs as well. You need clothing—it takes time to kill a leopard and to get its skin. You need shelter—it takes time to build a hut, and food to sustain you while you're building it. The satisfaction of your daily physical needs would absorb all of your time. Observe that time is the price of your survival, and that it has to be paid in advance.

Would it make any difference if there were ten of you, instead of one? If there were a hundred of you? A thousand? A hundred thousand? Do not let the numbers confuse you: in regard to nature, the facts will remain inexorably the same. Socially, the large numbers may enable some men to enslave others and to live without effort, but unless a sufficient number of men are able to hunt, all of you will perish and so will your rulers.

The issue becomes much clearer when you discover agriculture. You can survive more safely and comfortably by planting seeds and collecting a harvest months later—on condition that you comply with two absolutes of nature: you must save enough of your harvest to feed you until the next harvest, and, above all, you must save enough seeds to plant your next harvest. You may run short on your own food, you may have to skimp and go half-hungry, but, under penalty of death, you do not touch your stock seed; if you do, you're through.

Agriculture is the first step toward civilization, because it requires a significant advance in men's conceptual development: it requires that they grasp two cardinal concepts which the perceptual, concrete-bound mentality of the hunters could not grasp fully: *time* and *savings*. Once you grasp these, you have grasped the three essentials of human survival: time-savings-production. You have grasped the fact that production is not a matter confined to the immediate moment, but a continuous process, and that production is fueled by previous production. The concept of "stock seed" unites the three essentials and applies not merely to agriculture, but much, much more widely: to *all* forms of productive work. Anything above the level of a savage's precarious, hand-to-mouth existence requires *savings*. Savings buy *time*.

If you live on a self-sustaining farm, you save your grain: you need the saved harvest of your good years to carry you through the bad ones; you need your saved seed to expand your production—to plant a larger field. The safer your supply of food, the more time it buys for the upkeep or improvement of the other things you need: your clothing, your shelter, your water well, your livestock and, above all, your tools, such as your plow. You make a gigantic step forward when you discover that you can trade with other farmers, which leads you all to the discovery of the road to an advanced

civilization: the division of labor. Let us say that there are a
hundred of you; each learns to specialize in the production of
some goods needed by all, and you trade your products by
direct barter. All of you become more expert at your tasks—
therefore, more productive—therefore, your time brings you
better returns.

On a self-sustaining farm, your savings consisted mainly of
stored grain and foodstuffs; but grain and foodstuffs are
perishable and cannot be kept for long, so you ate what you
could not save; your time-range was limited. Now, your horizon has been pushed immeasurably farther. You don't have to
expand the storage of your food: you can trade your grain for
some commodity which will keep longer, and which you can
trade for food when you need it. But which commodity? It is
thus that you arrive at the next gigantic discovery: you devise
a tool of exchange—*money*.

Money is the tool of men who have reached a high level of
productivity and a long-range control over their lives. Money
is not merely a tool of exchange: much more importantly, it is
a tool of saving, which permits delayed consumption and buys
time for future production. To fulfill this requirement, money
has to be some material commodity which is imperishable,
rare, homogeneous, easily stored, not subject to wide fluctua-
tions of value, and always in demand among those you trade
with. This leads you to the decision to use gold as money.
Gold money is a tangible value in itself and a token of wealth
actually produced. When you accept a gold coin in payment
for your goods, you actually deliver the goods to the buyer;
the transaction is as safe as simple barter. When you store
your savings in the form of gold coins, they represent the
goods which you have actually produced and which have gone
to buy time for other producers, who will keep the productive
process going, so that you'll be able to trade your coins for
goods any time you wish.

Now project what would happen to your community of a
hundred hard-working, prosperous, forward-moving people, if

one man were allowed to trade on your market, not by means of gold, but by means of paper—i.e., if he paid you, not with a material commodity, not with goods he had actually produced, but merely with a promissory note on his future production. This man takes your goods, but does not use them to support his own production; he does not produce at all—he merely consumes the goods. Then, he pays you higher prices for more goods—again in promissory notes—assuring you that he is your best customer, who expands your market.

Then, one day, a struggling young farmer, who suffered from a bad flood, wants to buy some grain from you, but your price has risen and you haven't much grain to spare, so he goes bankrupt. Then, the dairy farmer, to whom he owed money, raises the price of milk to make up for the loss—and the truck farmer, who needs the milk, gives up buying the eggs he had always bought—and the poultry farmer kills some of his chickens, which he can't afford to feed—and the alfalfa grower, who can't afford the higher price of eggs, sells some of his stock seed and cuts down on his planting—and the dairy farmer can't afford the higher price of alfalfa, so he cancels his order to the blacksmith—and you want to buy the new plow you have been saving for, but the blacksmith has gone bankrupt. Then all of you present the promissory notes to your "best customer," and you discover that they were promissory notes not on *his* future production, but on *yours*—only you have nothing left to produce with. Your land is there, your structures are there, but there is no food to sustain you through the coming winter, and no stock seed to plant.

Would it make any difference if that community consisted of a thousand farmers? A hundred thousand? A million? Two hundred and eleven million? The entire globe? No matter how widely you spread the blight, no matter what variety of products and what incalculable complexity of deals become involved, *this*, dear readers, is the cause, the pattern, and the outcome of inflation.

There is only one institution that can arrogate to itself the power legally to trade by means of rubber checks: the government. And it is the only institution that can mortgage your future without your knowledge or consent: government securities (and paper money) are promissory notes on future tax receipts, i.e., on your future production.

Now project the mentality of a savage, who can grasp nothing but the concretes of the immediate moment, and who finds himself transported into the midst of a modern, industrial civilization. If he is an intelligent savage, he will acquire a smattering of knowledge, but there are two concepts he will not be able to grasp: "credit" and "market."

He observes that people get food, clothes, and all sorts of objects simply by presenting pieces of paper called checks—and he observes that skyscrapers and gigantic factories spring out of the ground at the command of very rich men, whose bookkeepers keep switching magic figures from the ledgers of one to those of another and another and another. This seems to be done faster than he can follow, so he concludes that *speed* is the secret of the magic power of paper—and that everyone will work and produce and prosper, so long as those checks are passed from hand to hand fast enough. If that savage breaks into print with his discovery, he will find that he has been anticipated by John Maynard Keynes.

Then the savage observes that the department stores are full of wonderful goods, but people do not seem to buy them. "Why is that?" he asks a floorwalker. "We don't have enough of a market," the floorwalker tells him. "What is that?" he asks. "Well," his new teacher answers, "goods are produced for people to consume, it's the consumers that make the world go 'round, but we don't have enough consumers." "Is that so?" says the savage, his eyes flashing with the fire of a new idea. Next day, he obtains a check from a big educational foundation, he hires a plane, he flies away—and comes back, a while later, bringing his entire naked, barefoot tribe along.

"You don't know how good they are at consuming," he tells his friend, the floorwalker, "and there's plenty more where these came from. Pretty soon you'll get a raise in pay." But the store, pretty soon, goes bankrupt.

The poor savage is unable to understand it to this day—because he had made sure that many, many people agreed with his idea, among them many noble tribal chiefs, such as Governor Romney, who sang incantations to "consumerism," and warrior Nader, who fought for the consumers' rights, and big business chieftains who recited formulas about serving the consumers, and chiefs who sat in Congress, and chiefs in the White House, and chiefs in every government in Europe, and many more professors than he could count.

Perhaps it is harder for us to understand that the mentality of that savage has been ruling Western civilization for almost a century.

Trained in college to believe that to look beyond the immediate moment—to look for causes or to foresee consequences—is impossible, modern men have developed context-dropping as their normal method of cognition. Observing a bad, small-town shopkeeper, the kind who is doomed to fail, they believe—as he does—that lack of customers is his only problem; and that the question of the goods he sells, or *where these goods come from*, has nothing to do with it. The goods, they believe, are here and will always be here. Therefore, they conclude, the consumer—not the producer—is the motor of an economy. Let us extend credit, i.e., our savings, to the consumers—they advise—in order to expand the market for our goods.

But, in fact, consumers *qua consumers* are not part of any one's market; qua consumers, they are *irrelevant* to economics. Nature does not grant anyone an innate title of "consumer"; it is a title that has to be earned—by production. Only *producers* constitute a market—only men who trade products or services for products or services. In the role of producers, they represent a market's "supply"; in the role of consumers, they represent a market's "demand." The law of supply and demand has an implicit subclause: that it involves the same people in both capacities. When this subclause is forgotten, ignored or evaded—you get the economic situation of today.

A successful producer can support many people, e.g., his children, by delegating to them his market power of consumer. Can that capacity be unlimited? How many men would you be able to feed on a self-sustaining farm? In more primitive times, farmers used to raise large families in order to obtain farm labor, i.e., productive help. How many *non-productive* people could you support by your own effort? If the number were unlimited, if demand became greater than supply—if demand were turned into a *command*, as it is today—you would have to use and exhaust your stock seed. *This* is the process now going on in this country.

There is only one institution that could bring it about: the government—with the help of a vicious doctrine that serves as a cover-up: altruism. The visible profiteers of altruism— the welfare recipients—are part victims, part window dressing for the statist policies of the government. But no government could have got away with it, if people had grasped the other concept which the savage was unable to grasp: the concept of "credit."

If you understand the function of stock seed—of *savings*—in a primitive farm community, apply the same principle to a complex industrial economy.

Wealth represents goods that have been produced, but not consumed. What would a man do with his wealth in terms of direct barter? Let us say a successful shoe manufacturer wants to enlarge his production. His wealth consists of shoes; he trades some shoes for the things he needs as a consumer, but he saves a large number of shoes and trades them for building materials, machinery and labor to build a new factory—and another large number of shoes, for raw materials and for the labor he will employ to manufacture more shoes. Money facilitates this trading, but does not change its nature. All the physical goods and services he needs for his project must actually exist and be available for trade—just as his payment for them must actually exist in the form of physical goods (in this case, shoes). An exchange of paper money (or even of gold coins) would not do any good to any of the parties involved, if the physical things they needed were not there and could not be obtained in exchange for the money.

If a man does not consume his goods at once, but saves them for the future, whether he wants to enlarge his production or to live on his savings (which he holds in the form of money)—in either case, he is counting on the fact that he will be able to exchange his money for the things he needs, when and as he needs them. This means that he is relying on a continuous process of production—which requires an uninterrupted flow of goods saved to fuel further and further production. This flow is "investment capital," the stock seed of industry. When a rich man lends money to others, what he lends to them is the goods which he has not consumed.

This is the meaning of the concept "investment." If you have wondered how one can start producing, when nature requires time paid in advance, this is the beneficent process that enables men to do it: a successful man lends his goods to a promising beginner (or to any reputable producer)—in exchange for the payment of interest. The payment is for the risk he is taking: nature does not guarantee man's success, neither on a farm nor in a factory. If the venture fails, it means that the goods have been consumed without a productive return, so the investor loses his money; if the venture succeeds, the producer pays the interest out of the new goods, the *profits*, which the investment enabled him to make.

Observe, and bear in mind above all else, that this process applies *only* to financing the needs of production, *not* of consumption—and that its success rests on the investor's judgment of men's productive ability, *not* on his compassion for their feelings, hopes or dreams.

Such is the meaning of the term "credit." In all its countless variations and applications, "credit" means money, i.e.,
unconsumed goods, loaned by one productive person (or
group) to another, to be repaid out of future production. Even
the credit extended for a consumption purpose, such as the
purchase of an automobile, is based on the productive record
and prospects of the borrower. Credit is not—as the savage
believed—a magic piece of paper that reverses cause and effect, and transforms consumption into a source of production.

Consumption is the *final*, not the *efficient*, cause of production. The efficient cause is savings, which can be said to
represent the opposite of consumption: they represent *unconsumed* goods. Consumption is the end of production, and a
dead end, as far as the productive process is concerned. The
worker who produces so little that he consumes everything he
earns, carries his own weight economically, but contributes
nothing to future production. The worker who has a modest
savings account, and the millionaire who invests a fortune
(and all the men in between), are those who finance the future. The man who consumes without producing is a parasite,
whether he is a welfare recipient or a rich playboy.

An industrial economy is enormously complex: it involves
calculations of time, of motion, of credit, and long sequences
of interlocking contractual exchanges. This complexity is the
system's great virtue and the source of its vulnerability. The
vulnerability is psycho-epistemological. No human mind and
no computer—and no planner—can grasp the complexity in
every detail. Even to grasp the principles that rule it, is a
major feat of abstraction. This is where the conceptual links
of men's integrating capacity break down: most people are
unable to grasp the working of their home-town's economy,
let alone the country's or the world's. Under the influence of
today's mind-shrinking, anti-conceptual education, most
people tend to see economic problems in terms of immediate
concretes: of their paychecks, their landlords, and the corner
grocery store. The most disastrous loss—which broke their

tie to reality—is the loss of the concept that money stands for existing, but unconsumed goods.

The system's complexity serves, occasionally, as a temporary cover for the operations of some shady characters. You have all heard of some manipulator who does not work, but lives in luxury by obtaining a loan, which he repays by obtaining another loan elsewhere, which he repays by obtaining another loan, etc. You know that his policy can't go on forever, that it catches up with him eventually and he crashes. But what if that manipulator is the government?

The government is not a productive enterprise. It produces nothing. In respect to its legitimate functions—which are the police, the army, the law courts—it performs a service needed by a productive economy. When a government steps beyond these functions, it becomes an economy's destroyer.

The government has no source of revenue, except the taxes paid by the producers. To free itself—for a while—from the limits set by reality, the government initiates a credit con game on a scale which the private manipulator could not dream of. It borrows money from you today, which is to be repaid with money it will borrow from you tomorrow, which is to be repaid with money it will borrow from you day after tomorrow, and so on. This is known as "deficit financing." It is made possible by the fact that the government cuts the connection between goods and money. It issues paper money, which is used as a claim check on actually existing goods—but that money is not backed by any goods, it is not backed by gold, it is backed by nothing. It is a promissory note issued to you in exchange for your goods, to be paid by you (in the form of taxes) out of your future production.

Where does your money go? Anywhere and nowhere. First, it goes to establish an altruistic excuse and window dressing for the rest: to establish a system of subsidized consumption—a "welfare" class of men who consume without producing—a growing dead end, imposed on a shrinking production. Then the money goes to subsidize any pressure

group at the expense of any other—to buy their votes—to
finance any project conceived at the whim of any bureaucrat
or his friends—to pay for the failure of that project, to start
another, etc. The welfare recipients are not the worst part of
the producers' burden. The worst part are the bureaucrats—
the government officials who are given the power to regulate
production. They are not merely unproductive consumers:
their job consists in making it harder and harder and, ultimately, impossible for the producers to produce. (Most of
them are men whose ultimate goal is to place all producers in
the position of welfare recipients.)

While the government struggles to save one crumbling
enterprise at the expense of the crumbling of another, it ac-
celerates the process of juggling debts, switching losses, pil-
ing loans on loans, mortgaging the future and the future's future. As things grow worse, the government protects itself not
by contracting this process, but by expanding it. The process
becomes global: it involves foreign aid, and unpaid loans to
foreign governments, and subsidies to other welfare states,
and subsidies to the United Nations, and subsidies to the
World Bank, and subsidies to foreign producers, and credits
to foreign consumers to enable them to consume our goods—
while, simultaneously, the American producers, who are paying for it all, are left without protection, and their properties
are seized by any sheik in any pesthole of the globe, and the
wealth they have created, as well as their energy, is turned
against them, as, for example, in the case of Middle Eastern
oil.

Do you think a spending orgy of this kind could be paid for
out of current production? No, the situation is much worse
than that. *The government is consuming this country's stock
seed*—the stock seed of industrial production: investment
capital, i.e., the savings needed to keep production going.
These savings were not paper, but actual goods. Under all the
complexities of private credit, the economy was kept going by
the fact that, in one form or another, in one place or another,

somewhere within it, actual material goods existed to back its financial transactions. It kept going long after that protection was breached. Today, the goods are almost gone.

A piece of paper will not feed you when there is no bread to eat. It will not build a factory when there are no steel girders to buy. It will not make shoes when there is no leather, no machines, no fuel. You have heard it said that today's economy is afflicted by sudden, unpredictable shortages of various commodities. These are the advance symptoms of what is to come.

You have heard economists say that they are puzzled by the nature of today's problem: they are unable to understand why inflation is accompanied by recession—which is contrary to their Keynesian doctrines; and they have coined a ridiculous name for it: "stagflation." Their theories ignore the fact that money can function only so long as it represents actual goods —and that at a certain stage of inflating the money supply, the government begins to consume a nation's investment capital, thus making production impossible.

The value of the total tangible assets of the United States at present, was estimated—in terms of 1968 dollars—at 3.1 trillion dollars. If government spending continues, that incredible wealth will not save you. You may be left with all the magnificent skyscrapers, the giant factories, the rich farmlands—but without fuel, without electricity, without transportation, without steel, without paper, without seeds to plant the next harvest.

If that time comes, the government will declare explicitly the premise on which it has been acting implicitly: that its only "capital asset" is *you*. Since you will not be able to work any longer, the government will take over and will make you work—on a slope descending to sub-industrial production. The only substitute for technological energy is the muscular labor of slaves. This is the way an economic collapse leads to dictatorship—as it did in Germany and in Russia. And if anyone thinks that government planning is a solution to the

problems of human survival, observe that after half a century
of total dictatorship, Soviet Russia is begging for American
wheat and for American industrial "know-how."

A dictatorship would find it impossible to rule this country
in the foreseeable future. What *is* possible is the blind chaos
of a civil war.

It is at a time like this, in the face of an approaching economic collapse, that the intellectuals are preaching egalitarian
notions. When the curtailment of government spending is imperative, they demand more welfare projects. When the need
for men of productive ability is desperate, they demand more
equality for the incompetents. When the country needs the
accumulation of capital, they demand that we soak the rich.
When the country needs more savings, they demand a "redistribution of income." They demand more jobs and less
profits—more jobs and fewer factories—more jobs and no
fuel, no oil, no coal, no "pollution"—but, above all, more
goods for free to more consumers, no matter what happens to
jobs, to factories, or to producers.

The results of their Keynesian economics are wrecking
every industrial country, but they refuse to question their
basic assumptions. The examples of Soviet Russia, of Nazi
Germany, of Red China, of Marxist Chile, of socialist England
are multiplying around them, but they refuse to see and to
learn. Today, production is the world's most urgent need, and
the threat of starvation is spreading through the globe; the
intellectuals know the only economic system that can and did
produce unlimited abundance, but they give it no thought and
keep silent about it, as if it had never existed. It is almost
irrelevant to blame them for their default at the task of intellectual leadership: the smallness of their stature is overwhelming.

Is there any hope for the future of this country? Yes, there
is. This country has one asset left: the matchless productive
ability of its people. If, and to the extent that, this ability is
liberated, we might still have a chance to avoid a collapse. We

cannot expect to reach the ideal overnight, but we must at least reveal its name. We must reveal to this country the secret which all those posturing intellectuals of any political denomination, who clamor for openness and truth, are trying so hard to cover up: that the name of that miraculous productive system is *Capitalism.*

As to such things as taxes and the rebuilding of a country, I will say that in his goals, if not his methods, the best economist in *Atlas Shrugged* was Ragnar Danneskjöld.

13

The Stimulus and the Response
1972

THE STIMULUS

There are occasions when a worthless, insignificant book acquires significance as a scrap of litmus paper exposing a culture's intellectual state. Such a book is *Beyond Freedom and Dignity* by B. F. Skinner.

"Skinner is the most influential of living American psychologists . . ." says *Time* magazine (September 20, 1971). "Skinner has remained a highly influential figure among U.S. college students for well over a decade," says *Newsweek* (September 20, 1971). "Burrhus Frederic Skinner is the most influential psychologist alive today, and he is second only to Freud as the most important psychologist of all time. This, at least, is the feeling of 56 percent of the members of the American Psychological Association, who were polled on the question. And it should be reason enough to make Dr. Skinner's new book, *Beyond Freedom and Dignity*, one of the most important happenings in 20th century psychology," says *Science News* (August 7, 1971).

One cannot evaluate the cultural significance of such statements until one identifies the nature of their object.

The book itself is like Boris Karloff's embodiment of Frankenstein's monster: a corpse patched with nuts, bolts and screws from the junkyard of philosophy (Pragmatism, Social Darwinism, Positivism, Linguistic Analysis, with some nails by Hume, threads by Russell, and glue by the *New York Post*). The book's voice, like Karloff's, is an emission of inarticulate, moaning growls—directed at a special enemy: "Autonomous Man."

"Autonomous Man" is the term used by Mr. Skinner to denote man's consciousness in all those aspects which distinguish it from the sensory level of an animal's consciousness—specifically: reason, mind, values, concepts, thought, judgment, volition, purpose, memory, independence, self-esteem. These, he asserts, do not exist; they are an illusion, a myth, a "prescientific" superstition. His term may be taken to include everything we call "man's inner world," except that Mr. Skinner would never allow such an expression; whenever he has to refer to man's inner world, he says: "Inside your skin."

"Inside his skin," man is totally determined by his environment (and by his genetic endowment, which was determined by his ancestors' environment), Mr. Skinner asserts, and totally malleable. By controlling the environment, "behavioral technologists" could—and should—control men inside out. If people were brought to give up individual autonomy and to join Mr. Skinner in proclaiming: "To man *qua* man we readily say good riddance" (p. 201), the behavioral technologists would create a new species and a perfect world. This is the book's thesis.

One expects that an assertion of this kind would be supported by some demonstration or indication of the methods these technologists will use in order to manipulate those nonautonomous bipeds. Curiously enough, there is no such indication in the book. I may be flattering Mr. Skinner, but it occurred to me that perhaps *the book itself* was intended to be a demonstration of the methods he envisions.

There are certain conditions which the book requires of its readers: (a) Being out of focus. (b) Skimming. (c) Self-doubt.

(d) The premise, when confronted with outrageous absurdity: "I don't get it, but he must have reasons for saying it."

These conditions will bring the reader to miss the main ingredients of the book's epistemological method, which are: 1. Equivocation. 2. Substituting metaphors for proof, and examples for definitions. 3. Setting up and knocking down straw men. 4. Mentioning a given notion as controversial, following it up with two or three pages of irrelevant small talk, then mentioning it again and treating it as if it had been proved. 5. Raising valid questions (to indicate that the author is aware of them) and, by the same technique, leaving them unanswered. 6. Overtalking and overloading the reader's consciousness with overelaborate discussions of trivia, then smuggling in enormous essentials without discussion, as if they were incontrovertible. 7. Assuming an authoritarian tone to enunciate dogmatic absolutes—and the more dubious the absolute, the more authoritarian the tone. 8. Providing a brief summary at the end of each chapter, which summary includes, as if they had been proved, notions not included or barely mentioned in the chapter's text.

All of this (and more) is done grossly, crudely, obviously, which leaves the book pockmarked with gaping craters of contradictions, like a moon landscape and as lifelessly dull.

In *Atlas Shrugged,* I discussed two variants of mysticism: the mystics of spirit and the mystics of muscle, "those who believe in consciousness without existence and those who believe in existence without consciousness. Both demand the surrender of your mind, one to their revelations, the other to their reflexes." I said that their aims are alike: "in matter— the enslavement of man's body, in spirit—the destruction oɪ his mind."

Mr. Skinner is a mystic of muscle—so extreme, complete, all-out a mystic of muscle that one could not use him in fiction: he sounds like a caricature.

At the start of his book, what he demands of his readers is: *faith.* "In what follows, these issues are discussed 'from a

scientific point of view,' but this does not mean that the
reader will need to know the details of a scientific analysis of
behavior. A mere interpretation will suffice. . . . The in-
stances of behavior cited in what follows are not offered as
'proof' of the interpretation. The proof is to be found in the
basic analysis. The principles used in interpreting the in-
stances have a plausibility which would be lacking in principles drawn entirely from casual observation." (Pp. 22–23.)

This means: the proof of Mr. Skinner's theory is inaccessible to laymen, who must take him on faith, substituting
"plausibility" for logic: if his "interpretation" sounds plausi-
ble, it means that he has valid ("non-casual") reasons for ex-
pounding it. This is offered as *scientific* epistemology.

(It must be noted that Mr. Skinner's interpretations of the
"scientific analysis of behavior" are rejected by a great many
experts initiated into its higher mysteries, not only by psy-
chiatrists and by psychologists of different schools, but even
by his own fellow-behaviorists.)

As a cover against criticism, Mr. Skinner resorts to the
mystics' usual scapegoat: language. "The text will often seem
inconsistent. English, like all languages, is full of prescientific
terms . . . but the issues are important to the nonspecialist
and need to be discussed in a nontechnical fashion." (Pp.
23–24.) The mystics of spirit accuse language of being "materialistic"; Mr. Skinner accuses it of being "mentalistic."
Both regard their own theories as *ineffable*, i.e., incommunicable in language.

Many psychologists are envious of the prestige—and the
achievements—of the physical sciences, which they try not to
emulate, but to imitate. Mr. Skinner is archetypical in this
respect: he is passionately intent on being accepted as a "scientist" and complains that only "Autonomous Man" stands in
the way of such acceptance (which, I am sure, is true). Mr.
Skinner points out scornfully that primitive men, who were
unable to see the difference between living beings and inanimate objects, ascribed the objects' motions to conscious gods

or demons, and that science could not begin until this belief was discarded. In the name of science, Mr. Skinner switches defiantly to the other side of the same basic coin: accepting the belief that consciousness is supernatural, he refuses to accept the existence of man's mind.

All human behavior, he asserts, is the product of a process called "operant conditioning"—and all the functions we ascribe to "Autonomous Man" are performed by a single agent called a "reinforcer." In view of the omnipotence ascribed to this agent throughout the book, a definition would have been very helpful, but here is all we get: "When a bit of behavior is followed by a certain kind of consequence, it is more likely to occur again, and a consequence having this effect is called a reinforcer. Food, for example, is a reinforcer to a hungry organism; anything the organism does that is followed by the receipt of food is more likely to be done again whenever the organism is hungry. . . . Negative reinforcers are called aversive in the sense that they are the things organisms 'turn away from.'" (P. 27.)

If you assume this means that a "reinforcer" is something which causes pleasure or pain, you will be wrong, because, on page 107, Mr. Skinner declares: "There is no important causal connection between the reinforcing effect of a stimulus and the feelings to which it gives rise. . . . What is maximized or minimized, or what is ultimately good or bad, are things, not feelings, and men work to achieve them or to avoid them not because of the way they feel but because they are positive or negative reinforcers." Then by what means or process do these "reinforcers" affect man's actions? In the whole of the book, no answer is given.

The only social difference between positive and negative "reinforcers" is the fact that the latter provoke "counterattack" or rebellion, and the former do not. Both are means of *controlling* man's behavior. "Productive labor, for example, was once the result of punishment: the slave worked to avoid the consequences of not working. Wages exemplify a different principle: a person is paid when he behaves in a given way so that he will continue to behave in that way." (P. 32.)

From this bit of package-dealing, context-dropping, and definition-by-nonessentials, Mr. Skinner slides to the assertion that slave-driving and wage-paying are both "techniques of control," then to the gigantic equivocation which underlies most of the others in his book: that every human relationship, every instance of men dealing with one another, is a form of *control.* You are "controlled" by the grocer across the street, because if he were not there, you would shop elsewhere. You are controlled by the person who praises you (praise is a "positive reinforcer"), and by the person who blames you (blame is an "aversive reinforcer"), etc., etc., etc.

Here Mr. Skinner revives the ancient saw to the effect that volition is an illusion, because one is not free if one has reasons for one's actions—and that true volition would consist in acting on *whim*, a causeless, unaccountable, inexplicable whim exercised in a vacuum, free of any contact with reality.

From this, Mr. Skinner's next step is easy: political freedom, he declares, necessitates the use of "aversive reinforcers," i.e., punishment for evil behavior. Since you are not free anyway, but controlled by everyone at all times, why not let specialists control you in a scientific way and design for you a world consisting of nothing but "positive reinforcers"?

What kind of world would that be? Here, Mr. Skinner seems to make a "Freudian slip": he is surprisingly explicit. ". . . it should be possible to design a world in which behavior likely to be punished seldom or never occurs. We try to design such a world for those who cannot solve the problem of punishment for themselves, such as babies, retardates, or psychotics, and if it could be done for everyone, much time and energy would be saved." (P. 66.)

" . . . there is no reason," he declares, "why progress toward a world in which people may be automatically good should be impeded." (P. 67.) No reason at all—provided you are willing to view yourself as a baby, a retardate or a psychotic.

"Dignity" is Mr. Skinner's odd choice of a designation for what is normally called *"moral worth"*—and he disposes of it by asserting that it consists in gaining the admiration of other people. Through a peculiar jumble of examples, which includes unrequited love, heroic deeds, and scientific (i.e., *intellectual*) achievements, Mr. Skinner labors to convince us that: " . . . we are likely to admire behavior more as we understand it less" (p. 53), and: " . . . the behavior we admire is the behavior we cannot yet explain." (P. 58.) It is mere vanity, he asserts, that makes our heroes cling to "dignity" and resist "scientific" analysis, because, once their achievements are explained, they will deserve no greater admiration—and *no greater credit*—than anyone else.

This last is the core, essence and purpose of his jumbled argument; the rest of the verbiage is merely a haphazard cover. There is a kind of veiled, subterranean intensity in Mr. Skinner's tired prose whenever he stresses the point that *men should be given no credit for their virtues or their achievements*. The behavior of a creative genius (my expression, not Mr. Skinner's) is determined by "contingencies of reinforcement," just like the behavior of a criminal, and neither of them can help it, and neither should be admired or blamed. Unlike other modern determinists, Mr. Skinner is not concerned primarily with the elimination of blame, but with the elimination of credit.

This sort of concern is almost self-explanatory. But I did find it surprising that Mr. Skinner includes achievement among the roots of *moral worth* (of "dignity"). He and I are probably the only two theoreticians who understand—from opposite moral poles—how much depends on this issue.

In reason, one would expect that so thorough a determinist as Mr. Skinner would not deal with questions of morality; but his abolition of reason frees him from concern with contradictions. *Beyond Freedom and Dignity* is a normative tract, prescribing the actions men *ought to* take (even though they have no volition), and the motives and beliefs they *ought to* adopt (even though there are no such things).

From the casual observation that "ethos and mores refer to the customary practices of a group" (pp. 112–113), Mr. Skinner slides to the assertion that morality is exclusively social, that moral principles are inculcated through socially designed contingencies of reinforcement "under which a person is induced to behave for the good of others," (p. 112)—then to the notion, smuggled in as an undiscussed absolute, that morality *is* behavior for the good of others—and then to the following remarkable passage: "The value or validity of the reinforcers used by other people and by organized agencies may be questioned: 'Why should I seek the admiration or avoid the censure of my fellow men?' 'What can my government—or any government—really do to me?' 'Can a church actually determine whether I am to be eternally damned or blessed?' 'What is so wonderful about money—do I need all the things it buys?' 'Why should I study the things set forth in a college catalogue?' In short, 'Why should I behave "for the good of others"?'" (Pp. 117–118.)

Yes, read that quotation over again. I had to, before I realized what Mr. Skinner means: he means that the asking of such questions is a violation of the good of others, because it challenges socially inculcated principles of behavior (so that even the pursuit of money or of a college education represents, not one's own good, but the good of others). And wider: all principles of long-range action, moral or practical, represent the good of others, because all principles are a social product.

This is supported by the statements immediately following the above quotation: "When the control exercised by others is thus evaded or destroyed, only the personal reinforcers are left. The individual turns to immediate gratification, possibly through sex or drugs." (P. 118.) Just as altruism is the primeval moral code of all mystics, of spirit or muscle, so this view of an individual's self-interest is their primordial cliché. But Mr. Skinner adds some epistemological "explanations" of his own.

Man, he asserts, is aware of nothing but the immediate moment: he has no capacity to form abstractions, to act by intention, to project the future. "Behavior is shaped and maintained by its consequences" (p. 18), and: "Behavior cannot really be affected by anything which follows it, but if a 'consequence' is immediate, it may overlap the behavior." (P. 120.) Evolution, he asserts, did the rest. "The process of operant conditioning presumably evolved when those organisms which were more sensitively affected by the consequences of their behavior were better able to adjust to the environment and survive." (P. 120.) What is this "sensitivity" and through what organ or faculty does it operate? No answer.

Claiming that man's first discoveries (such as banking a fire) were purely accidental (pp. 121–122), Mr. Skinner concludes that other men learned, somehow, to imitate those lucky practices. "One advantage in being a social animal is that one need not discover practices for oneself." (P. 122.) As to the time-range of man's awareness, Mr. Skinner asserts: "Probably no one plants in the spring simply because he then harvests in the fall. Planting would not be adaptive or 'reasonable' if there were no connection with a harvest, but one plants in the spring because of more immediate contingencies, most of them arranged by the social environment." (P. 122.) How is this done by a social environment consisting of men who are unable to think long-range? No answer.

The phenomenon of language is a problem to a mystic of muscle. Mr. Skinner gets around it semantically, by calling it "verbal behavior." "Verbal behavior presumably arose under contingencies involving practical social interactions . . ." (P. 122.) How? No answer. "Verbal behavior" is a means of controlling men, because words, somehow, become associated with physical "reinforcers." To be exact, one cannot use the word "words" in Mr. Skinner's context: it is sounds or marks on paper that acquire an associational link with the omnipotent "reinforcers" and stick inside a man's skin, forming "a repertoire of verbal behavior." This would require an incredible feat of memorizing. But Mr. Skinner denies the existence of memory—he calls it "storage" and declares: "Evolutionary and environmental histories change an organism, but they are not stored within it." (Pp. 195–196.) His view of the nature of language, therefore, is as simple as the views of black-magic practitioners: verbal incantations have a mystic power to effect physical changes in a living organism.

"The verbal community" (i.e., society), Mr. Skinner asserts, is the source and cause of man's self-awareness and introspection. How? This time an answer is given: "It [the verbal community] asks such questions as: What did you do yesterday? What are you doing now? What will you do tomorrow? Why did you do that? Do you really want to do that? How do you feel about that? The answers help people to adjust to each other effectively. And it is because such questions are asked that a person responds to himself and his behavior in the special way called knowing or being aware. *Without the help of a verbal community all behavior would be unconscious. Consciousness is a social product.*" (P. 192; emphasis added.) But how did such questions occur to men who were incapable of discovering introspection? No answer.

Apparently to appease man's defenders, Mr. Skinner offers the following: "In shifting control from autonomous man to the observable environment we do not leave an empty organism. A great deal goes on inside the skin, and physiology will eventually tell us more about it." (P. 195.) This means: No, man is not empty, he is a solid piece of meat.

Inexorably, like all mystics, Mr. Skinner reverts to a mystic dualism—to an equivalent of the mind-body split, which becomes a body-bodies split. In Mr. Skinner's version, it is not a conflict between God and the Devil, but between man's two conditioners: social environment and genetic endowment. The conflict takes place inside man's skin, in the form of *two selves*. "A self is a repertoire of behavior appropriate to a given set of contingencies." (P. 199.) The conflict, therefore, is between two repertoires. "The controlling self (the con-

science or superego) is of social origin, but the controlled self
is more likely to be the product of genetic susceptibilities to
reinforcement (the id, or the Old Adam). The controlling self
generally represents the interests of others, the controlled self
the interests of the individual." (P. 199.)

Where have we heard this before, and for how many
"prescientific" millennnia?

Mr. Skinner's voice is loud and clear when he declares: "To
be for oneself is to be almost nothing." (P. 123.) As proof, he
revives another ancient saw: the capacity of the human species to transmit knowledge deprives man of any claim to in-
dividuality (or to *individual achievement*) because he has to
start by learning from others. "The great individualists so
often cited to show the value of personal freedom have owed
their successes to earlier social environments. The involuntary individualism of a Robinson Crusoe and the voluntary
individualism of a Henry David Thoreau show obvious debts
to society. If Crusoe had reached the island as a baby, and if
Thoreau had grown up unattended on the shores of Walden
Pond, their stories would have been different. We must all
begin as babies, and no degree of self-determination, self-
sufficiency, or self-reliance will make us individuals in any
sense beyond that of single members of the human species."
(Pp. 123–124.)

This means: we all begin as babies and remain in that state;
since a baby is not self-sufficient, neither is an adult; nothing
has happened in between. Observe also the same method of
setting up a straw man that was used in regard to volition:
setting it up outside of reality. E.g., in order to be an individual, Thomas A. Edison would have had to appear in the jungle
by parthenogenesis, as an infant without human parents, then
rediscover, all by himself, the entire course of the science of
physics, from the first fire to the electric light bulb. Since no
one has done this, there is no such thing as individualism.

From a foundation of this kind, Mr. Skinner proceeds to
seek "justice or fairness" or a "reasonable balance" in the

"exchange between the individual and his social environment." (P. 124.) But, he announces, such questions "cannot be answered simply by pointing to what is personally good or what is good for others. There is another kind of value to which we must now turn." (P. 125.)

Now we come to the payoff.

A mystic code of morality demanding self-sacrifice cannot be promulgated or propagated without a supreme ruler that becomes the collector of the sacrificing. Traditionally, there have been two such collectors: either God or society. The collector had to be inaccessible to mankind at large, and his authority had to be revealed only through an elite of special intermediaries, variously called "high priests," "commissars," "Gauleiters," etc. Mr. Skinner follows the same pattern, but he has a new collector and supreme ruler to hoist: *the culture.*

A culture, he explains, is "the customs, the customary *behaviors* of people." (P. 127.) "A culture, like a species, is selected by its adaptation to an environment: to the extent that it helps its members to get what they need and avoid what is dangerous, it helps them to survive and transmit the culture. The two kinds of evolution are closely interwoven. The same people transmit both a culture and a genetic endowment—though in very different ways and for different parts of their lives." (P. 129.) "A culture is not the product of a creative 'group mind' or the expression of a 'general will.' . . . A culture evolves when new practices further the survival of those who practice them." (Pp. 133–134.) Thus we owe our survival to the culture. Therefore, Mr. Skinner announces, to the two values discussed—personal good and the good of others—"we must now add a third, the good of the culture." (P. 134.)

What is the good of a culture? *Survival.* Whose survival? Its own. A culture is an end in itself. "When it has become clear that a culture may survive or perish, some of its members may begin to act to promote its survival." (P. 134.)

Which members? By what means are they able to grasp such
a goal? No answer.

Mr. Skinner stresses repeatedly that the survival of a culture is a value different from, and superior to, the survival of
its members, of oneself or of others—a value one ought to
live and die for. Why? Mr. Skinner is suddenly explicit:
"None of this will explain what we might call a pure concern
for the survival of a culture, but we do not really need an
explanation. . . . The simple fact is that a culture which *for
any reason* induces its members to work for its survival, or for
the survival of some of its practices, is more likely to survive.
Survival is the only value according to which a culture is
eventually to be judged, and any practice that furthers survival has survival value by definition." (P. 136.) *Whose* survival?
No answer. Mr. Skinner lets it ride on an equivocation of this
kind.

If survival "is the only value according to which a culture is
eventually to be judged," then the Nazi culture, which lasted
twelve years, had a certain degree of value—the Soviet culture, which has lasted fifty-five years, has a higher value—
the feudal culture of the Middle Ages, which lasted five centuries, had a still higher value—but the highest value of all
must be ascribed to the culture of ancient Egypt, which, with
no variations or motion of any kind, lasted *unchanged* for
thirty centuries.

A "culture," in Mr. Skinner's own terms, is not a thing, not
an idea, not even people, but a collection of *practices*, a "behavior," a disembodied behavior that supersedes those who
behave—i.e., a way of acting to which the actors must be
sacrificed. This is *mysticism* of a kind that makes God or society seem sensibly realistic rulers by comparison. It is also
conservatism of a metaphysical kind that makes political conservatism seem innocuously childish. It demands that we live,
work and die not for ourselves or for others, but for the sake
of preserving and transmitting to yet unborn generations and
in perpetuity the way we dress, the way we ride the subway,

the way we get drunk, the way we deal with baseball or religion or economics, etc.

Thus Mr. Skinner, the arch-materialist, ends up as a worshipper of disembodied motion—and the arch-revolutionary, as a guardian of the status quo, *any* status quo.

In order to be induced to sacrifice for the good of the culture, the victims are promised "deferred advantages" (*indeterminately* deferred). "But what is its [an economic system's] answer to the question: 'Why should I be concerned about the survival of a particular kind of economic system?' The only honest answer to that kind of question seems to be this: 'There is no good reason why you should be concerned, but if your culture has not convinced you that there is, so much the worse for your culture.'" (P. 137.) This means: in order to survive, a culture must convince its members that there *is* a good reason to be concerned with its survival, even though there is none.

This is *Social Darwinism* of a kind that Herbert Spencer would not dream of. The nearest approach to an exponent in practice was Adolf Hitler who "reinforced" his followers by demanding sacrifices for the survival of the German *Kultur*.

But Mr. Skinner envisions a grander scale. He advocates "a single culture for all mankind," which, he admits, is difficult to explain to the sacrificial victims. "We can nevertheless point to many reasons why people should now be concerned for the good of all mankind. The great problems of the world today are all global. . . . But pointing to consequences is not enough. We [who?] must arrange contingencies under which consequences have an effect." (Pp. 137–138.) This "arranger of contingencies" is to be a single totalitarian world state, serving the survival of a single culture, ruling every cell of every man's brain and every moment of his life.

What are the "great problems" this state would solve? What are the "terrifying possibilities" from which we must be saved—at the price of giving up our freedom, dignity, reason, mind, values, self-esteem? Mr. Skinner answers: "Overpopulation, the depletion of resources, the pollution of the environment, and the possibility of a nuclear holocaust—these are the not-so-remote consequences of present courses of action." (P. 138.)

If lightning struck Mount Sinai, and Moses appeared on the mountaintop, carrying sacred tablets, and silenced the lost, frightened, desperate throng below in order to read a revelation of divine wisdom, and read a third-rate editorial from a random tabloid—the dramatic, intellectual and moral effect would be similar (except that Moses was less pretentious).

Mr. Skinner's book falls to pieces in its final chapters. The author's "verbal behavior" becomes so erratic that he sounds as if he has lost all interest in his subject. Tangled in contradictions, equivocations and non sequiturs, he seems to stumble wearily in circles, seizing any rationalization at random—not to defend his thesis, but to attack his critics, throwing feeble little jabs, projecting an odd kind of stale, lethargic, perfunctory malice, almost a "reflex-malice." He sounds like a man filling empty pages with something, anything, in order to circumvent the accumulated weight of unanswered questions—or like a man who resents being questioned.

Who will be the "designers" of his proposed global culture and the rulers of mankind? He answers unequivocally: the "technologists of behavior." What qualifies them for such a job? They are "scientists." What is science? In the whole of the book, no definition is given, as if the term were a self-evident, mystically hallowed primary.

Since man, according to Mr. Skinner, is biologically unable to project a time span of three months—from spring planting to fall harvest—how are these technologists able to see the course and plan the future of a global culture? No answer. What sort of men are they? The closest approach to an answer is: "those who have been induced by their culture to act to further its survival. . . ." (P. 180.)

It is futile to ask by what means and through what agencies

the culture (i.e., the *behavior*) of birdbrained creatures can accomplish such a feat, because here we are obviously dealing with a standard requirement of mysticism: Mr. Skinner is establishing an opportunity for the high priesthood to "hear voices"—not the voice of God or of the people, but the voice of the culture *inducing* them to act. But the culture "induces" a great many people to different courses of action, including the people who paint prophecies of doom on rocks by the side of highways. How are the culture-designers (and the rest of us) to know that theirs is the true voice of the culture? No answer. One must assume that they *feel* it.

Now we come to the grand cashing-in on the book's basic equivocation. Mr. Skinner keeps stressing that mankind needs "more controls, not less"; in a polemical passage, he quotes his critics asking: "Who is to control?"—and answers them as follows: "The relation between the controller and the controlled is reciprocal The scientist in the laboratory, studying the behavior of a pigeon, designs contingencies and observes their effects. His apparatus exerts a conspicuous control on the pigeon, but we must not overlook the control exerted by the pigeon. The behavior of the pigeon has determined the design of the apparatus and the procedures in which it is used. Some such reciprocal control is characteristic of all science. . . . [Here I omit one sentence, which is an unconscionable misuse of a famous statement.] The scientist who designs a cyclotron is under the control of the particles he is studying. The behavior with which a parent controls his child, either aversively or through positive reinforcement, is shaped and maintained by the child's responses. A psychotherapist changes the behavior of his patient in ways which have been shaped and maintained by his success in changing that behavior. A government or religion prescribes and imposes sanctions selected by their effectiveness in controlling citizen or communicant. An employer induces his employees to work industriously and carefully with wage systems determined by their effects on behavior. The classroom practices of the teacher are shaped and maintained by the effects on his students. In a very real sense, then, the slave controls the slave driver, the child the parent, the patient the therapist, the citizen the government, the communicant the priest, the employee the employer, and the student the teacher." (P. 169.)

To this, I shall add just one more example: the victim controls the torturer, because if the victim screams very loudly at a particular method of torture, this is the method the torturer will select to use.

The above quotation is sufficient to convey the book's intellectual stature, the logic of its arguments, and the validity of its thesis.

As far as one can judge the book's purpose, the establishment of a dictatorship does not seem to be Mr. Skinner's *personal* ambition. If it were, he would have been more clever about it. His goal seems to be: 1. to clear the way for a dictatorship by eliminating its enemies; 2. to see how much he can get away with.

The book's motive power is hatred of man's mind and virtue (with everything they entail: reason, achievement, independence, enjoyment, moral pride, self-esteem)—so intense and consuming a hatred that it consumes itself, and what we read is only its gray ashes, with feeble, snickering obscenities (such as the title) as a few last, smoking, stinking coals. To destroy "Autonomous Man"—to strike at him, to punch, to stab, to jab, and, if all else fails, to spit at him—is the book's apparent purpose, and it is precisely the long-range, *cultural* consequences that the author does not seem to give a damn about.

The passages dealing with the Global State are so rambling, incoherent and diffuse, that they sound, not like a plan, but like a daydream—the kind of daydream Mr. Skinner, apparently, finds "reinforcing." But he remains unoriginal even in his fantasy: borrowing Plato's notion of a philosopher-king, Mr. Skinner fancies a world ruled by a psychologist-king—in terms which sound as if a small-time manipulator were tempted by the image of a big shot.

If only we would abolish "Autonomous Man"—Mr. Skinner declares with a kind of growling wistfulness—we would be able to turn "from the miraculous to the natural, from the *inaccessible* to the *manipulable*." (P. 201; emphasis added.) This, I submit, is the secret behind the book—and behind the modern intellectuals' response to it.

In *Les Misérables*, describing the development of an independent young man, Victor Hugo wrote: " . . . and he blesses God for having given him these two riches which many of the rich are lacking: work, which gives him freedom, and thought, which gives him dignity."

I doubt that B. F. Skinner ever did or could read Victor Hugo—he wouldn't know what it's all about—but it is not a mere coincidence that made him choose the title of his book. Victor Hugo knew the two essentials that man's life requires. B. F. Skinner knows the two essentials that have to be destroyed if man qua man is to be destroyed.

THE RESPONSE

"The attention lavished on Harvard psychologist B. F. Skinner and his new book has been nothing short of remarkable," states *The New York Times Book Review* (October 24, 1971), in a special box on its front page. After citing a long list of Mr. Skinner's press interviews and television appearances, the statement continues: "The American Psychological Association gave him its annual award in September and hailed him as 'a pioneer in psychological research, leader in theory, master in technology, who has revolutionized the study of behavior in our time. A superlative scholar, scientist, teacher and writer.'"

Bear in mind the fact that the above testimonial was given to a theoretician whose theory consists in proclaiming that man is a mindless automaton—to a technologist whose technology consists in urging people to accept totalitarian control—to a scholar who substitutes the oldest of old wives' tales for a knowledge of philosophy—to a scientist who commits the kinds of logical fallacies for which a freshman would be flunked.

It would be unfair to assume that that testimonial represents the intellectual level of the entire psychological profession. Obviously, it does not—and we all know how such testimonials (or resolutions or protests) are put over by a special clique on a busy, confused, indifferent majority. But which is worse: a profession that actually subscribes to that testimonial—or a profession that does not, yet permits this sort of thing to be issued in its name? I think the latter is worse. Manipulators, such as Mr. Skinner's clique, do not seek to persuade, but to put something over on people. The fact that Mr. Skinner got away with the mere title of the book (let alone its thesis) indicates that the cultural field is empty, that no serious opposition is to be expected, that anything goes.

To be exact, I would say: not quite anything and not quite yet, but the cultural prognosis is pretty bleak. Mr. Skinner's trial balloon has been punctured by many different people, including some able sharpshooters, but if he studies the shreds, he will notice that only buckshot was used. The book deserves no heavier ammunition; its thesis does.

With a few exceptions, the superlatives hailing the book's importance came from press agents or blurb writers, not from reviewers. Most of the reviews were mixed or negative. As a whole, they conveyed an odd feeling, not the violence of a storm, but the sadness of a steady drizzle, as if exhausted men were still unable to accept the evil brazenly offered to them for appraisal, but unable without knowing why, their reasons long since forgotten, moved by some remnant of decency as by a faint echo from a very distant past. What deserved a scream of indignation, was received with a sigh.

The two best—i.e., thoroughly unfavorable—reviews appear in *The New Republic* and *The New York Review of Books.*

The rest of them attack Mr. Skinner, but concede his case. They accept him as an exponent of reason and science—and seize the opportunity to damn reason and science.

The review in *The New Republic* (October 16, 1971) is quietly firm and civilized. Its primary target is Mr. Skinner's—and behaviorism's—view of man, which it describes as "psychology without a psyche." As an example of its approach: Skinner's argument "goes like this: physics used to attribute human characteristics to physical objects (such as growing more jubilant as they approached their natural places); only when it stopped doing this did scientific progress follow. Would not scientific progress follow in psychology if we could stop attributing human characteristics to human beings? He does not, naturally, put it quite in those terms, but I have given the structural essence of the matter." As an example of its appraisal of other aspects: " . . . the argumentation is often sloppy, the sensibility often philistine, the language often eccentric." As an apparent rebuke for Mr. Skinner's expression "inside man's skin": "And something inside my skull is reluctant to accept the simple, unproblematic world that Skinner offers, not just because it doesn't like it but because it thinks it all wrong for people whose skulls contain similarly complex apparatus." In all the reviews I read, this is the only passage that defends *intelligence*.

A cautious little piece in the *Saturday Review* (October 9, 1971) praises the book for the following: "First of all, Dr. Skinner pays admirable attention to social problems. . . . Skinner's sharp critique of punishment as largely ineffectual control is pertinent to the pressing question of prisons." In the context of the profound philosophical fundamentals that Mr. Skinner challenges, this sort of comment cannot even be classified as journalistic or range-of-the-moment: this is range-of-the-split-second. After which, the reviewer proceeds gently to blame Mr. Skinner for "his lust to objectivize everything." This, he complains, destroys the "mystery of man." Therefore, he concludes placatingly: "Another dream of reason has ended as a nightmare of an eminent psychologist, in this case perhaps the most influential of living American psychologists. But was it a good dream to begin with? Was it even an especially rational one? [I.e.: Is it rational to use reason?] We all know some of the devastating results of following the old imperative to control and subdue nature outside man, of adopting the dictum of Skinner's spiritual forebear, Francis Bacon, that 'knowledge is power.' Are we about to try the same experiment with 'manipulable man'?" This means that Mr. Skinner is a man of reason and a great scientist, whose theory would lead us to triumphs as brilliant as those achieved by the physical sciences, but we must not try it. The reviewer concludes sweetly: "Thus only if the views of this book are for the most part rejected will it really have a good effect on the social environment." (I suppose, on prison reform.) This sort of mealy-mouthed insult is unfair to any book, even Mr. Skinner's.

The review in *Psychotherapy & Social Science Review* (January 1972) is of a much higher caliber. It blasts many aspects of Mr. Skinner's notions, competently and effectively—then blasts itself by the following indications of its own viewpoint: "But what in individual terms may be a struggle between narcissism and object-love, between indulgence in self and love of others, in societal terms becomes a struggle between anarchy and overcontrol. It is hard to know what the remedy should be." The reviewer mentions "the vicissitudes of the personal and social super ego"—and "the slowly accumulating evidence that man will *always* have to struggle with his dual and decisive nature" (which consists of the capacity to think and to feel). He concludes: "But to pursue the last path, to attempt to turn pure instinct into pure reason is to fly in the face of the ambivalent nature of man . . ." (This means that Mr. Skinner is an advocate or representative of pure reason.) And: "Perhaps to be able to face these unresolvable dilemmas and painful paradoxes without recourse to either impotence *or* grandiosity may finally deserve the name of dignity."

If behaviorism declares, through Mr. Skinner: "I can resolve anything (somehow)," and its major rival school of psychology, Freudianism, advises: "Resign yourself to unresolvable dilemmas," behaviorism will win.

The review in *The Atlantic* (October 1971) is a peculiar mixture. The reviewer (properly) condemns Mr. Skinner for his "love of power over others." He attacks Mr. Skinner on a crucial issue: the destruction of language and, therefore, of judgment. But observe the following statement: "Let us be clear: it is not the sublime dumbness of mysticism [?!] toward which Skinner's idealism [?] moves. It is rather closer to the societies of *1984* and their Newspeak—the atrophy of consciousness through the shriveling of language." In his best paragraph, the reviewer states that Skinner's "own gospel of environmental determinism is one of the most serious threats conceivable to human survival. By eroding the sense of responsibility, it licenses people to shift the blame from themselves to 'the system.' It provides universal exoneration for atrocity after atrocity, or for compliance after compliance. It works to *increase* the amount of evil in the world." This is eminently true. But a few paragraphs earlier the reviewer said: "Determinism may be true, false, or both. But whatever it is, if it is used as Skinner uses it, the doom of conscious life is announced." How else can determinism "be used"? If a man cannot help what he does, how can he be held responsible for it? And if a given idea could be "true, false, or both" (at the same time and in the same respect), what sort of conscious life would be possible?

The mystery of that reviewer's stand is solved in his last paragraph: "Skinner believes that we can survive only if we allow a gigantic simplification of life. By that he means—he must finally mean—the atrophy of consciousness. He does not think that introspective, complex, self-doubting, self-torturing, self-indulgent, dissident, wordy people are *efficient*. He can set things up, he is sure, so that fewer such people occur. Does he not see that only silly geese lay golden eggs?"

This means: Mr. Skinner represents reason, order, efficiency, but it is the emotion-ridden, contradiction-riddled, self-confessedly silly and sloppy souls who give value or meaning to life.

The review in *The New Leader* (January 10, 1972) is cruder and more open. It declares: "'The reasonable man,' Shaw said, 'tries to adapt himself to the world' (certainly the behaviorist's approach), 'the unreasonable one persists in trying to adapt the world to himself. Therefore all progress depends on the unreasonable man.'" Also: "And behaviorism is still, thank God, a science, not a technology." Also: "History, no less than behavioristic experiments, proves that man is innately selfish. The manipulation of mankind is unacceptable not because man is a noble being, but precisely because he is not. Those with power have always used it for their own ends, and there is no reason to suppose that their selfish preoccupations will diminish." (This means, one must assume, that the totalitarian control and manipulation of noble, selfless beings by noble, selfless beings would be all right.)

Then there is a batch of small-fry reviews which echo similar sentiments or no sentiments at all, make feeble objections, carefully miss the point, and do not commit themselves to anything. An astonishing one is a piece in *Science News* (August 7, 1971), which seems to be written by a teen-ager and makes a remarkable statement. Mr. Skinner's new book, it announces, may be one of the most important of the century: "Not only because it represents the summation of the Harvard psychologist's behavioristic approach to psychology, but because it goes beyond psychology into philosophy. And because Dr. Skinner's philosophy will probably be insulting to a great many people." Further, this particular expert declares that "Dr. Skinner makes [his] arguments logically and rationally . . ."

After a collection of this kind, it is a relief to read the essay in *The New York Review of Books* (December 30, 1971), entitled "The Case Against B. F. Skinner." The essay is neither apologetic nor sentimental. It is bright and forceful. It is a demolition job. What it demolishes is Mr. Skinner's scientific pretensions—and, to this extent, it is a defense of science.

"His [Skinner's] speculations are devoid of scientific content and do not even hint at general outlines of a possible science of human behavior." In regard to Skinner's claims: "Claims . . . must be evaluated according to the evidence presented for them. In the present instance, this is a simple task, since no evidence is presented . . . In fact, the question of evidence is beside the point, since the claims dissolve into triviality or incoherence under analysis."

The reviewer employs one of the best methods of dealing with a false theory: he takes it literally. "If Skinner's thesis is false, then there is no point in his having written the book or our reading it. But if his thesis is true, then there is also no point in his having written the book or our reading it. For the only point could be to modify behavior, and behavior, according to the thesis, is entirely controlled by arrangement of reinforcers. Therefore reading the book can modify behavior only if it is a reinforcer, that is, if reading the book will increase the probability of the behavior that led to reading the book (assuming an appropriate state of deprivation). At this point, we seem to be reduced to gibberish."

There are many other notable passages in that review. But its author is Noam Chomsky who, philosophically, is a Cartesian linguist advocating a theory to the effect that man's mental processes are determined by innate ideas—and who, politically, belongs to the New Left.

I shall [discuss shortly] the two significant reviews that appeared in *The New York Times*. But the picture of our cultural devastation is clear. There are no defenders of *reason*—in the country that was created not by historical accident, but by philosophical design. There are no defenders of *freedom*—in what had once been the only moral social system on earth. There are no defenders of man's *mind*—in the world's

greatest scientific-technological civilization. All that is left is a
battle between the mystics of spirit and the mystics of
muscle—between men guided by their *feelings* and men
guided by their *reflexes*.

We are passengers on a plane flying at tremendous speed
One of these days, we will discover that its cockpit is empty.

Newspapers do not create a culture, they are its product.
They are transmission belts that carry ideas from the universities to the general public. *The New York Times* is one of the
most influential newspapers in this country and a good indi-
cator of our cultural trends. It published two reviews of Mr.
Skinner's book, which—in different ways—are the most objectionable ones of the lot.

"There is just no gainsaying the profound importance of B.
F. Skinner's new book, *Beyond Freedom and Dignity*. If you
plan to read only one book this year, this is probably the one
you should choose." This is the opening of the review in the
daily *Times* (September 22, 1971)—the only essentially favorable review I have found.

"Dr. Skinner's message is hard to take," the reviewer
claims, but warns that "it cannot be dismissed so frivolously
. . ." Then, without protective evasions, he summarizes accu-
rately the brutal essentials of Mr. Skinner's thesis, and declares: "All of which is *logically unassailable . . .*" (Emphasis
added.) Attempting, apparently, to resist the thesis, he states
that "one tries reviewing the traditional criticisms of behaviorism. But even here, Skinner is not nearly so vulnerable as he
once seemed. For he has confronted his many critics with telling counterarguments. . . . To those who call his program totalitarian, he replies that 'the relation between the controller
and the controlled is reciprocal' . . ." This refers to the passage on page 169 of Mr. Skinner's book, which is quoted
[above, pages 182–183]. Please reread it in order to judge
whether *that* is a "telling counterargument."

"No, none of the familiar objections to behaviorism will
suffice to demolish *Beyond Freedom and Dignity*," the re-

viewer sighs. " . . . the book remains logically tenable. I don't like it, which is to say that it doesn't reinforce me in the manner to which I am accustomed." To make a concession of this kind is to confess that one has no grounds for one's convictions, and that one is not aware of one's own mental processes. The concession is followed by an odd statement: "But for the moment the only retort that I can think of is that conceived by Dostoyevsky's 'underground man'—to 'deliberately go mad to prove' that all behavior cannot be predicted or controlled. But such a response might not prove very useful to me or the culture. . . . So we may indeed be trapped in a Skinnerian maze." What is odd here is the fact that the quotation from Dostoyevsky's "underground man" is not a retort the reviewer thought of spontaneously: this very quotation is discussed by Mr. Skinner on pages 164–165 of his book and is, properly, dismissed.

At first glance, the review creates the impression that it was written by an earnest intellectual who struggled desperately against the necessity of accepting a totalitarian state, but failed to find counterarguments and gave in, reluctantly, to the power of unanswerable logic. After one has read the book, one asks: Is that the reviewer's case? Or is it the case of a man eager to convince us that Mr. Skinner's thesis is unanswerable?

The review in *The New York Times Book Review* (October 24, 1971) is different. It is unfavorable. It declares that Skinner has a secret motive (a "hidden agenda") which is unknown to him, but known to the reviewer. "The actual text of Skinner's new book reveals a man desperately in search of some way to preserve the old-fashioned virtues associated with 19th-century individualism in a world where self-reliance no longer makes sense." Which virtues? Hard work, believe it or not. "First, behavior control appears to him a way to get people hard at work again in an age where indolence is rife." If hard work is the essential characteristic of individualism, then the Nazi and Soviet forced labor camps are examples of individualism unmatched in the nineteenth or any other century. But there is no discussion or advocacy of "hard work" in Mr. Skinner's book, and nothing to justify the allegation that this is his *first* concern.

"This hidden agenda can first be detected in the way Skinner talks about controlling behavior. All his attention is centered on situations where one person is being controlled; he employs such phrases as 'a person's behavior' or 'operant conditioning of the subject.' He seldom refers to different controls for different kinds of social groups." Even Mr. Skinner does not deserve a reviewer of this kind. Many people are unable to deal with metaphysical questions, but this one is militantly aggressive about it. He is so rabid a collectivist that he will not tolerate any concern with the individual, even for the purpose of destroying him. He does not see that if his own beliefs are to be put into practice, it is Mr. Skinner who is laying the necessary foundation.

If a doctor stated that man needs food, and were criticized as follows: "Which man does he mean, Smith or Jones? Different men need different foods. And he hasn't said anything about the poor, the black, the young, and the women"—the *Skedunk Gazette* would not publish it. Yet this type of mentality is published on the front page of *The New York Times Book Review*. If you think I am exaggerating, judge the following. The reviewer picks on a passage in which Mr. Skinner attempts to teach us behaviorist language by describing a young man's emotional states in behaviorist terms—e.g., Mr. Skinner translates "he feels uneasy or anxious" into "his behavior frequently has unavoidable aversive consequences which have emotional effects." The reviewer's comment: "But Professor, there's a war on! Why aren't you talking about the social cause of his behavior? Why do you treat him as if he lives in a vacuum?"

Mr. Skinner is not only too individualistic, the reviewer claims, but also *too rational*. "While Heisenberg contemplated the unpredictable behavior of matter, Skinner insists that we must find unambiguous facts about human behavior; the difference is between wanting to explore the world as it is and wanting to possess knowledge. The possession of knowledge, of hard facts you can act on, is an echo of 19th-century positivistic science, just as Skinner's beliefs are an echo of that century's small-town society."

If "the possession of knowledge" is unattainable, what do you acquire when you "explore the world as it is"—and why do you explore it? What is a "soft" fact? What do you act on, when you cannot act on knowledge or facts? (That review may be an example of such action.) But I shall borrow a phrase from Noam Chomsky's essay, and say that these are questions "which I happily leave to others to decode."

The daily *Times* reviewer may be taken as typical of the present—a frightened liberal trying to convince us (and himself) that Mr. Skinner's totalitarian state is the wave of the future. But the Sunday *Times* reviewer *is* the future—the future of Mr. Skinner's theories, their successful product and embodiment, who has been molded by the "contingencies of reinforcement" in our universities, who sees reason, individualism and "autonomy" as incontrovertibly nonexistent, sees no point in arguing about them, sees nothing beyond the range of the immediate moment, regards Mr. Skinner as old-fashioned, and goes on from there. If you have read *The Fountainhead*, you will understand the relationship: he is the Gus Webb to Mr. Skinner's Ellsworth Toohey.

The *Times* chose the publication of *Beyond Freedom and Dignity* as an occasion to go beyond B. F. Skinner. A different push in the same direction was provided by *Time* magazine. The headline on its cover (September 20, 1971) announced: "B. F. Skinner Says: WE CAN'T AFFORD FREEDOM"—not a very original statement, but regarded, apparently, as important or valuable enough to justify placing Mr. Skinner's picture on the cover, and giving him a lengthy story. The story, however, is flattering only in its length; otherwise, it is noncommittal and empty, playing both sides of the fence in the "safe" modern manner, i.e., praising Mr. Skinner, and insulting him by quoting his enemies.

If you wonder what motives could bring Mr. Skinner to his theories, what frustration could lead him to so profound a hatred of mankind, and who would be his first victims, the *Time* story offers three passages that provide eloquent clues. The first is a quotation from Mr. Skinner's novel *Walden Two*. The speaker, *Time* explains, "is T. E. Frazier, a character in *Walden Two* and the fictional founder of the utopian community described in that novel. He is also an alter ego of the author . . ." The quotation: "I've had only one idea in my life—a true *idée fixe*. To put it as bluntly as possible—the idea of having my own way. 'Control!' expresses it. The control of human behavior. In my early experimental days it was a frenzied, selfish desire to dominate. I remember the rage I used to feel when a prediction went awry. I could have shouted as the subjects of my experiments, 'Behave, damn you! Behave as you ought!'"

The second passage deals with Mr. Skinner's youth. In his college days, he wrote short stories and "sent three of them to Robert Frost, who praised them warmly. That encouragement convinced Fred Skinner that he should become a writer. The decision, he says, was 'disastrous.'. . . In his own words, he 'failed as a writer' because he 'had nothing important to say.'"

The third passage is about Twin Oaks, a real-life commune founded on a farm in Virginia, and "governed by Skinner's laws of social engineering." "Private property is forbidden, except for such things as books and clothing. . . . No one is allowed to boast of individual accomplishments . . . What is considered appropriate behavior—cooperating, showing affection, turning the other cheek and working diligently—is, on the other hand, applauded, or 'reinforced,' by the group." "The favorite sports are 'cooperation volleyball' and skinny-dipping in the South Anna River—false modesty is another of the sins that are not reinforced—and there is plenty of folk

singing and dancing." In regard to the consequences: "After
starting with only $35,000, Twin Oaks, four years later, still
finds survival a struggle. The farm brings more emotional
than monetary rewards; members would find it cheaper to
work at other jobs and buy their food at the market. . . .
Beyond economics, there are serious psychological problems
at Twin Oaks, and few members have stayed very long.
[Emotional rewards?] Turnover last year was close to 70 percent. The ones who leave first, in fact, are often the most
competent members, who still expect special recognition for
their talents. 'Competent people are hard to get along with,'
says Richard Stutsman, one of Twin Oaks' trained psychologists. 'They tend to make demands, not requests. We cannot
afford to reinforce ultimatum behavior, although we recognize
our need for their competence. . . . ' When they leave, the
community not only loses their skills but also sacrifices a
potential rise in its standard of living."

For my comments on this, see *Atlas Shrugged*.

The cultural establishment has pushed *Beyond Freedom
and Dignity* to the best-seller lists. The most dangerous part
of its potential impact—particularly on young readers—is not
that the book is convincing or eloquent, but that it is so bad.
If it were less crudely irrational and inept, a reader could give
the benefit of the doubt to those who were taken in by some
trickily complex arguments. But if so evil a thesis as the advocacy of totalitarian dictatorship is offered in such illogical,
unconvincing terms, yet is acclaimed as "important," what is
one to think of the intellectual and moral state of our culture?
A rational reader may become paralyzed—not by fear, fear is
not his psychological danger—but by disgust, contempt, discouragement and, ultimately, withdrawal from the realm of
the intellect (which, perhaps, is Mr. Skinner's hope).

But before you draw the "malevolent-universe" conclusion
that falsehood always wins over truth, or that men prefer irrationality to reason, and dictatorship to freedom (and, therefore, "What's the use?")—consider the following. *Human*

Events (January 15, 1972) reports that "the National Institutes
of Mental Health had granted $283,000 to Dr. B. F. Skinner
. . ." which, apparently, financed the writing of his book. *The
New Republic* (January 28, 1972) gives some details: the Skinner grant "was one of 20 Senior Research Career Awards,
that is, plums for scientific leaders in 'mental health' across
the board rather than a unique grant. . . . The particular
award was made for the purpose of 'integrating and con-
solidating' Skinner's findings and 'considering the application
of the science of behavior to the problems of society' [!]. . . ."

This is the way an "establishment" is formed and placed
beyond the reach of dissent. What chance would a beginner,
a nonconformist, an opponent of behaviorism, have against
the entrenched power of a clique supported by government
funds? This is not a free marketplace of ideas any longer.
Evil, falsehood, irrationality are not winning in free competition with virtue, truth, reason. Today's culture is ruled by intellectual pressure groups which have become intellectual
monopolies backed, like all monopolies, by the government's
gun and the money of the victims.

(The solution, of course, is not to censor research projects,
but to *abolish* all government subsidies in the field of the social sciences and, eventually, in all fields. But this is a different subject, which I shall discuss [in the next chapter].)

The significance of B. F. Skinner's book lies in its eloquent
demonstration of the results of philosophical collapse and
governmental power: when the intellectual default of the victims permits the dead hand of the government to get a
stranglehold on the field of ideas, a nation will necessarily be
pushed beyond freedom and dignity.

14

The Establishing of
an Establishment
1972

Staleness is the dominant characteristic of today's culture—and, at first glance, it may appear to be a puzzling phenomenon.

There is an air of impoverished drabness, of tired routine, of stagnant monotony in all our cultural activities—from stage and screen, to literature and the arts, to the allegedly intellectual publications and discussions. There is nothing to see or to hear. Everything produces the effect of *déjà vu* or *déjà entendu.* How long since you have read anything startling, different, fresh, unexpected?

Intellectually, people are wearing paste jewelry copied from paste jewelry by artisans who have never seen the original gems. Originality is a forgotten experience. The latest fads are withering at birth. The substitutes for daring and vitality—such as the screeching hippies—are mere camouflage, like too much make-up on the lined face of an aging slut.

The symptoms of today's cultural disease are: conformity, with nothing to conform to—timidity, expressed in a self-shrinking concern with trivia—a kind of obsequious anxiety to please the unknown standards of some nonexistent authority—and a pall of fear without object. Psychologically, this is the cultural atmosphere of a society living under censorship.

But there is no censorship in the United States.

I have said that the fundamental cause of a culture's disintegration is the collapse of philosophy, which leaves men without intellectual guidance. But this is the *fundamental* cause, its consequences are not always direct or obvious, and its working may raise many questions. By what intermediary processes does this cause affect men's lives? Does it work only by psychological means, from within, or is it assisted, from without, by practical, existential measures? When philosophy collapses, why are there no thinkers to step into the vacuum and rebuild a system of thought on a new foundation? Since there was no philosophical unanimity, why did the collapse of falsehoods paralyze the men who had never believed them? Why do the falsehoods linger on, unchallenged—like a cloud of dust over the rubble? Philosophy affects education, and a false philosophy can cripple men's minds in childhood; but it cannot cripple them all, nor does it cripple most men irreparably—so what becomes of those who manage to survive? Why are they not heard from? What—except physical force—can silence active minds?

The answer to this last question is: nothing. Only the use of physical force can protect falsehoods from challenge and perpetuate them. Only the intrusion of force into the realm of the intellect—i.e., only the action of a government—can silence an entire nation. But then how does the cultural wreckage maintain its power over the United States? There is no governmental repression or suppression of ideas in this country.

As a mixed economy, we are chained by an enormous tangle of government controls; but, it is argued, they affect our incomes, not our minds. Such a distinction is not tenable; a chained aspect of a man's—or a nation's—activity will gradually and necessarily affect the rest. But it is true that the government, so far, has made no overt move to repress or control the intellectual life of this country. Anyone is still free to say, write and publish anything he pleases. Yet men keep silent—while their culture is perishing from an entrenched, institutionalized epidemic of mediocrity. It is not possible that mankind's intellectual stature has shrunk to this extent. And it is not possible that all talent has vanished suddenly from this country and this earth.

If you find it puzzling, the premise to check is the idea that governmental repression is the only way a government can destroy the intellectual life of a country. It is not. There is another way: *governmental encouragement.*

Governmental encouragement does not order men to believe that the false is true: it merely makes them indifferent to the issue of truth or falsehood.

Bearing this preface in mind, let us consider an example of the methods, processes and results of that policy.

In December 1971, Representative Cornelius E. Gallagher (D.-N.J.) declared in the House that "the National Institute of Mental Health has granted to Dr. B. F. Skinner the sum of $283,000 for the purpose of writing *Beyond Freedom and Dignity.*" On further inquiry, he discovered that "this merely represents the tip of the iceberg." (*Congressional Record*, December 15, 1971, H12623.)

Human Events (January 15, 1972) summarized his findings as follows: "When Gallagher sought information about the Skinner grant and the scope and amount of government spending in the behavioral research field, the General Accounting Office reported back that the task was virtually impossible. Agency officials stated that there were tens of thousands of behavioral research projects being financed by government agencies. A preliminary check turned up 70,000 grants and contracts at the Department of Health, Education and Welfare and 10,000 within the Manpower Administration of the Labor Department. Thousands of additional behavioral projects, costing millions of dollars, also are being financed by the Defense Department, National Aeronautics and Space Administration, and the Atomic Energy Commission, according to the General Accounting Office's survey."

In his speech to the House, Representative Gallagher declared: "The Congress has authorized and appropriated every single dollar in these grants and contracts yet, for the most part, we are unaware of how they are being spent." And further: " . . . the Federal grant and contract system has inextricably intertwined colleges and universities with moneys authorized and appropriated by the Congress. I mean to imply no suggestion of a lessening of academic freedom in the Nation, but I do suggest that the Congress should at the very least be fully informed and, if need be, have the tools and expertise at our own disposal to counter antidemocratic thoughts launched with Federal funds." (*Congressional Record*, H12624.)

Mr. Gallagher stated that he believes in Dr. Skinner's right to advocate his ideas. "But what I question is whether he should be subsidized by the Federal Government [—] especially since, in my judgment, he is advancing ideas which threaten the future of our system of government by denigrating the American traditions of individualism, human dignity, and self-reliance." (*Ibid.*, H12623.)

If Mr. Gallagher were a consistent supporter of the American traditions he describes in the second half of his sentence, he would have stopped after its first half. But, apparently, he was not aware of the contradiction, because his solution was a proposal to create "a Select Committee on Privacy, Human Values, and Democratic Institutions. . . . designed to deal specifically with the type of threats to our Constitution, our Congress, and our constituents which are contained in the thoughts of B. F. Skinner." (*Ibid.*, H12624.)

Nothing could be as dangerous a threat to our institutions as a proposal to establish a government committee to deal with "antidemocratic thoughts" or B. F. Skinner's thoughts or anyone's *thoughts*. The liberal *New Republic* was quick to sense the danger and to protest (January 28, 1972). But, not questioning the propriety of government grants, it merely expounded the other side of the same contradiction: it objected to the notion of the government determining which ideas are right or acceptable and thus establishing a kind of intellectual orthodoxy.

Yet both contentions are true: it is viciously improper for the government to subsidize the enemies of our political system; it is also viciously improper for the government to assume the role of an ideological arbiter. But neither Representative Gallagher nor *The New Republic* chose to see the answer: that those evils are inherent in the vicious impropriety of the government subsidizing ideas. Both chose to ignore the fact that any intrusion of government into the field of ideas, for or against anyone, withers intellectual freedom and creates an official orthodoxy, a privileged elite. Today, it is called an "Establishment."

Ironically enough, it is *The New Republic* that offered an indication of the mechanics by which an Establishment gets established—apparently, without realizing the social implications of its own argument. Objecting to Gallagher's contention that a deliberate policy may be favoring the behaviorist school of psychology, *The New Republic* stated: "The Gallagher account did not note that the Skinner grant was one of 20 Senior Research Career Awards, that is, plums for scientific leaders in 'mental health' across the board rather than a unique grant. No new awards of this kind have been made by NIMH since 1964, but 18 of them, which were originally for five years, have been renewed. Skinner's was renewed in 1969, so his $283,000 amounts to $28,300 a year ending in 1974. . . . Skinner has continued to teach roughly one seminar a year at Harvard since 1964 . . . In other words, his Harvard salary will be paid by the feds until [1974], a bonanza perhaps more rewarding to Harvard than to him, since he could command at least as large a salary . . . in a number of other places."

Consider the desperate financial plight of private universities, then ask yourself what a "bonanza" of this kind will do to them. It is generally known that most universities now depend on government research projects as one of their major sources of income. The government grants to those "Senior" researchers establish every recipient as an unofficially official power. It is *his* influence—his ideas, his theories, his prefer-

ences in faculty hiring—that will come to dominate the
school, in a silent, unadmitted way. What debt-ridden college
administrator would dare antagonize the carrier of the
bonanza?

Now observe that these grants were given to *senior* researchers, that they were "plums"—as *The New Republic*
calls them coyly and cynically—for "scientific leaders." How
would Washington bureaucrats—or Congressmen, for that
matter—know which scientist to encourage, particularly in so
controversial a field as social science? The safest method is to
choose men who have achieved some sort of reputation.
Whether their reputation is deserved or not, whether their
achievements are valid or not, whether they rose by merit,
pull, publicity or accident, are questions which the awarders
do not and cannot consider. When personal judgment is in-
operative (or forbidden), men's first concern is not how to
choose, but how to justify their choice. This will necessarily
prompt committee members, bureaucrats and politicians to
gravitate toward "prestigious names." The result is to help
establish those already established—i.e., to entrench the
status quo.

The worst part of it is the fact that this method of selection
is not confined to the cowardly or the corrupt, that the *honest*
official is obliged to use it. The method is forced on him by
the terms of the situation. To pass an informed, independent
judgment on the value of every applicant or project in every
field of science, an official would have to be a universal scholar. If he consults "experts" in the field, the dilemma remains:
either he has to be a scholar who knows which experts to
consult—or he has to surrender his judgment to men trained
by the very professors he is supposed to judge. The awarding
of grants to famous "leaders," therefore, appears to him as
the only fair policy—on the premise that "somebody made
them famous, somebody knows, even if I don't."

(If the officials attempted to bypass the "leaders" and give
grants to promising beginners, the injustice and irrationality

of the situation would be so much worse that most of them have the good sense not to attempt it. If universal scholarship is required to judge the value of the actual in every field, nothing short of omniscience would be required to judge the value of the potential—as various privately sponsored contests to discover future talent, even in limited fields, have amply demonstrated.)

Furthermore, the terms of the situation actually forbid an honest official to use his own judgment. He is supposed to be "impartial" and "fair"—while considering awards in the social sciences. An official who does not have some knowledge and some convictions in *this* field, has no moral right to be a public official. Yet the kind of "fairness" demanded of him means that he must suspend, ignore or evade his own convictions (these would be challenged as "prejudices" or "censorship") and proceed to dispose of large sums of public money, with incalculable consequences for the future of the country—without judging the nature of the recipients' ideas, i.e., without using any judgment whatever.

The awarders may hide behind the notion that, in choosing recognized "leaders," they are acting "democratically" and rewarding men chosen by the public. But there is no "democracy" in this field. Science and the mind do not work by vote or by consensus. The best-known is not necessarily the best (nor is the least-known, for that matter). Since no rational standards are applicable, the awarders' method leads to concern with personalities, not ideas; pull, not merit; "prestige," not truth. The result is: rule by press agents.

The profiteers of government grants are usually among the loudest protesters against "the tyranny of money": science and the culture, they cry, must be liberated from the arbitrary private power of the rich. But there is this difference: the rich can neither buy an entire nation nor *force* one single individual. If a rich man chooses to support cultural activities, he can do so only on a very limited scale, and he bears the consequences of his actions. If he does not use his judgment, but merely indulges his irrational whims, he achieves the opposite of his intention: his projects and his protégés are ignored or despised in their professions, and no amount of money will buy him any influence over the culture. Like vanity publishing, his venture remains a private waste without any wider significance. The culture is protected from him by three invincible elements: choice, variety, competition. If he loses his money in foolish ventures, he hurts no one but himself. And, above all: *the money he spends is his own;* it is not extorted by force from unwilling victims.

The fundamental evil of government grants is the fact that men are forced to pay for the support of ideas diametrically opposed to their own. This is a profound violation of an individual's integrity and conscience. It is viciously wrong to take the money of rational men for the support of B. F. Skinner— or vice versa. The Constitution forbids a governmental establishment of religion, properly regarding it as a violation of individual rights. Since a man's beliefs are protected from the intrusion of force, the same principle should protect his reasoned convictions and forbid governmental establishments in the field of thought.

Socially, the most destructive consequences of tyranny are spread by an indeterminate, unofficial class of rulers: the officials' favorites. In the histories of absolute monarchies, it was the king's favorites who perpetrated the worst iniquities. Even an absolute monarch was restrained, to some minimal extent, by the necessity to pretend to maintain some semblance of justice, in order to protect his image from the people's indignation. But the recipients of his arbitrary, capricious favor held all the privileges of power without any of the restraints. It was among the scrambling, conniving, bootlicking, backstabbing climbers of a royal court that the worst exponents of power for power's sake were to be found. This holds true in any political system that leaves an opportunity open to them: in an absolute monarchy, in a totalitarian dictatorship, in a mixed economy.

Today, what we see in this country's intellectual field is one of the worst manifestations of political power: rule by favorites, by the unofficially privileged—by *private groups with governmental power, but without governmental responsibility.* They are shifting, switching groups, often feuding among themselves, but united against outsiders; they are scrambling to catch momentary favors, their precise status unknown to their members, their rivals, or their particular patrons among the hundreds of Congressmen and the thousands of bureaucrats—who are now bewildered and intimidated by these Frankensteinian creations. As in any other game devoid of objective rules, success and power in this one depend on barkers (press agents) and bluff.

Private cliques have always existed in the intellectual field, particularly in the arts, but they used to serve as checks and balances on one another, so that a nonconformist could enter the field and rise without the help of a clique. Today, the cliques are consolidated into an Establishment.

The term "Establishment" was not generally used or heard in this country until about a decade ago. The term originated in Great Britain, where it was applied to the upper-class families which traditionally preempted certain fields of activity. The British aristocracy is a politically created caste—an institution abolished and forbidden by the political system of the United States. The origin of an aristocracy is the king's power to confer on a chosen individual the privilege of receiving an unearned income from the involuntary servitude of the inhabitants of a given district.

Now, the same policy is operating in the United States—only the privileges are granted not in perpetuity, but in a lump sum for a limited time, and the involuntary servitude is imposed not on a group of serfs in a specific territory, but on all the citizens of the country. This does not change the nature of the policy or its consequences.

Observe the character of our intellectual Establishment. It is about a hundred years behind the times. It holds as dogma the basic premises fashionable at the turn of the century: the mysticism of Kant, the collectivism of Marx, the altruism of street-corner evangelists. Two world wars, three monstrous dictatorships—in Soviet Russia, Nazi Germany, Red China —plus every lesser variant of devastating socialist experimentation in a global spread of brutality and despair, have not prompted modern intellectuals to question or revise their dogma. They still think that it is daring, idealistic and unconventional to denounce the rich. They still believe that money is the root of all evil—except government money, which is the solution to all problems. The intellectual Establishment is frozen on the level of those elderly "leaders" who were prominent when the system of governmental "encouragement" took hold. By controlling the schools, the "leaders" perpetuated their dogma and gradually silenced the opposition.

Dissent still exists among the intellectuals, but it is a nit-picking dissent over trivia, which never challenges fundamental premises. This sort of dissent is permitted even in the Catholic Church, so long as it does not challenge the dogma—or in the "self-criticism" sessions of Soviet institutions, so long as it does not challenge the tenets of communism. A disagreement that does not challenge fundamentals serves only to reinforce them. It is particularly in this respect that the collapse of philosophy and the growth of government power work together to entrench the Establishment.

Rule by unofficially privileged private groups spreads a special kind of fear, like a slow poison injected into the culture. It is not fear of a specific ruler, but of the unknown power of anonymous cliques, which grows into a chronic fear of unknowable enemies. Most people do not hold any firm convictions on fundamental issues; today, people are more confused and uncertain than ever—yet the system demands of them a heroic kind of integrity, which they do not possess: they are destroyed by means of fundamental issues which they are unable to recognize in seemingly inconsequential concretes. Many men are capable of dying on the barricades for a big issue, but few—very few—are able to resist the gray suction of small, unheralded, day-by-day surrenders. Few want to start trouble, make enemies, risk their position and, perhaps, their livelihood over such issues as a colleague's objectionable abstract notions (which should be opposed, but are not), or the vaguely improper demands of a faculty clique (which should be resisted, but are not), or the independent attitude of a talented instructor (who should be hired, but is not). If a man senses that he ought to speak up, he is stopped by the routine "Who am I to know?" of modern skepticism—to which another, paralyzing clause is added in his mind: "Whom would I displease?"

Most men are quick to sense whether truth does or does not matter to their superiors. The atmosphere of cautious respect for the recipients of undeserved grants awarded by a mysterious governmental power, rapidly spreads the conviction that truth does not matter because *merit* does not matter, that something takes precedence over both. (And the issue of grants is only one of the countless ways in which the same arbitrary power intrudes into men's lives.) From the cynical notion: "Who cares about justice?" a man descends to: "Who cares about truth?" and then to: "Who cares?" Thus most men succumb to an intangible corruption, and sell their souls on the installment plan—by making small compromises, by cutting small corners—until nothing is left of their minds except the fear.

In business, the rise of the welfare state froze the status quo, perpetuating the power of the big corporations of the pre-income-tax era, placing them beyond the competition of the tax-strangled newcomers. A similar process took place in the welfare state of the intellect. The results, in both fields, are the same.

If you talk to a typical business executive or college dean or magazine editor, you can observe his special, modern quality: a kind of flowing or skipping evasiveness that drips or bounces automatically off any fundamental issue, a gently noncommittal blandness, an ingrained cautiousness toward everything, as if an inner tape recorder were whispering: "Play it safe, don't antagonize—whom?—anybody."

Whom would these men fear most, psychologically—and least, existentially? The brilliant loner—the beginner, the young man of potential genius and innocently ruthless integrity, whose only weapons are talent and truth. They reject him "instinctively," saying that "he doesn't belong" (to what?), sensing that he would put them on the spot by raising issues they prefer not to face. He might get past their protective barriers, once in a while, but he is handicapped by his virtues—in a system rigged against intelligence and integrity.

We shall never know how many precociously perceptive youths sensed the evil around them, before they were old enough to find an antidote—and gave up, in helplessly indignant bewilderment; or how many gave in, stultifying their minds. We do not know how many young innovators may exist today and struggle to be heard—but we will not hear of them because the Establishment would prefer not to recognize their existence and not to take any cognizance of their ideas.

So long as a society does not take the ultimate step into the abyss by establishing censorship, some men of ability will always succeed in breaking through. But the price—in effort, struggle and endurance—is such that only exceptional men can afford it. Today, originality, integrity, independence have become a road to martyrdom, which only the most dedicated will choose, knowing that the alternative is much worse. A society that sets up these conditions as the price of achievement, is in deep trouble.

The following is for the consideration of those "humanitarian" Congressmen (and their constituents) who think that a few public "plums" tossed to some old professors won't hurt anyone: it is the moral character of decent average men that has no chance under the rule of entrenched mediocrity. The genius can and will fight to the last. The average man cannot and does not.

In *Atlas Shrugged*, I discussed the "pyramid of ability" in the realm of economics. There is another kind of social pyramid. The genius who fights "every form of tyranny over the mind of man" is fighting a battle for which lesser men do not have the strength, but on which their freedom, their dignity, and their integrity depend. It is the pyramid of moral endurance.

15

Censorship:
Local and Express
1973

I have been saying, for many years, that statism is winning by default—by the intellectual default of capitalism's alleged defenders; that freedom and capitalism have never had a firm, philosophical base; that today's conservatives share all the fundamental premises of today's liberals and thus have paved, and are still paving, the road to statism. I have also said repeatedly that the battle for freedom is primarily philosophical and cannot be won by any lesser means—because philosophy rules human existence, including politics.

But philosophy is a science that deals with the broadest abstractions and, therefore, many people do not know how to observe its influence in practice or how to grasp the process by which it affects the conditions of their daily life. A recent event, however, offers a clear, striking illustration of that process. It shows philosophy's influence in action, and reveals the essence (and the contradictions) of both the conservative and the liberal ideologies. This event is the decision of the Supreme Court in five recent "obscenity" cases.

In [*The Ayn Rand Letter*] of November 20, 1972, I expressed hope in regard to the four men appointed to the Supreme Court by President Nixon, even though it was too early to tell the exact nature of their views. "But," I said, "if they live up to their enormous responsibility, we may forgive Mr.

Nixon a great many of his defaults: the Supreme Court is the last remnant of a philosophical influence in this country." Today, less than a year later, the evidence is sufficient to indicate that there are no intellectual grounds left for forgiving Mr. Nixon.

Since inconsistent premises lead to inconsistent actions, it is not impossible that the present Supreme Court may make some liberating decisions. For instance, the Court made a great contribution to justice and to the protection of individual rights when it legalized abortion. I am not in agreement with all of the reasoning given in that decision, but I am in enthusiastic agreement with the result—i.e., with the recognition of a woman's right to her own body. But the Court's decision in regard to obscenity takes an opposite stand: it denies a man's (or a woman's) right to the exercise of his own mind—by establishing the legal and intellectual base of *censorship*.

Before proceeding to discuss that decision, I want to state, for the record, my own view of what is called "hard-core" pornography. I regard it as unspeakably disgusting. I have not read any of the books or seen any of the current movies belonging to that category, and I do not intend ever to read or see them. The descriptions provided in legal cases, as well as the "modern" touches in "soft-core" productions, are sufficient grounds on which to form an opinion. The reason of my opinion is the opposite of the usual one: I do *not* regard sex as evil—I regard it as *good*, as one of the most important aspects of human life, too important to be made the subject of public *anatomical* display. But the issue here is not one's view of sex. The issue is freedom of speech and of the press—i.e., the right to hold *any* view and to express it.

It is not very inspiring to fight for the freedom of the purveyors of pornography or their customers. But in the transition to statism, every infringement of human rights has begun with the suppression of a given right's least attractive practitioners. In this case, the disgusting nature of the offenders makes it a good test of one's loyalty to a principle.

In the five "obscenity" cases decided on June 21, 1973, the Court was divided five to four. In each case, the majority opinion was written by Chief Justice Burger, joined by Justices Blackmun, Powell, Rehnquist (all four appointed by Nixon) and Justice White (appointed by Kennedy); in each case, the dissenting opinion was written by Justice Brennan, joined by Justices Stewart and Marshall; Justice Douglas, in each case, wrote a separate dissenting opinion. The two most important cases are Miller v. California and Paris Adult Theater I v. Slaton.

The Miller case involves a man who was convicted in California of mailing unsolicited, sexually explicit material, which advertised pornographic books. It is in the Miller decision that Chief Justice Burger promulgated the new criteria for judging whether a given work is obscene or not. They are as follows:

"The basic guidelines for the trier of fact must be: (a) whether 'the average person, applying contemporary community standards' would find that the work, taken as a whole, appeals to the prurient interest . . . (b) whether the work depicts or describes, in a patently offensive way, sexual conduct specifically defined by the applicable state law, and (c) whether the work, taken as a whole, lacks serious literary, artistic, political, or scientific value."

These criteria are based on previous Supreme Court decisions, particularly on Roth v. United States, 1957. Nine years later, in the case of Memoirs v. Massachusetts, 1966, the Supreme Court introduced a new criterion: "A book cannot be proscribed unless it is found to be *utterly* without redeeming social value." This was bad enough, but the present decision emphatically rejects that particular notion and substitutes a horrendous criterion of its own: "whether the work, taken as a whole, lacks serious literary, artistic, political, or scientific value."

Morally, this criterion, as well as the rest of Chief Justice Burger's decision, *taken as a whole*, is a proclamation of collectivism—not so much political as specifically *moral* collectivism. The intellectual standard which is here set up to rule an individual's mind—to prescribe what an individual may write, publish, read or see—is the judgment of an *average* person applying *community* standards. Why? No reason is given—which means that the will of the collective is here taken for granted as the source, justification and criterion of value judgments.

What is a *community?* No definition is given—it may, therefore, be a state, a city, a neighborhood, or just the block you live on. What are *community standards?* No definition is given. In fact, the standards of a community, when and if they can be observed as such, as distinguished from the standards of its individual citizens, are a product of chance, lethargy, hypocrisy, second-handedness, indifference, fear, the manipulations of local busybodies or small-time power-lusters—and, occasionally, the traditional acceptance of some decent values inherited from some great mind of the past. But the great mind is now to be outlawed by the ruling of the Supreme Court.

Who is the *average person?* No definition is given. There is some indication that the term, in this context, means a person who is neither particularly susceptible or sensitive nor totally insensitive in regard to sex. But to find a *sexually* average person is a more preposterously impossible undertaking than to find the average representative of any other human characteristic—and, besides, this is not what the Court decision says. It says simply "average"—which, in an issue of judgment, means *intellectually* average: average in intelligence, in ability, in ideas, in feelings, in tastes, which means: a conformist or a nonentity. Any proposition concerned with establishing a human "average" necessarily eliminates the top and the bottom, i.e., the best and the worst. Thus the standards of a genius and the standards of a moron are automatically eliminated, suppressed or prohibited—and both are ordered to subordinate their own views to those of the average. Why is the average person to be granted so awesome a privilege? By reason of the fact that he possesses no special distinction. Nothing can justify such a notion, except the theory of collectivism, which is itself unjustifiable.

The Court's decision asserts repeatedly—just *asserts*—that this ruling applies only to hard-core pornography or obscenity, i.e., to certain ideas dealing with sex, not to any other kinds of ideas. Other kinds of ideas—it keeps asserting—are protected by the First Amendment, but ideas dealing with sex are not. Apart from the impossibility of drawing a line between these two categories (which we shall discuss later), this distinction is contradicted and invalidated right in the text of this same decision: the trial judges and juries are empowered to determine whether a work that contains sexual elements "lacks *serious literary, artistic, political, or scientific value*."

This means—and can mean nothing else—that the government is empowered to judge literary, artistic, political, and scientific values, and to permit or suppress certain works accordingly.

The alleged limits on that power, the conditions of when, where and by whom it may be exercised, are of no significance—once the principle that the government holds such a power has been established. The rest is only a matter of details—and of time. The present Supreme Court may seek to suppress only sexual materials; on the same basis (the will of the community), a future Court may suppress "undesirable" *scientific* discussions; still another Court may suppress *political* discussions (and a year later all discussions in all fields would be suppressed). The law functions by a process of deriving logical consequences from established precedents.

The "average person's community standards" criterion, was set up in the Roth case. But the Roth criterion, of "utterly without redeeming social value" was too vague to be immediately dangerous—anything may be claimed to have some sort of "social value." So, logically, on the basis of that precedent, the present Court took the next step toward censorship. It gave to the government the power of entry into four *specific* intellectual fields, with the power to judge whether the values of works in these fields are serious or not.

"Serious" is an *unserious* standard. Who is to determine what is serious, to whom, and by what criterion? Since no definition is given, one must assume that the criterion to apply is the only one promulgated in those guidelines: what the average person would find serious. Do you care to contemplate the spectacle of the average person as the ultimate authority—the censor—in the field of literature? In the field of art? In the field of politics? In the field of science? An authority whose edict is to be imposed by *force* and is to determine what will be permitted or suppressed in all these fields? I submit that no pornographic movie can be as morally obscene as a prospect of this kind.

No first-rate talent in any of those fields will ever be willing to work by the intellectual standards and under the orders of any authority, even if it were an authority composed of the best brains in the world (who would not accept the job), let alone an authority consisting of "average persons." And the greater the talent, the less the willingness.

As to those who *would* be willing, observe the moral irony of the fact that they *do* exist today in large numbers and are generally despised: they are the hacks, the box-office chasers, who try to please what they think are the tastes—and the standards—of the public, for the sake of making money. Apparently, intellectual prostitution is evil, if done for a "selfish" motive—but noble, if accepted in selfless service to the "moral purity" of the community.

In another of the five "obscenity" cases (U.S. v. 12 200-Ft. Reels of Super 8mm. Film), but in a totally different context, Chief Justice Burger himself describes the danger created by the logical implications of a precedent: "The seductive plausibility of single steps in a chain of evolutionary development of a legal rule is often not perceived until a third, fourth or fifth 'logical' extension occurs. Each step, when taken, appeared a reasonable step in relation to that which preceded it,

although the aggregate or end result is one that would never
have been seriously considered in the first instance. This kind
of gestative propensity calls for the 'line drawing' familiar in
the judicial, as in the legislative process: 'thus far but not
beyond.'"

I would argue that since a legal rule is a principle, the
development of its logical consequences cannot be cut off,
except by repealing the principle. But assuming that such a
cutoff were possible, *no line of any sort is drawn* in the Miller
decision: the community standards of average persons are
explicitly declared to be a sovereign power over sexual matters and over the works that deal with sexual matters.

In the same Miller decision, Chief Justice Burger admits
that no such line can be drawn. "Nothing in the First
Amendment requires that a jury must consider hypothetical
and unascertainable 'national standards' when attempting to
determine whether certain materials are obscene as a matter
of fact." He quotes Chief Justice Warren saying in an earlier
case: "I believe that there is no provable 'national standard.'
. . . At all events, this Court has not been able to enunciate
one, and it would be unreasonable to expect local courts to
divine one."

By what means are local courts to divine a *local* one? Actually, the only *provable* standard of what constitutes obscenity would be an *objective* standard, philosophically proved and
valid for all men. Such a standard cannot be defined or
enforced in terms of law: it would require the formulation of
an entire philosophic system; but even this would not grant
anyone the right to enforce that standard on others. When the
Court, however, speaks of a "provable national standard," it
does not mean an *objective* standard; it substitutes the *collective* for the objective, and seeks to enunciate a standard held
by all the average persons of the nation. Since even a guess at
such a concept is patently impossible, the Court concludes
that what is impossible (and improper) nationally, is permissible locally—and, in effect, passes the buck to state legisla-

tures, granting them the power to enforce arbitrary (*unprovable*) local standards.

Chief Justice Burger's arguments, in the Miller decision, are not very persuasive. "It is neither realistic nor constitutionally sound to read the First Amendment as requiring that the people of Maine or Mississippi accept public depiction of conduct found tolerable in Las Vegas, or New York City." I read the First Amendment as not requiring any person anywhere to accept any depiction he does not wish to read or see, but forbidding him to abridge the rights and freedom of those who do wish to read or see it.

In another argument against a national standard of what constitutes obscenity, the decision declares: "People in different States vary in their tastes and attitudes, and this diversity is not to be strangled by the absolutism of imposed uniformity." What about the absolutism of imposed uniformity *within* a state? What about the non-conformists in that state? What about communication between citizens of different states? What about the freedom of a *national* marketplace of ideas? No answers are given.

The following argument, offered in a footnote, is unworthy of a *serious* tribunal: "The mere fact juries may reach different conclusions as to the same material does not mean that constitutional rights are abridged. As this Court observed in Roth v. United States . . . 'It is common experience that different juries may reach different results under any criminal statute. That is one of the consequences we accept under our jury system. . . .' " In a criminal case, the jury's duty is only to determine whether a particular defendant committed the crime which is clearly and specifically defined by the statute. Under the new "obscenity" ruling, a jury is expected to determine whether the defendant committed an undefined crime and, simultaneously, to determine what that crime is.

Thus the Nixon Court's notion of censorship-sharing by diffusing it at random over the entire country, is as illusory as Nixon's notion of returning power to the states by means of revenue-sharing. While the public rides on the creaking train of local censorship, with delays, derailments and chaos at every whistle stop—the express of statism is flying full speed on an unobstructed track.

Four of the Justices who handed down the Miller decision, are regarded as conservatives; the fifth, Justice White, is regarded as middle-of-the-road. On the other hand, Justice Douglas is the most liberal or the most leftward-leaning member of the Court. Yet his dissent in the Miller case is an impassioned cry of protest and indignation. He rejects the notion that the First Amendment allows an implied exception in the case of obscenity. "I do not think it does and my views on the issue have been stated over and over again." He declares: "Obscenity—which even we cannot define with precision—is a hodge-podge. To send men to jail for violating standards they cannot understand, construe, and apply is a monstrous thing to do in a Nation dedicated to fair trials and due process."

What about the antitrust laws, which are responsible for precisely this kind of monstrous thing? Justice Douglas does not mention them—but antitrust, as we shall see later, is a chicken that comes home to roost on *both* sides of this issue.

On the subject of censorship, however, Justice Douglas is eloquently consistent: "The idea that the First Amendment permits punishment for ideas that are 'offensive' to the particular judge or jury sitting in judgment is astounding. No greater leveler of speech or literature has ever been designed. To give the power to the censor, as we do today, is to make a sharp and radical break with the traditions of a free society. The First Amendment was not fashioned as a vehicle for dispensing tranquilizers to the people. Its prime function was to keep debate open to 'offensive' as well as to 'staid' people. The tendency throughout history has been to subdue the individual and to exalt the power of government. The use of the standard 'offensive' gives authority to government that cuts the very vitals out of the First Amendment. As is intimated by the Court's opinion, the materials before us may be garbage. But so is much of what is said in political campaigns, in the daily press, on TV or over the radio. By reason of the First Amendment—and solely because of it—speakers and publishers have not been threatened or subdued because their thoughts and ideas may be 'offensive' to some."

I can only say "Amen" to this statement.

Observe that such issues as the individual against the State are never mentioned in the Supreme Court's majority decision. It is Justice Douglas, the arch-liberal, who defends individual rights. It is the conservatives who speak as if the individual did not exist, as if the *unit* of social concern were the collective—the *"community."*

A profound commitment to moral collectivism does not occur in a vacuum, as a causeless primary: it requires an epistemological foundation. The Supreme Court's majority decision in the case of Paris Adult Theater I v. Slaton reveals that foundation.

This case involves two movie theaters in Atlanta, Georgia, which exhibited allegedly obscene films, admitting only adults. The local trial court ruled that this was constitutionally permissible, but the Georgia Supreme Court reversed the decision—on the grounds that hard-core pornography is not protected by the First Amendment. Thus the issue before the U.S. Supreme Court was whether it is constitutional to abridge the freedom of consenting adults. The Court's majority decision said: "Yes."

Epistemologically, this decision is a proclamation of *non-objectivity:* it supports and defends explicitly the most evil of social phenomena: non-objective law.

The decision, written by Chief Justice Burger, declares: "we hold that there are legitimate state interests at stake in stemming the tide of commercialized obscenity . . . These include *the interest of the public in the quality of life and the total community environment,* the tone of commerce in the great city centers, and, possibly, the public safety itself."

(Emphasis added.) Try to find a single issue or action that would be exempt from this kind of "legitimate" state interest.

Quoting a book by Professor Bickel, the decision declares: "A man may be entitled to read an obscene book in his room . . . But if he demands a right to obtain the books and pictures he wants in the market . . . then to grant him his right is to affect the world about the rest of us, and to impinge on other privacies. . . . what is commonly read and seen and heard and done intrudes upon us all, want it or not." Which human activity would be exempt from a declaration of this kind? And what advocate of a totalitarian dictatorship would not endorse that declaration?

Mr. Burger concedes that "there is no scientific data which conclusively demonstrates that exposure to obscene materials adversely affects men and women or their society." But he rejects this as an argument against the suppression of such materials. And there follows an avalanche of statements and of quotations from earlier Court decisions—all claiming (in terms broader than the issue of pornography) that *scientific knowledge* and *conclusive proof* are not required as a basis for legislation, that the State has the right to enact laws on the grounds of what does or *might* exist.

"Scientific data" (in the proper, literal sense of these words) means knowledge of *reality*, reached by a process of *reason;* and "conclusive demonstration" means that the content of a given proposition is proved to be a fact of reality. It is reason and reality that are here being removed as a limitation on the power of the State. It is the right to legislate on the basis of any assumption, any hypothesis, any guess, any feeling, any *whim*—on any grounds or none—that is here being conferred on the government.

"We do not demand of legislatures 'scientifically certain criteria of legislation,'" the decision affirms. "Although there is no conclusive proof of a connection between antisocial behavior and obscene material, the legislature of Georgia could quite reasonably determine that such a connection does or might exist. In deciding Roth, this Court implicitly accepted that a legislature could legitimately act on such a conclusion to protect *'the social interest in order and morality.'"*

If the notion that something *might* be a threat to the "social interest" is sufficient to justify suppression, then the Nazi or the Soviet dictatorship is justified in exterminating anyone who, in its belief, *might* be a threat to the "social interest" of the Nazi or the Soviet "community."

Whatever theory of government such a notion represents, it is *not* the theory of America's Founding Fathers. Strangely enough, Chief Justice Burger seems to be aware of it, because he proceeds to call on a pre-American precedent. "From the beginning of civilized societies, legislators and judges have acted on various unprovable assumptions. Such assumptions underlie much lawful state regulation of commercial and business affairs."

This is preeminently true—and look at the results. Look at the history of *all* the governments in the world prior to the birth of the United States. Ours was the first government based on and strictly limited by a written document—the Constitution—which specifically forbids it to violate individual rights or to act on whim. The history of the atrocities perpetrated by all the other kinds of governments—unrestricted governments acting on unprovable assumptions—demonstrates the value and validity of the original political theory on which this country was built. Yet here is the Supreme Court citing all those bloody millennia of tyranny, as a precedent for us to follow.

If this seems inexplicable, the very next sentence of Mr. Burger's decision gives a clue to the reasons—and a violently clear demonstration of the role of precedent in the development of law. That next sentence seems to unleash a whirling storm of feathers, as chickens come flying home from every direction to roost on everyone's coop, perch or fence—in retribution for every evasion, compromise, injustice, and violation of rights perpetrated in past decades.

That next sentence is: "The same [a basis of unprovable assumptions] is true of the federal securities, antitrust laws and a host of other federal regulations."

Formally, I would have to say: "Oh, Mr. Chief Justice!" Informally, I want to say: "Oh, brother!"

"On the basis of these assumptions," Mr. Burger goes on, "both Congress and state legislatures have, for example, drastically restricted associational rights by adopting antitrust laws, and have strictly regulated public expression by issuers of and dealers in securities, profit sharing 'coupons,' and 'trading stamps,' commanding what they must and may not publish and announce. . . . Understandably those who entertain an absolutist view of the First Amendment find it uncomfortable to explain why rights of association, speech, and press should be severely restrained in the marketplace of goods and money, but not in the marketplace of pornography."

On the collectivist premise, there is, of course, no answer. The only answer, in today's situation, is to check that premise and reject it—and start repealing all those catastrophically destructive violations of individual rights and of the Constitution. But this is not what the Court majority has decided. Forgetting his own warning about the "gestative propensity" of the judicial and legislative processes, Chief Justice Burger accepts the precedent as an irrevocable absolute and pushes the country many steps further toward the abyss of statism.

"Likewise," the decision continues, "when legislatures and administrators act to protect the physical environment from pollution and to preserve our resources of forests, streams and parks, they must act on such imponderables as the impact of a new highway near or through an existing park or wilderness area. . . . Thus the Federal-Aid Highway Act of 1968 . . . and the Department of Transportation Act of 1966 . . . have been described by Mr. Justice Black as 'a solemn determination of the highest law-making body of this Nation that beauty and health-giving facilities of our parks are not to be taken away for public roads without hearings, fact-findings, and policy determinations under the supervision of a Cabinet officer. . . . ' The fact that a congressional directive reflects unprovable assumptions about what is good for the people, including imponderable aesthetic assumptions, is not a sufficient reason to find that statute unconstitutional."

Isn't it? If it is not, then *the imponderable aesthetic assumptions* of government officials are entitled to invade the field of literature and art—as Mr. Burger's decision is inviting them to do.

The ugly hand of altruism slithers into the decision, in a passage that sideswipes the concept of free will. "We have just noted, for example, that neither the First Amendment nor 'free will' precludes States from having 'blue sky' laws to regulate what sellers of securities may write or publish about their wares. . . . Such laws are to protect the weak, the uninformed, the unsuspecting, and the gullible from the exercise of their own volition." It is for this kind of purpose that the rest of us—who are not weak, uninformed, unsuspecting, and gullible—are to be *protected* from *our* volition and deprived of the right to exercise it. So much for the relation of altruism to rights and to freedom.

Here is another chicken flying home: "States are told by some that they must await a 'laissez-faire' market solution to the obscenity-pornography problem, paradoxically 'by people who have never otherwise had a kind word to say for laissez-faire,' particularly in solving urban, commercial, and environmental pollution problems."

The decision contains many other homing chickens of this kind—an entire barnyard of them—many more than I have space to quote. But these are sufficient to give you the nature, style and spirit of that ruling.

In his dissenting opinion, Justice Brennan, joined by Justices Stewart and Marshall, offers some good arguments to support the conclusion that censorship in regard to consenting adults is unconstitutional. But he wavers, hesitates to go that far, and tries to compromise, to strike "a better balance between the guarantee of free expression and the States' legitimate interests."

He concedes the notion that obscene material is not protected by the First Amendment, but expresses an anxious concern over the Court's failure to draw a clear line between protected and unprotected speech. He cites the chaotic, contradictory record of the Court's decisions in "obscenity" cases, but sidesteps the issue by saying, in a footnote: "Whether or not a class of 'obscene' and thus entirely unprotected speech does exist, I am forced to conclude that the class is incapable of definition with sufficient clarity to withstand attack on vagueness grounds. Accordingly, it is on principles of the void-for-vagueness doctrine that this opinion exclusively relies."

Justice Brennan speaks eloquently about the danger of vague laws, and quotes Chief Justice Warren, who said that "the constitutional requirement of definiteness is violated by a criminal statute that fails to give a person of ordinary intelligence fair notice that his contemplated conduct is forbidden by the statute." But Justice Brennan does not mention the antitrust laws, which do just that. He states: "The resulting level of uncertainty is utterly intolerable, not alone because it makes 'bookselling . . . a hazardous profession,' . . . but as well because it invites arbitrary and erratic enforcement of the law." He deplores the fact that "obscenity" judgments are now made on "a case-by-case, sight-by-sight" basis. He observes that the Court has been struggling "to fend off legislative attempts 'to pass to the courts—and ultimately to the Supreme Court—the awesome task of making case by case at once the criminal and the constitutional law.'" But he does not mention the living hell of antitrust, the grim monument to law made case by case.

However, a greater respect for principles and a greater understanding of their consequences are revealed in Justice Brennan's dissenting opinion than in the majority decision.

He declares that on the basis of that majority decision: "it is hard to see how state-ordered regimentation of our minds can ever be forestalled. For if a State may, in an effort to maintain or create a particular moral tone, prescribe what its citizens cannot read or cannot see, then it would seem to follow that in pursuit of that same objective a State could decree that its citizens must read certain books or must view certain films."

The best statement, however, is made again by Justice Douglas, who ends his forceful dissent with the words: "But our society—unlike most in the world—presupposes that freedom and liberty are in a frame of reference that make the individual, not government, the keeper of his tastes, beliefs, and ideas. That is the philosophy of the First Amendment; and it is the article of faith that sets us apart from most nations in the world."

I concur—except that it is not an "article of *faith*," but a *provable*, rational conviction.

In the life of a nation, the law plays the same role as a decision-making process of thought does in the life of an individual. An individual makes decisions by applying his basic premises to a specific choice—premises which he can change, but seldom does. The basic premises of a nation's laws are set by its dominant political philosophy and implemented by the courts, whose task is to determine the application of broad principles to specific cases; in this task, the equivalent of basic premises is *precedent*, which can be challenged, but seldom is.

How far a loosely worded piece of legislation can go in the role of precedent, is horrifyingly demonstrated by the Supreme Court's majority decision in another one of the five "obscenity" cases, U.S. v. Orito. This case involves a man charged with knowingly transporting obscene material by common carrier in interstate commerce.

The clause giving Congress the power to regulate interstate commerce is one of the major errors in the Constitution. That clause, more than any other, was the crack in the Constitution's foundation, the entering wedge of statism, which permitted the gradual establishment of the welfare state. But I would venture to say that the framers of the Constitution could not have conceived of what that clause has now become. If, in writing it, one of their goals was to facilitate the flow of trade and prevent the establishment of trade barriers among the states, that clause has reached the opposite destination. You may now expect fifty different frontiers inside this country, with customs officials searching your luggage and pockets for books or magazines permitted in one state but prohibited in another.

Chief Justice Burger's decision declares, quoting an earlier Court decision: "The motive and purpose of a regulation of interstate commerce are matters for the legislative judgment upon the exercise of which the Constitution places no restriction and over which the courts are given no control." Such an interpretation means that legislative judgment is given an absolute power, beyond the restraint of any principle, beyond the reach of any checks or balances. This is an outrageous instance of context-dropping: the Constitution, taken as a whole, *is* a fundamental restriction on the power of the government, whether in the legislative or in any other branch.

"It is sufficient to reiterate," Mr. Burger declares, "the well-settled principle that Congress may impose relevant conditions and requirements on those who use the channels of interstate commerce in order that those channels will not become the means of promoting or spreading evil, whether of a physical, moral or economic nature." As if this were not clear enough, a footnote is added: "Congress can certainly regulate interstate commerce to the extent of forbidding and punishing the use of such commerce as an agency to promote immorality, dishonesty, or the spread of any evil or harm to the people of other states from the state of origin." Immorality, evil and harm—by what standard?

The only rights which the five majority decisions leave you are the right to read and see what you wish in your own room, but not outside it—and the right to think whatever you please in the privacy of your own mind. But this is a right which even a totalitarian dictatorship is unable to suppress. (You are free to *think* in Soviet Russia, but not to *act* on your thinking.) Again, Justice Douglas's dissent is the only voice raised in desperate protest: "Our whole constitutional heritage rebels at the thought of giving government the power to control men's minds."

The division between the conservative and the liberal viewpoints in the opinions of the Supreme Court, is sharper and clearer than in less solemn writings or in purely political debates. By the nature of its task, the Supreme Court has to and does become the voice of philosophy.

The necessity to deal with principles makes the members of the Supreme Court seem archetypical of the ideas—almost, of the soul—of the two political camps they represent. They were not chosen as archetypes: in the undefined, indeterminate, contradictory chaos of political views loosely labeled "conservative" and "liberal," it would be impossible to choose an essential characteristic or a typical representative. Yet, as one reads the Supreme Court's opinions, the essential premises stand out with an oddly bright, revealing clarity— and one grasps that under all the lesser differences and inconsistencies of their followers, *these* are the basic premises of one political camp or of the other. It is almost as if one were seeing not these antagonists' philosophy, but their sense of life.

The subject of the five "obscenity" cases was not obscenity as such—which is a marginal and inconsequential matter— but a much deeper issue: the sexual aspect of man's life. Sex is not a separate nor a purely physical attribute of man's character: it involves a complex integration of all his fundamental values. So it is not astonishing that cases dealing with sex (even in its ugliest manifestations) would involve the influence of all the branches of philosophy. We have seen the influence of ethics, epistemology, politics, esthetics (this last as the immediate victim of the debate). What about the fifth branch of philosophy, the basic one, the fundamental of the science of fundamentals: metaphysics? Its influence is revealed in—and explains—the inner contradictions of each camp. The metaphysical issue is their view of man's nature.

Both camps hold the same premise—*the mind-body dichotomy*—but choose opposite sides of this lethal fallacy.

The conservatives want freedom to act in the material realm; they tend to oppose government control of production, of industry, of trade, of business, of physical goods, of material wealth. But they advocate government control of man's spirit, i.e., man's consciousness; they advocate the State's right to impose censorship, to determine moral values, to create and enforce a governmental establishment of morality, to rule the intellect. The liberals want freedom to act in the spiritual realm; they oppose censorship, they oppose government control of ideas, of the arts, of the press, of education (note their concern with "academic freedom"). But they advocate government control of material production, of business, of employment, of wages, of profits, of all physical property—they advocate it all the way down to total expropriation.

The conservatives see man as a body freely roaming the earth, building sand piles or factories—with an electronic computer inside his skull, controlled from Washington. The liberals see man as a soul freewheeling to the farthest reaches of the universe—but wearing chains from nose to toes when he crosses the street to buy a loaf of bread.

Yet it is the conservatives who are predominantly religionists, who proclaim the superiority of the soul over the body, who represent what I call the "mystics of spirit." And it is the liberals who are predominantly materialists, who regard man as an aggregate of meat, and who represent what I call the "mystics of muscle."

This is merely a paradox, not a contradiction: *each camp wants to control the realm it regards as metaphysically impor-*

tant; each grants freedom only to the activities it despises. Observe that the conservatives insult and demean the rich or those who succeed in material production, regarding them as morally inferior—and that the liberals treat ideas as a cynical con game. "Control," to both camps, means the power to rule by physical force. Neither camp holds freedom as a value. The conservatives want to rule man's consciousness; the liberals, his body.

On that premise, neither camp has permitted itself to observe that force is a killer in both realms. The conservatives, frozen in their mystic dogmas, are paralyzed, terrified and impotent in the realm of ideas. The liberals, waiting for the unearned, are paralyzed, terrified and, frequently, incompetent in or hostile to the realm of material production (observe the ecology crusade).

Why do both camps cling to blind faith in the power of physical force? I quote from *Atlas Shrugged:* "Do you observe what human faculty that doctrine [the mind-body dichotomy] was designed to destroy? It was man's mind that had to be negated in order to make him fall apart." Both camps, conservatives and liberals alike, are united in their hatred of man's mind—i.e., of *reason.* The conservatives reject reason in favor of faith; the liberals, in favor of emotions. The conservatives are either lethargically indifferent to intellectual issues, or actively anti-intellectual. The liberals are smarter in this respect: they use intellectual weapons to destroy and negate the intellect (they call it "to redefine"). When men reject reason, they have no means left for dealing with one another —except brute, physical force.

I quote from *Atlas Shrugged:* " . . . the men you call materialists and spiritualists are only two halves of the same dissected human, forever seeking completion, but seeking it by swinging from the destruction of the flesh to the destruction of the soul and vice versa . . . seeking any refuge against reality, any form of escape from the mind." Since the two camps are only two sides of the same coin—the same *counterfeit* coin

—they are now moving closer and closer together. Observe the fundamental similarity of their philosophical views: in metaphysics—the mind-body dichotomy; in epistemology—irrationalism; in ethics—altruism; in politics—statism.

The conservatives used to claim that they were loyal to tradition—while the liberals boasted of being "progressive." But observe that it is Chief Justice Burger, a conservative, who propounds a militant collectivism, and formulates general principles that stretch the power of the State way beyond the issue of pornography—and it is Justice Douglas, a liberal, who invokes "the traditions of a free society" and pleads for "our constitutional heritage."

If someone had said in 1890 that antitrust laws for the businessmen would, sooner or later, lead to censorship for the intellectuals, no one would have believed it. You can see it today. When Chief Justice Burger declares to the liberals that they cannot explain why rights "should be severely restrained in the marketplace of goods and money, but not in the marketplace of pornography," I am tempted to feel that it serves them right—except that all of us are the victims.

If this censorship ruling is not revoked, the next step will be more explicit: it will replace the words "marketplace of pornography" with the words "marketplace of ideas." This will serve as a precedent for the liberals, enabling them to determine which ideas *they* wish to suppress—in the name of the "social interest"—when their turn comes. No one can win a contest of this kind—except the State.

I do not know how the conservative members of the Supreme Court can bear to look at the Jefferson Memorial in Washington, where his words are engraved in marble: "I have sworn . . . eternal hostility to every form of tyranny over the mind of man."

Permit me to add without presumptuousness: "So have I."

16

Fairness Doctrine for Education
1972

The "Fairness Doctrine" is a messy little makeshift of the mixed economy, and a poor substitute for freedom of speech. It has, however, served as a minimal retarder of the collectivist trend: it has prevented the Establishment's total takeover of the airwaves. For this reason—as a temporary measure in a grave national emergency—the fairness doctrine should now be invoked in behalf of education.

The doctrine is a typical product of the socialist sentimentality that dreams of combining government ownership with intellectual freedom. As applied to television and radio broadcasting, the fairness doctrine demands that equal opportunity be given to all sides of a controversial issue—on the grounds of the notion that "the people owns the airwaves" and, therefore, all factions of "the people" should have equal access to their communal property.

The trouble with the fairness doctrine is that it cannot be applied fairly. Like any ideological product of the mixed economy, it is a vague, indefinable approximation and, therefore, an instrument of pressure-group warfare. Who determines which issues are controversial? Who chooses the representatives of the different sides in a given controversy? If there are too many conflicting viewpoints, which are to be given a voice and which are to be kept silent? Who *is* "the people" and who *is not*?

It is clear that the individual's views are barred altogether and that the "fairness" is extended only to groups. The formula employed by the television stations in New York declares that they recognize their obligation to provide equal time to *"significant* opposing viewpoints." Who determines which viewpoint is "significant"? Is the standard qualitative or quantitative? It is obviously this last, as one may observe in practice: whenever an answer is given to a TV editorial, it is given by a representative of some group involved in the debated subject.

The fairness doctrine (as well as the myth of public ownership) is based on the favorite illusion of the mushy socialists, i.e., those who want to combine force and freedom, as distinguished from the bloody socialists, i.e., the communists and the fascists. That illusion is the belief that the people ("the masses") would be essentially unanimous, that dissenting groups would be rare and easily accommodated, that a monolithic majority-will would prevail, and that any injustice done would be done only to recalcitrant individuals, who, in socialist theory, do not count anyway. (For a discussion of why the airwaves should be private property, see "The Property Status of Airwaves" in my book *Capitalism: The Unknown Ideal*.)

In practice, the fairness doctrine has led to the precarious rule of a "centrist" attitude: of timidity, compromise and fear (with the "center" slithering slowly, inexorably to the left)—i.e., control by the Establishment, limited only by the remnants of a tradition of freedom: by lip service to "impartiality," by fear of being caught at too obvious an "unfairness," and by the practice of "window dressing," which consists in some occasional moments of air time tossed to some representatives of extreme and actually significant opposing viewpoints. Such a policy, by its very nature, is temporary. Nevertheless, this "window dressing" is the last chance that the advocates of freedom have, as far as the airwaves are concerned.

There is no equivalent of the fairness doctrine in the field which is much more important to a nation's future than its airwaves—the field which determines a country's intellectual trends, i.e., the dominant ideas in people's minds, in the culture, in the Establishment, in the press and, ultimately, on the air: the field of higher education.

So long as higher education was provided predominantly by private colleges and universities, no problem of unfairness existed. A private school has the right to teach any ideas of its owners' choice, and to exclude all opposing ideas; but it has no power to force such exclusion on the rest of the country. The opponents have the right to establish schools of their own and to teach their ideas or a wider spectrum of viewpoints, if they so choose. The competition of the free marketplace of ideas does the rest, determining every school's success or failure—which, historically, was the course of the development of the great private universities. But the growth of government power, of state universities, and of taxation brought the private universities under a growing control by and dependence on the government. [On this point, see also "Tax Credits for Education," in *The Ayn Rand Letter* of March 13, 1972.] The current bill providing Federal "aid" to higher education will make the control and dependence all but total, thus establishing a governmental monopoly on education.

The most ominously crucial question now hanging over this country's future is: *what* will our universities teach at our expense and without our consent? What ideas will be propagated or excluded? (This question applies to all public and semi-public institutions of learning. By "semi-public" I mean those formerly private institutions which are to be supported in part by public funds and controlled in full by the government.)

The government has no right to set itself up as the arbiter of ideas and, therefore, its establishments—the public and semi-public schools—have no right to teach a single viewpoint, excluding all others. They have no right to serve the beliefs of any one group of citizens, leaving others ignored and silenced. They have no right to impose inequality on the citizens who bear equally the burden of supporting them.

As in the case of governmental grants to science, it is viciously wrong to force an individual to pay for the teaching of ideas diametrically opposed to his own; it is a profound violation of his rights. The violation becomes monstrous if *his* ideas are excluded from such public teaching: this means that he is forced to pay for the propagation of that which he regards as false and evil, and for the suppression of that which he regards as true and good. If there is a viler form of injustice, I challenge any resident of Washington, D.C., to name it.

Yet *this* is the form of injustice committed by the present policy of an overwhelming majority of our public and semi-public universities.

There is a widespread impression that television and the press are biased and slanted to the left. But they are models of impartiality and fairness compared to the ferocious intolerance, the bias, the prejudices, the distortions, the savage obscurantism now running riot in most of our institutions of higher learning—in regard to matters deeper than mere politics. With rare exceptions, each of the various departments and disciplines is ruled by its own particular clique that gets in and virtually excludes the teaching of any theory or viewpoint other than its own. If a private school permits this, it has the right to do so; a public or semi-public school has not.

Controversy is the hallmark of our age; there is no subject, particularly in the humanities, which is not regarded in fundamentally different ways by many different schools of thought. (This is not to say that all of them are valid, but merely to observe that they exist.) Yet most university departments, particularly in the leading universities, offer a single viewpoint (camouflaged by minor variations) and maintain their monopoly by the simple means of evasion: by ignoring anything that does not fit their viewpoint, by pretending that no others exist, and by reducing dissent to trivia, thus leaving fundamentals unchallenged.

Most of today's philosophy departments are dominated by Linguistic Analysis (the unsuccessful product of crossbreeding between philosophy and grammar, a union whose offspring is less viable than a mule), with some remnants of its immediate progenitors, Pragmatism and Logical Positivism, still clinging to its bandwagon. The more "broadminded" departments include an opposition—the other side of the same Kantian coin, Existentialism. (One side claims that philosophy is grammar, the other that philosophy is feelings.)

Psychology departments have a sprinkling of Freudians, but are dominated by Behaviorism, whose leader is B. F. Skinner. (Here the controversy is between the claim that man is moved by innate ideas, and the claim that he has no ideas at all.)

Economics departments are dominated by Marxism, which is taken straight or on the rocks, in the form of Keynesianism.

What the political science departments and the business administration schools are dominated by is best illustrated by the following example: in a distinguished Ivy League university, a dean of the School of Business recently suggested that it be renamed "School of Management," explaining that profit-making is unpopular with students and that most of them want to work for non-profit institutions, such as government or charities.

Sociology departments are dominated by the fact that no one has ever defined what sociology is.

English departments are dominated by *The New York Times Book Review*.

I do not know the state of the various departments in the physical sciences, but we have seen an indication of it: the "scientific" writings of the ecologists.

As a result of today's educational policies, the majority of college graduates are virtually illiterate, in the literal and the wider sense of the word. They do not necessarily accept their teachers' views, but they do not know that any other views exist or have ever existed. There are philosophy majors who graduate without having taken a single course on Aristotle (except as part of general surveys). There are economics majors who have no idea of what capitalism is or was, theoretically or historically, and not the faintest notion of the mechanism of a free market. There are literature majors who have never heard of Victor Hugo (but have acquired a full vocabulary of four-letter words).

So long as there were variations among university departments in the choice of their dominant prejudices—and so long as there were some distinguished survivors of an earlier, freer view of education—non-conformists had some chance. But with the spread of "unpolarized" unity and Federal "encouragement"—the spread of the same gray, heavy-footed, deaf-dumb-and-blind, hysterically stagnant dogma—that chance is vanishing. It is becoming increasingly harder for an independent mind to get or keep a job on a university faculty—or for the independent mind of a student to remain independent.

This is the logical result of generations of post-Kantian statist philosophy and of the vicious circle which it set up: as philosophy degenerates into irrationalism, it promotes the growth of government power, which, in turn, promotes the degeneration of philosophy.

It is a paradox of our age of skepticism—with its proliferation of bromides to the effect that "Man can be certain of nothing," "Reality is unknowable," "There are no hard facts or hard knowledge—everything is soft [except the point of a gun]"—that the overbearing dogmatism of university departments would make a medieval enforcer of religious dogma squirm with envy. It is a paradox but not a contradiction, because it is the necessary consequence—and purpose—of skepticism, which disarms its opponents by declaring: "How can you be sure?" and thus enables its leaders to propound absolutes at whim.

It is this kind of intellectual atmosphere and these types of cynical, bigoted, envy-ridden, decadent cliques that the Federal Government now proposes to support with public funds, and with the piously reiterated assurance that the profiteering institutions will retain their full freedom to teach whatever they please, that there will be "no strings attached."

Well, there is one string which all the opponents of the intellectual status quo now have the right to expect and demand: the fairness doctrine.

If the public allegedly owns universities, as it allegedly owns the airwaves, then for all the same reasons *no specific ideology can be permitted to hold a monopoly in any department of any public or semi-public university.* In all such institutions, every "significant viewpoint" must be given representation. (By "ideology," in this context, I mean a system of ideas derived from a theoretical base or frame of reference.)

The same considerations that led to the fairness doctrine in broadcasting, apply to educational institutions, only more crucially, more urgently, more desperately so, because much more is involved than some ephemeral electronic sounds or images, because the mind of the young and the future of human knowledge are at stake.

Would this doctrine work in regard to universities? It would work as well—and as badly—as it has worked in broadcasting. It would work not as a motor of freedom, but as a brake on total regimentation. It would not achieve actual fairness, impartiality or objectivity. But it would act as a temporary impediment to intellectual monopolies, a retarder of the Establishment's takeover, a breach in the mental lethargy of the status quo, and, occasionally, an opening for a brilliant dissenter who would know how to make it count.

Remember that *dissenters*, in today's academic world, are not the advocates of mysticism-altruism-collectivism, who are the dominant cliques, the representatives of the entrenched status quo. The dissenters are the advocates of reason-individualism-capitalism. (If there are universities somewhere that bar the teaching of overtly vicious theories, such as communism, the advocates of these theories would be entitled to the protection of the fairness doctrine, so long as the university received government funds—because there are taxpaying citizens who are communists. The protection would apply to the right to teach ideas—*not* to criminal actions, such as campus riots or any form of physical violence.)

Since the fairness doctrine cannot be defined objectively, its application to specific cases would depend in large part on subjective interpretations, which would often be arbitrary and, at best, approximate. But there is no such approximation in the universities of Soviet Russia, as there was not in the universities of Nazi Germany. The purpose of the approximation is to preserve, to keep alive in men's minds, the principle of intellectual freedom—until the time when it can be implemented fully once more, in free, i.e., private, universities.

The main function of the fairness doctrine would be a switch of the burden of fear, from the victim to the entrenched gang—and a switch of moral right, from the entrenched gang to the victim. A dissenter would not have to be in the position of a martyr facing the power of a vast Establishment with all the interlockings of unknowable cliques, with the mysterious lines of secret pull leading to omnipotent governmental authorities. He would have the protection of a recognized *right*. On the other hand, the Establishment's hatchet men would have to be cautious, knowing that there is a limitation (at least, in principle) on the irresponsible power granted by the use of public funds "with no strings attached."

But the fight for the fairness doctrine would require intellectual clarity, objectivity, and good, i.e., contextual, judgment—because the elements to consider are extremely complex. For instance, the concept of "equal time" would not be entirely relevant: an hour in the class of an able professor can undo the harm done by a semester in the classes of the incompetent ones. And it would be impossible to burden the students with courses on every viewpoint in every subject.

There is no precise way to determine which professors' viewpoints are the appropriate opposites of which—particularly in the midst of today's prevalent eclecticism. The policy of lip service to impartiality and of window dressing is practiced in many schools; and the eclecticism in some of the smaller colleges is such that no specific viewpoint can be discerned at all. It is the cases of extremes, of ideological unity on the faculty and monopolistic monotony in teaching—particularly in the leading universities (which set the trends for all the rest)—that require protest by an informed public opinion, by the dissenting faculty members, and by the main victims: the students.

Intellectual diversity and ideological opposites can be determined only in terms of essentials—but it is an essential of modern philosophy to deny the existence or validity of essentials (which are called "oversimplification"). The result is that some advocates of a guaranteed minimum income are regarded as defenders of capitalism, advocates of theories of innate ideas are regarded as champions of reason, the tribal conformity of hippies is regarded as an expression of individualism, etc. And most college students have lost or never developed the ability to think in terms of essentials.

But—as in the case of political election campaigns, in which essentials are evaded more stringently than in modern universities—everyone knows implicitly which side he is for or against, though no public voices care to identify the issues explicitly. The consistency of such politicians' or professors' followers is remarkable for men who claim man's inability to distinguish essentials. (Which is one clue to the motives of the advocates of the "non-simplified," i.e., concrete-bound, approach.)

The ability explicitly to identify the essentials of any subject he studies, is the first requirement of a student who would want to fight for the fairness doctrine. Then, if he sees that he is offered only one viewpoint on a given *fundamental* issue —and knows that other "significant" viewpoints exist—he can protest, on the grounds of his right to know and to make an informed choice.

"Significance," in this context, should be gauged by one of two standards: the degree of historical influence achieved by a given theory or, if the theory is contemporary, its value in providing original answers to fundamental questions. As in the case of broadcasting, it would be impossible to present every individual's viewpoint. But if the great historical schools of thought were presented, the fairness doctrine would achieve its purpose (or perform its "trustbusting" function, if you will): the breakup of that one-sided indoctrination which is the hallmark of government-controlled schools.

In all fields that the government enters (outside of its proper sphere), two motives—one vicious, the other virtuous—produce the same results. In the case of schools, the vicious motive is power-lust, which prompts a teacher or an educational bureaucrat to indoctrinate students with a single viewpoint (of the kind that disarms them mentally, stunts their critical faculty, and conditions them to the passive acceptance of memorized dogma). The virtuous motive is a teacher's integrity: a man of integrity has firm convictions about what he regards as true; he teaches according to his convictions, and he does not propagate or support the theories which he regards as false (though he is able to present them objectively, when necessary). Such a teacher would be invaluable in a private university; but in a government-controlled school, his monopolistic position makes him as tyrannical an indoctrinator as the power-luster. (The solution is not what the opponents of any firm convictions suggest: that the honest teacher turn into a flexible pragmatist who'll switch his ideas from moment to moment, or into a skeptical pig who'll eat anything.) The consequences of any attempt to rule or *to support* intellectual activities by means of force will be evil, regardless of motives. (This does not mean that dissent is essential to intellectual freedom; the *possibility* of dissent, is.)

Who would enforce the fairness doctrine in education? Not the executive branch of the government, which is the dis-

tributor of the funds and has a vested interest in uniformity,
i.e., conformity. The doctrine has to be invoked and upheld
by private individuals and groups. This is another opportunity
for those who wish to take practical action against the growth
of statism. This issue could become the goal of an ad hoc
movement, uniting all men of good will, appealing (in the
name of intellectual justice) to whatever element of nineteenth-century liberalism still exists in the minds of academic
liberals—as distinguished from the Marcuseans, who openly
propose to drive all dissenters off the university faculties. (Is
the Marcuseans' goal to be achieved at public expense and
with government support?)

If a fairness movement enlisted the talents of some intelligent young lawyers, it could conceivably find support in the
courts of law, which are still supposed to protect an individual's civil rights. The legal precedent for a fairness doctrine is
to be found in the field of broadcasting. The practical implementation, i.e., the challenge to the Establishment in
specific cases, is up to the voluntary effort, the dedication,
and the persuasiveness of individuals.

It must be remembered firmly that a fairness doctrine is not
a string on the universities' freedom, but a string on the government's power to distribute public funds. That power has
already demonstrated its potential for fantastically evil and
blatantly unconstitutional control over the universities. Under
threat of withholding government funds and contracts, the
Department of Health, Education and Welfare is now imposing racial and sexual quotas on university faculties, demanding that some unspecified number of teachers consist of
ethnic minority-members and women. To add insult to injury,
HEW insists that this is not a demand for quotas, nor a demand to place racial considerations above merit, but a demand for "proof" that a university (e.g., Columbia) has made
an effort "to find" teachers of equal merit among those
groups. Try and prove it. Try and prove that you have
"searched." Try to measure and prove the various applicants'

merit—when no precise, objective standards of comparison are given or known. The result is that almost any female or minority-member is given preference over anyone else. The consequence is a growing anxiety about their future among young teachers who are male and do not belong to an ethnic minority: they are now the victims of the most obscenely vicious discrimination—obscene, because perpetrated in the name of fighting discrimination.

If the rights of various physiological minorities are so loudly claimed today, what about the rights of intellectual minorities?

I have said that the fairness doctrine is a product of the mixed economy. The whole precarious structure of a mixed economy, in its transition from freedom to totalitarian statism, rests on the power of pressure groups. But pressure-group warfare is a game that two (or more) ideological sides can play as well as one. The disadvantage of the statists is the fact that up to the last minute (and even beyond it) they have to play under cover of the slogans of individual rights and freedom. The advocates of freedom can beat them at their own game—by taking them at their word, but playing it straight. The time is right for it. The Establishment is not very popular at present, neither politically nor intellectually, neither with the country at large nor with many of its own members. A movement of the serious students and of the better teachers, defending the rights of intellectual minorities and demanding a fairness doctrine for education, would have a good chance to grow and to succeed. But taking part in such a movement would be much more difficult and demanding (and rewarding) than chanting slogans and dancing ring-around-a-rosy on some campus lawn.

If student minorities have succeeded in demanding that they be given courses on such subjects as Zen Buddhism, guerrilla warfare, Swahili, and astrology, then an intellectual student minority can succeed in demanding courses on, for instance, Aristotle in philosophy, von Mises in economics,

Montessori in education, Hugo in literature. At the very least, such courses would save the students' mind; potentially, they would save the culture.

No, the fairness doctrine would not reform the universities' faculties and administrations. There would be a great deal of hypocrisy, of compromising, of cheating, of hiring weak advocates to teach the unfashionable theories, of "tokenism," of window dressing.

But think of what one window can do for a sealed, airless, lightless room.

17

What Can One Do?
1972

This question is frequently asked by people who are concerned about the state of today's world and want to correct it. More often than not, it is asked in a form that indicates the cause of their helplessness: "What can *one person* do?"

I was in the process of preparing this article when I received a letter from a reader who presents the problem (and the error) still more eloquently: "How can an individual propagate your philosophy on a scale large enough to effect the immense changes which must be made in every walk of American life in order to create the kind of ideal country which you picture?"

If this is the way the question is posed, the answer is: he can't. No one can change a country single-handed. So the first question to ask is: why do people approach the problem this way?

Suppose you were a doctor in the midst of an epidemic. You would not ask: "How can one doctor treat millions of patients and restore the whole country to perfect health?" You would know, whether you were alone or part of an organized medical campaign, that you have to treat as many people as you can reach, according to the best of your ability, and that nothing else is possible.

It is a remnant of mystic philosophy—specifically, of the

mind-body split—that makes people approach intellectual issues in a manner they would not use to deal with physical problems. They would not seek to stop an epidemic overnight, or to build a skyscraper single-handed. Nor would they refrain from renovating their own crumbling house, on the grounds that they are unable to rebuild the entire city. But in the realm of man's consciousness, the realm of ideas, they still tend to regard knowledge as irrelevant, and they expect to perform instantaneous miracles, somehow—or they paralyze themselves by projecting an impossible goal.

(The reader whose letter I quoted was doing the right things, but felt that some wider scale of action was required. Many others merely ask the question, but do nothing.)

If you are seriously interested in fighting for a better world, begin by identifying the nature of the problem. The battle is primarily intellectual (*philosophical*), not political. Politics is the last consequence, the practical implementation, of the fundamental (metaphysical-epistemological-ethical) ideas that dominate a given nation's culture. You cannot fight or change the consequences without fighting and changing the cause; nor can you attempt any practical implementation without knowing what you want to implement.

In an intellectual battle, you do not need to convert everyone. History is made by minorities—or, more precisely, history is made by intellectual movements, which are created by minorities. Who belongs to these minorities? Anyone who is able and willing actively to concern himself with intellectual issues. Here, it is not quantity, but *quality*, that counts (the quality—and consistency—of the ideas one is advocating).

An intellectual movement does not start with organized action. Whom would one organize? A philosophical battle is a battle for men's minds, not an attempt to enlist blind followers. Ideas can be propagated only by men who understand them. An organized movement has to be preceded by an *educational* campaign, which requires trained—*self-trained*—teachers (self-trained in the sense that a philospher can offer

you the material of knowledge, but it is your own mind that
has to absorb it). Such training is the first requirement for
being a doctor during an ideological epidemic—and the precondition of any attempt to "change the world."

"The immense changes which must be made in every walk
of American life" cannot be made singly, piecemeal or "re-
tail," so to speak; an army of crusaders would not be enough
to do it. But the factor that underlies and determines every
aspect of human life is philosophy; teach men the right
philosophy—and their own minds will do the rest. Philosophy
is the wholesaler in human affairs.

Man cannot exist without some form of philosophy, i.e.,
some comprehensive view of life. Most men are not intellectual innovators, but they are receptive to ideas, are able to
judge them critically and to choose the right course, when and
if it is offered. There are also a great many men who are indifferent to ideas and to anything beyond the concrete-bound
range of the immediate moment; such men accept subconsciously whatever is offered by the culture of their time, and
swing blindly with any chance current. They are merely social
ballast—be they day laborers or company presidents—and,
by their own choice, irrelevant to the fate of the world.

Today, most people are acutely aware of our cultural-
ideological vacuum; they are anxious, confused, and groping
for answers. Are *you* able to enlighten them?

Can *you* answer their questions? Can *you* offer them a
consistent case? Do *you* know how to correct their errors? Are
you immune from the fallout of the constant barrage aimed at
the destruction of reason—and can *you* provide others with
antimissile missiles? A political battle is merely a skirmish
fought with muskets; a philosophical battle is a nuclear war.

If you want to influence a country's intellectual trend, the
first step is to bring order to your own ideas and integrate
them into a consistent case, to the best of your knowledge and
ability. This does not mean memorizing and reciting slogans
and principles, Objectivist or otherwise: knowledge necessar-

ily includes the ability to apply abstract principles to concrete
problems, to recognize the principles in specific issues, to
demonstrate them, and to advocate a consistent course of action. This does not require omniscience or omnipotence; it is
the subconscious expectation of automatic omniscience in
oneself and in others that defeats many would-be crusaders
(and serves as an excuse for doing nothing). What is required
is *honesty*—intellectual honesty, which consists in knowing
what one does know, constantly expanding one's knowledge,
and *never* evading or failing to correct a contradiction. This
means: the development of an *active* mind as a permanent
attribute.

When or if your convictions are in your conscious, orderly
control, you will be able to communicate them to others. This
does not mean that you must make philosophical speeches
when unnecessary and inappropriate. You need philosophy to
back you up and give you a consistent case when you deal
with or discuss specific issues.

If you like condensations (provided you bear in mind their
full meaning), I will say: when you ask "What can one
do?"—the answer is "SPEAK" (provided you know what you
are saying).

A few suggestions: do not wait for a national audience.
Speak on any scale open to you, large or small—to your
friends, your associates, your professional organizations, or
any legitimate public forum. You can never tell when your
words will reach the right mind at the right time. You will see
no immediate results—but it is of such activities that public
opinion is made.

Do not pass up a chance to express your views on important
issues. Write letters to the editors of newspapers and magazines, to TV and radio commentators and, above all, to your
Congressmen (who depend on their constituents). If your letters are brief and rational (rather than incoherently emotional), they will have more influence than you suspect.

The opportunities to speak are all around you. I suggest
that you make the following experiment: take an ideological

"inventory" of one week, i.e., note how many times people utter the wrong political, social and *moral* notions as if these were self-evident truths, with *your* silent sanction. Then make it a habit to object to such remarks—no, not to make lengthy speeches, which are seldom appropriate, but merely to say: "I don't agree." (And be prepared to explain why, if the speaker wants to know.) This is one of the best ways to stop the spread of vicious bromides. (If the speaker is innocent, it will help him; if he is not, it will undercut his confidence the next time.) Most particularly, *do not keep silent* when your own ideas and values are being attacked.

Do not "proselytize" indiscriminately, i.e., do not force discussions or arguments on those who are not interested or not willing to argue. It is not your job to save everyone's soul. If you do the things that are in your power, you will not feel guilty about not doing—"somehow"—the things that are not.

Above all, do not join the wrong *ideological* groups or movements, in order to "do something." By "ideological" (in this context), I mean groups or movements proclaiming some vaguely generalized, undefined (and, usually, contradictory) *political* goals. (E.g., the Conservative Party, which subordinates reason to faith, and substitutes theocracy for capitalism; or the "libertarian" hippies, who subordinate reason to whims, and substitute anarchism for capitalism.) To join such groups means to reverse the philosophical hierarchy and to sell out fundamental principles for the sake of some superficial political action which is bound to fail. It means that you help the defeat of *your* ideas and the victory of your enemies. (For a discussion of the reasons, see "The Anatomy of Compromise" in my book *Capitalism: The Unknown Ideal*.)

The only groups one may properly join today are *ad hoc* committees, i.e., groups organized to achieve a single, specific, clearly defined goal, on which men of differing views can agree. In such cases, no one may attempt to ascribe *his* views to the entire membership, or to use the group to serve some hidden ideological purpose (and *this* has to be watched very, very vigilantly).

I am omitting the most important contribution to an intellectual movement—writing—because this discussion is addressed to men of every profession. Books, essays, articles are a movement's permanent fuel, but it is worse than futile to attempt to become a writer solely for the sake of a "cause." Writing, like any other work, is a profession and must be approached as such.

It is a mistake to think that an intellectual movement requires some special duty or self-sacrificial effort on your part. It requires something much more difficult: a profound conviction that ideas are important to *you* and to your own life. If you integrate that conviction to every aspect of your life, you will find many opportunities to enlighten others.

The reader whose letter I quoted, indicates the proper pattern of action: "As a teacher of astronomy, for several years, I have been actively engaged in demonstrating the power of reason and the absolutism of reality to my students . . . I have also made an effort to introduce your works to my associates, following their reading with discussion when possible; and have made it a point to insist on the use of reason in all of my personal dealings."

These are some of the right things to do, as often and as widely as possible.

But that reader's question implied a search for some shortcut in the form of an organized movement. No shortcut is possible.

It is too late for a movement of people who hold a conventional mixture of contradictory philosophical notions. It is too early for a movement of people dedicated to a philosophy of reason. But it is never too late or too early to propagate the right ideas—except under a dictatorship.

If a dictatorship ever comes to this country, it will be by the default of those who keep silent. We are still free enough to speak. Do we have time? No one can tell. But time is on our side—because we have an indestructible weapon and an invincible ally (if we learn how to use them): reason and reality.

18

Don't Let It Go
1971

In order to form a hypothesis about the future of an individual, one must consider three elements: his present course of action, his conscious convictions, and his sense of life. The same elements must be considered in forming a hypothesis about the future of a nation.

A sense of life is a pre-conceptual equivalent of metaphysics, an emotional, subconsciously integrated appraisal of man and of existence. It represents an individual's unidentified philosophy (which can be identified—and corrected, if necessary); it affects his choice of values and his emotional responses, influences his actions, and, frequently, clashes with his conscious convictions. (For a detailed discussion, see "Philosophy and Sense of Life" in my book *The Romantic Manifesto*.)

A nation, like an individual, has a sense of life, which is expressed not in its formal culture, but in its "life style"—in the kinds of actions and attitudes which people take for granted and believe to be self-evident, but which are produced by complex evaluations involving a fundamental view of man's nature.

A "nation" is not a mystic or supernatural entity: it is a large number of individuals who live in the same geographical locality under the same political system. A nation's culture is the sum of the intellectual achievements of individual men, which their fellow-citizens have accepted in whole or in part, and which have influenced the nation's way of life. Since a culture is a complex battleground of different ideas and influences, to speak of a "culture" is to speak only of the *dominant* ideas, always allowing for the existence of dissenters and exceptions.

(The dominance of certain ideas is not necessarily determined by the number of their adherents: it may be determined by majority acceptance, or by the greater activity and persistence of a given faction, or by default, i.e., the failure of the opposition, or—when a country is free—by a combination of persistence and truth. In any case, ideas and the resultant culture are the product and active concern of a minority. Who constitutes this minority? Whoever chooses to be concerned.)

Similarly, the concept of a nation's sense of life does not mean that every member of a given nation shares it, but only that a dominant majority shares its essentials in various degrees. In this matter, however, the dominance is numerical: while most men may be indifferent to cultural-ideological trends, no man can escape the process of subconscious integration which forms his sense of life.

A nation's sense of life is formed by every individual child's early impressions of the world around him: of the ideas he is taught (which he may or may not accept) and of the way of acting he observes and evaluates (which he may evaluate correctly or not). And although there are exceptions at both ends of the psychological spectrum—men whose sense of life is better (truer philosophically) or worse than that of their fellow-citizens—the majority develop the essentials of the same subconscious philosophy. This is the source of what we observe as "national characteristics."

A nation's political trends are the equivalent of a man's course of action and are determined by its culture. A nation's culture is the equivalent of a man's conscious convictions. Just as an individual's sense of life can clash with his conscious convictions, hampering or defeating his actions, so a nation's sense of life can clash with its culture, hampering or defeating its political course. Just as an individual's sense of life can be better or worse than his conscious convictions, so can a nation's. And just as an individual who has never translated his sense of life into conscious convictions is in terrible danger—no matter how good his subconscious values—so is a nation.

This is the position of America today.

If America is to be saved from destruction—specifically, from dictatorship—she will be saved by her sense of life.

As to the two other elements that determine a nation's future, one (our political trend) is speeding straight to disaster, the other (culture) is virtually nonexistent. The political trend is pure statism and is moving toward a totalitarian dictatorship at a speed which, in any other country, would have reached that goal long ago. The culture is worse than nonexistent: it is operating below zero, i.e., performing the opposite of its function. A culture provides a nation's intellectual leadership, its ideas, its education, its moral code. Today, the concerted effort of our cultural "Establishment" is directed at the obliteration of man's rational faculty. Hysterical voices are proclaiming the impotence of reason, extolling the "superior power" of irrationality, fostering the rule of incoherent emotions, attacking science, glorifying the stupor of drugged hippies, delivering apologias for the use of brute force, urging mankind's return to a life of rolling in primeval muck, with grunts and groans as means of communication, physical sensations as means of inspiration, and a club as means of argumentation.

This country, with its magnificent scientific and technological power, is left in the vacuum of a pre-intellectual era, like the wandering hordes of the Dark Ages—or in the position of an adolescent before he has fully learned to conceptualize. But an adolescent has his sense of life to guide his choices. So has this country.

What is the specifically American sense of life?

A sense of life is so complex an integration that the best way to identify it is by means of concrete examples and by contrast with the manifestations of a different sense of life.

The emotional keynote of most Europeans is the feeling that man belongs to the State, as a property to be used and disposed of, in compliance with his natural, metaphysically determined fate. A typical European may disapprove of a given State and may rebel, seeking to establish what he regards as a better one, like a slave who might seek a better master to serve—but the idea that *he* is the sovereign and the government is his servant, has no emotional reality in his consciousness. He regards service to the State as an ultimate moral sanction, as an *honor,* and if you told him that his life is an end in itself, he would feel insulted or rejected or lost. Generations brought up on statist philosophy and acting accordingly, have implanted this in his mind from the earliest, formative years of his childhood.

A typical American can never fully grasp that kind of feeling. An American is an independent entity. The popular expression of protest against "being pushed aroung" is emotionally unintelligible to Europeans, who believe that to be pushed around is their natural condition. Emotionally, an American has no concept of service (or of servitude) to anyone. Even if he enlists in the army and hears it called "service to his country," his feeling is that of a generous aristocrat who *chose* to do a dangerous task. A European soldier feels that he is doing his duty.

"Isn't my money as good as the next fellow's?" used to be a popular American expression. It would not be popular in Europe: a fortune, to be good, must be old and derived by special favor from the State; to a European, money earned by personal effort is vulgar, crude or somehow disreputable.

Americans admire achievement; they know what it takes. Europeans regard achievement with cynical suspicion and envy. Envy is not a widespread emotion in America (not yet); it is an overwhelmingly dominant emotion in Europe.

When Americans feel respect for their public figures, it is the respect of equals; they feel that a government official is a human being, just as they are, who has chosen this particular line of work and has earned a certain distinction. They call celebrities by their first names, they refer to Presidents by their initials (like "F.D.R." or "J.F.K."), not in insolence or egalitarian pretentiousness, but in token of affection. The custom of addressing a person as "Herr Doktor Doktor Schmidt" would be impossible in America. In England, the freest country of Europe, the achievement of a scientist, a businessman or a movie star is not regarded as fully real until he has been clunked on the head with the State's sword and declared to be a knight.

There are practical consequences of these two different attitudes.

An American economist told me the following story. He was sent to England by an American industrial concern, to investigate its European branch: in spite of the latest equipment and techniques, the productivity of the branch in England kept lagging far behind that of the parent-factory in the U.S. He found the cause: a rigidly circumscribed mentality, a kind of psychological caste system, on all the echelons of British labor and management. As he explained it: in America, if a machine breaks down, a worker volunteers to fix it, and usually does; in England, work stops and people wait for the appropriate department to summon the appropriate engineer. It is not a matter of laziness, but of a profoundly ingrained feeling that one must keep one's place, do one's prescribed duty, and never venture beyond it. It does not occur to the British worker that he is free to assume responsibility for anything beyond the limits of his particular job. *Initiative* is an "instinctive" (i.e., automatized) American characteristic; in an American consciousness, it occupies the place which, in a European one, is occupied by *obedience*.

As to the differences in the social atmosphere, here is an example. An elderly European woman, a research biochemist from Switzerland, on a visit to New York, told me that she wanted to buy some things at the five-and-ten. Since she could barely speak English, I offered to go with her; she hesitated, looking astonished and disturbed, then asked: "But wouldn't that embarrass you?" I couldn't understand what she meant: "Embarrass—how?" "Well," she explained, "you are a famous person, and what if somebody sees you in the five-and-ten?" I laughed. She explained to me that in Switzerland, by unwritten law, there are different stores for different classes of people, and that she, as a professional, has to shop in certain stores, even though her salary is modest, that better goods at lower prices are available in the workingmen's stores, but she would lose social status if she were seen shopping there. Can you conceive of living in an atmosphere of that kind? (We did go to the five-and-ten.)

A European, on any social level, lives emotionally in a world made by others (he never knows clearly by whom), and seeks or accepts his place in it. The American attitude is best expressed by a line from a poem: "The world began when I was born and the world is mine to win." ("The Westerner" by Badger Clark.)

Years ago, at a party in Hollywood, I met Eve Curie, a distinguished Frenchwoman, the daughter of Marie Curie. Eve Curie was a best-selling author of non-fiction books and, politically, a liberal; at the time, she was on a lecture tour of the United States. She stressed her astonishment at American audiences. "They are so happy," she kept repeating, "so *happy*. . . ." She was saying it without disapproval and without admiration, with only the faintest touch of amusement; but her astonishment was genuine. "People are not like that in Europe. . . . Everybody is happy in America—except the intellectuals. Oh, the intellectuals are unhappy everywhere."

This incident has remained in my mind because she had named, unwittingly, the nature of the breach between the American people and the intellectuals. The culture of a worn, crumbling Europe—with its mysticism, its lethargic resignation, its cult of suffering, its notion that misery and impotence are man's fate on earth, and that unhappiness is the hallmark of a sensitive spirit—of what use could it be to a country like America?

It was a European who discovered America, but it was Americans who were the first nation to discover this earth and man's proper place in it, and man's potential for happiness, and the world which is man's to win. What they failed to discover is the words to name their achievement, the concepts to identify it, the principles to guide it, i.e., the appropriate philosophy and its consequence: an *American* culture.

America has never had an *original* culture, i.e., a body of ideas derived from her philosophical *(Aristotelian)* base and expressing her profound difference from all other countries in history.

American intellectuals were Europe's passive dependents and poor relatives almost from the beginning. They lived on Europe's drying crumbs and discarded fashions, including even such hand-me-downs as Freud and Wittgenstein. America's sole contribution to philosophy—Pragmatism— was a bad recycling of Kantian-Hegelian premises.

America's best minds went into science, technology, industry—and reached incomparable heights of achievement. Why did they neglect the field of ideas? Because it represented Augean stables of a kind no joyously active man would care to enter. America's childhood coincided with the rise of Kant's influence in European philosophy and the consequent disintegration of European culture. America was in the position of an eager, precocious child left in the care of a scruffy, senile, decadent guardian. The child had good reason to play hooky.

An adolescent can ride on his sense of life for a while. But by the time he grows up, he must translate it into conceptual knowledge and conscious convictions, or he will be in deep trouble. A sense of life is not a substitute for explicit knowledge. Values which one cannot identify, but merely senses implicitly, are not in one's control. One cannot tell what they depend on or require, what course of action is needed to gain and/or keep them. One can lose or betray them without knowing it. For close to a century, this has been America's tragic predicament. Today, the American people is like a sleepwalking giant torn by profound conflicts. (When I speak of "the American people," in this context, I mean every group, including scientists and businessmen—except the intellectuals, i.e., those whose professions deal with the humanities. The intellectuals are a country's guardians.)

Americans are the most reality-oriented people on earth. Their outstanding characteristic is the childhood form of reasoning: common sense. It is their only protection. But common sense is not enough where theoretical knowledge is required: it can make simple, concrete-bound connections—it cannot integrate complex issues, or deal with wide abstractions, or forecast the future.

For example, consider the statist trend in this country. The doctrine of collectivism has never been submitted explicitly to the American voters; if it had been, it would have sustained a landslide defeat (as the various socialist parties have demonstrated). But the welfare state was put over on Americans piecemeal, by degrees, under cover of some undefined "Americanism"—culminating in the absurdity of a President's declaration that America owes its greatness to "the willingness for self-sacrifice." People sense that something has gone wrong; they cannot grasp what or when. This is the penalty they pay for remaining a silent (and deaf) majority.

Americans are anti-intellectual (with good grounds, in view of current specimens), yet they have a profound respect for knowledge and education (which is being shaken now). They are self-confident, trusting, generous, enormously benevolent and innocent. " . . . that celebrated American 'innocence' [is] a quality which in philosophical terms is simply an ignorance of how questionable a being man really is and which strikes the European as alien . . ." declares an existentialist (William Barrett, *Irrational Man*). The word "questionable" is a euphemism for miserable, guilty, impotent, groveling, evil—which is the European view of man. Europeans do believe in Original Sin, i.e., in man's innate depravity; Americans do not. Americans see man as a value—as clean, free, creative, rational. But the American view of man has not been expressed or upheld *in philosophical terms* (not since the time of our first Founding Father, Aristotle; see his description of the "magnanimous man").

Barrett continues: "Sartre recounts a conversation he had with an American while visiting in this country. The American insisted that all international problems could be solved if men would just get together and be rational; Sartre disagreed and after a while discussion between them became impossible. 'I believe in the existence of evil,' says Sartre, 'and he does not.'" This, again, is a euphemism: it is not merely the existence but the *power* of evil that Europeans believe in. Americans do not believe in the power of evil and do not understand its nature. The first part of their attitude is (philosophically) true, but the second makes them vulnerable. On the day when Americans grasp the cause of evil's impotence—its mindless, fear-ridden, envy-eaten smallness—they will be free of all the man-hating manipulators of history, foreign and domestic.

So far, America's protection has been a factor best expressed by a saying attributed to con men: "You can't cheat an honest man." The innocence and common sense of the American people have wrecked the plans, the devious notions, the tricky strategies, the ideological traps borrowed by the intellectuals from the European statists, who devised them to fool and rule Europe's impotent masses. There have never been any "masses" in America: the poorest American is an individual and, subconsciously, an individualist. Marxism, which has conquered our universities, is a dismal failure as far as the people are concerned: Americans cannot be sold on any sort of class war; American workers do not see themselves as a "proletariat," but are among the proudest of property owners. It is professors and businessmen who advocate cooperation with Soviet Russia—American labor unions do not.

The enormous propaganda effort to make Americans fear fascism but not communism, has failed: Americans hate them both. The terrible hoax of the United Nations has failed. Americans were never enthusiastic about that institution, but they gave it the benefit of the doubt for too long. The current polls, however, indicate that the majority have turned against the U.N. (better late than never).

The latest assault on human life—the ecology crusade— will probably end in defeat for its ideological leadership: Americans will enthusiastically clean their streets, their rivers, their backyards, but when it comes to giving up progress, technology, the automobile, and their standard of living, Americans will prove that the man-haters "ain't seen nothing yet."

The sense-of-life emotion which, in Europe, makes people uncertain, malleable and easy to rule, is unknown in America: fundamental guilt. No one, so far, has been able to infect America with that contemptible feeling (and I doubt that anyone ever will). Americans cannot begin to grasp the kind of corruption implied and demanded by that feeling.

But an honest man can cheat himself. His trusting innocence can lead him to swallow sugar-coated poisons—the deadliest of which is *altruism*. Americans accept it—not for what it is, not as a vicious doctrine of self-immolation—but in the spirit of a strong, confident man's overgenerous desire to relieve the suffering of others, whose character he does not understand. When such a man awakens to the betrayal of his trust—to the fact that his generosity has brought him within reach of a permanent harness which is about to be slipped on him by his sundry beneficiaries—the consequences are unpredictable.

There are two ways of destroying a country: dictatorship or chaos, i.e., immediate rigor mortis or the longer agony of the collapse of all civilized institutions and the breakup of a nation into roving armed gangs fighting and looting one another, until some one Attila conquers the rest. This means: chaos as a prelude to tyranny—as was the case in Western Europe in the Dark Ages, or in the three hundred years preceding the Romanoff dynasty in Russia, or under the war lords regime in China.

A European is disarmed in the face of a dictatorship: he may hate it, but he feels that he is wrong and, metaphysically, the State is right. An American would rebel to the bottom of his soul. But this is all that his sense of life can do for him: it cannot solve his problems.

Only one thing is certain: a dictatorship cannot take hold in America today. This country, as yet, cannot be ruled—but it can explode. It can blow up into the helpless rage and blind violence of a civil war. It cannot be cowed into submission, passivity, malevolence, resignation. It cannot be "pushed around." Defiance, not obedience, is the American's answer to overbearing authority. The nation that ran an underground railroad to help human beings escape from slavery, or began drinking *on principle* in the face of Prohibition, will not say "Yes, sir," to the enforcers of ration coupons and cereal prices. Not yet.

If America drags on in her present state for a few more generations (which is unlikely), dictatorship will become possible. A sense of life is not a permanent endowment. The characteristically American one is being eroded daily all around us. Large numbers of Americans have lost it (or have never developed it) and are collapsing to the psychological level of Europe's worst rabble.

This is prevalent among the two groups that are the main supporters of the statist trend: the very rich and the very poor—the first, because they want to rule; the second, because they want to be ruled. (The leaders of the trend are the intellectuals, who want to do both.) But this country has never had an unearned, hereditary "elite." America is still the country of self-made men, which means: the country of the middle class—the most productive and exploited group in any modern society.

The academia–jet set coalition is attempting to tame the American character by the deliberate breeding of helplessness and resignation—in those incubators of lethargy known as "Progressive" schools, which are dedicated to the task of crippling a child's mind by arresting his cognitive development. (See "The Comprachicos" in my book *The New Left: The Anti-Industrial Revolution.*) It appears, however, that the "progressive" rich will be the first victims of their own social theories: it is the children of the well-to-do who emerge from expensive nursery schools and colleges as hippies, and destroy the remnants of their paralyzed brains by means of drugs.

The middle class has created an antidote which is perhaps the most hopeful movement of recent years: the spontaneous, unorganized, grass-roots revival of the Montessori system of education—a system aimed at the development of a child's cognitive, i.e., rational, faculty. But that is a long-range prospect.

At present, even so dismal a figure as President Nixon is a hopeful sign—precisely because he is so dismal. If any other country were in as desperately precarious a state of confusion as ours, a dozen flamboyant Führers would have sprung up overnight to take it over. It is to America's credit that no such Führer has appeared, and if any did, it is doubtful that he would have a chance.

Can this country achieve a peaceful rebirth in the foreseeable future? By all precedents, it is not likely. But America is an unprecedented phenomenon. In the past, American perseverance became, on occasion, too long-bearing a patience. But when Americans turned, *they turned.* What may happen to the welfare state is what happened to the Prohibition Amendment.

Is there enough of the American sense of life left in

people—under the constant pressure of the cultural-political efforts to obliterate it? It is impossible to tell. But those of us who hold it, must fight for it. We have no alternative: we cannot surrender this country to a zero—to men whose battle cry is mindlessness.

We cannot fight against collectivism, unless we fight against its moral base: altruism. We cannot fight against altruism, unless we fight against its epistemological base: irrationalism. We cannot fight *against* anything, unless we fight *for* something—and what we must fight for is the supremacy of reason, and a view of man as a rational being.

These are philosophical issues. The philosophy we need is a conceptual equivalent of America's sense of life. To propagate it, would require the hardest intellectual battle. But isn't that a magnificent goal to fight for?

Index

Frank, Anne, 86, 87
Freedom, 80, 183, 210
  censorship and, 211
  fairness doctrine and, 231, 232,
    238, 242
  Skinner and, 171, 176, 189
"From the Horses Mouth," 93–99
Future, the, 250–62
  anti-conceptual mentality and,
    46–47
  determinants of, 252

Gallagher, Cornelius E., 199–201
Gans, Herbert, 146–47, 150
General Accounting Office, 199
Gibson, William 109, 112
Goals and final causation, 119–20
God, 30, 177
Gold, 154–55
Government
  controls of, 198–199, 214, 218,
    221, 227
  establishing an establishment by,
    197–209
  inflation and, 156, 157, 158,
    161–63
  private, 53
  socialism and, 82–84
  subsidizing of ideas by, 195–96,
    199–09, 233–43
  Supreme Court, 210–30
"Growl to Me Softly and I'll Under-
  stand," 105–106
Guilt
  Age of, 73
  sense-of-life, 259

Hegel, Georg Wilhelm Friedrich, 5,
  10, 23–24, 139
Hitler, Adolf, 179
Honesty, 247
  in ethics, 15
  intellectual, 19
Hugo, Victor, 183, 236
Human Events, 195–96, 199
Humanities, 31–32, 234
  breach between science and, 97

Hume, David, 5, 167

"I can't prove it, but I feel that it's
  true," 5, 22
Identity, 29, 32
  personal, 37
  see also Law of Identity
Imagination, 31
*Immanuel Kant: His Life and Doc-
  trine* (Paulsen), 93–99
Imperialism, 10
Independence, 253
Individualism, 53, 125–26, 239
  Skinner and, 173–74, 176–77
Individual rights, 15, 27, 34, 51
  Supreme Court and, 218–19, 221,
    222
Industrial revolution, 76, 79
Inflation, 97–98
  credit and, 158
  egalitarianism and, 145–65
  government and, 156, 157, 158,
    161–63
  psycho-epistemological precondi-
    tion of, 152–55
Instinct, 89–90
Intellectual honesty, 19
Intellectuals
  American, 129–30, 252
  change and, 245–49
  culture and, 252
  government and, 196, 206
  "majority will" and, 137–38
  sense of life and, 255–56, 257
  socialism and, 82, 83, 84, 85
Intelligence, 39, 185, 229
*Introduction to Objectivist Epis-
  temology* (Rand), 108
Introspection, 20–21
  failure of, 35
Investment capital, 159
Irrationalism, 66, 68–69, 108, 236,
  262
  technique for selling, 141
  tribalism and, 52
Irreducible primary, 15–16
  anti-conceptual mentality and, 46

Metaphysical absolutism, 63
Metaphysically given, 30–31
acceptance of, 32–34, 39
man-made facts and, 37–38
natural phenomenon as, 33–34
rejection of, 33–36
volition and, 38, 39
"Metaphysical Versus the Man-Made, The," 28–41
egalitarian movement and, 40–41
man-made facts and, 37–38
man's nature and, 38–40
obliteration of the differences between, 34–37
volition and, 29–32, 37–38
see also Metaphysically given;
Primacy of consciousness
Metaphysics, 26
anti-conceptual mentality and, 49
irreducible primaries and, 15–16
man's nature and, 228–30
philosophy and, 3, 4, 14
Mill, John Stuart, 82, 138
Miller v. California, 212, 216, 217, 218
Mind, 88, 189–90
cognitive efficacy of, 108
hatred of, 229
self as, 60
Mind-body dichotomy, 228–30, 244–45
Miracle Worker, The (Gibson), 109–13
"Missing Link, The," 55
Mitchell, Edgar, 97
Mixed economy, 231, 242
Money, 154–56, 159, 161
credit and, 160
gold, 154–55
intellectuals and, 206
Montessori schools, 243, 261
Moral autonomy, 8
Moral endurance, pyramid of, 209
Morality
altruism and, 61–62, 73–75, 78–92

defined, 73–74
desire to escape, 21–22
duty and, 115–21
faith and, 95–99
Kant and, 78–79, 95–99, 115–21
man's life and, 90
Objectivism and, 88–92
reason and, 87–88, 90
Skinner and, 172–73
theories of, 19–20
see also Ethics
More Equality (Gans), 146–47
Mysticism
culture and, 73, 177–79
defined, 75–76
duty and, 115–21
justification of altruism via, 74–75, 139
motivation for, 123
of muscle, 168–69, 173, 174, 190, 228–30
of spirit, 168, 169, 173, 190, 228–30
philosophy, science and, 93–99
problem of universals and, 108
reason versus, 75–77, 80, 85, 93–99
violence and, 85

Nader, Ralph, 157
National characteristics, 251
National Institute of Mental Health, 195–96, 199, 201
Naturalists, 43
Nature, 30
metaphysically given and, 30–31, 33, 39
penalizing those favored by, 132–44
rules of, 69
"Nature, to be commanded, must be obeyed," 31, 34, 38
Nazi Germany, 83, 97, 138, 164, 206, 221, 238
Nero, 145
Neurotic anxiety, 72

61089 115